THE THREE RICHARDS

The reverse of the second great seal of Richard I

The Three Richards

Richard I, Richard II and Richard III

Nigel Saul

hambledon
continuum

Hambledon Continuum

The Tower Building,
11 York Road,
London SE1 7NX

80 Maiden Lane,
Suite 704,
New York, NY 10038

First Published 2005 in hardback

This edition published 2006

ISBN 978 1 85285 521 5

Reprinted 2008

Typeset by Carnegie Publishing, Lancaster,
and printed in Great Britain by Biddles Ltd., King's Lynn, Norfolk

Contents

Illustrations

Plates

Between Pages 116 and 117

Text Illustrations

Illustration Acknowledgements

The author and publishers are grateful to the following for permission
to reproduce illustrations: British Library Board, plates 1, 4, 5 and p. 65;
National Gallery, London, plate 2; Dean and Chapter of Westminster
Abbey, plate 3; National Portrait Gallery, London, plate 6; Society of
Antiquaries of London, plate 7; Royal Holloway, University of London,
plate 8; A. F. Kersting, pp. 20, 33, 230; Shrewsbury Museums Service,
p. 48.

Acknowledgements

The idea of writing this book was suggested to me by Tony Morris. I am very grateful to him for his initiative. The inspiration for the title is Michael Prestwich's study *The Three Edwards*, published in 1980. Prestwich's book offered a continuous history of England for the period of the three Edwards from 1272 to 1377. A continuous history of the same sort cannot be undertaken for the three Richards because of the long gaps between the reigns. Instead, a decision has been taken to adopt a comparative approach. Attention is focused on a set of themes common to all three reigns. These are the kings' piety, their lack of legitimate surviving issue and their violent deaths. At the same time, and perhaps unexpectedly, an overarching theme emerges. This is the influence of the first Richard's-example and fame on the careers of the other two – indeed, on the development of English medieval kingship more generally. There is a sense in which all medieval English kings lived under the first Richard's long shadow.

I am very grateful to John Gillingham for reading the entire book in manuscript. His searching eye not only rooted out a host of errors and inconsistencies but also highlighted many issues which I had overlooked. Whatever merits the book may have are, in large measure, attributable to his stimulating criticism.

The dedication, as usual, is to those who have shown such understanding while I have been at work.

For Jane, Dominic and Louise

There were three Richards whose fortunes were alike in three respects, but otherwise the fate of each was his own. Thus they had in common an end without issue of their body; a life of greed and a violent fall; but it was the greater glory of the first that he fought in the Holy Land; and returning home he was struck down, in a foreign land, by the bolts from a crossbow. The second, deposed from his kingdom, after he had been shut up in prison for some months, actually chose to die from hunger of his own will rather than bear the dishonour of ill fame. The third, after exhausting the ample store of Edward's wealth, was not content until he suppressed his brother's progeny and proscribed their supporters; at last, two years after taking violent possession of the kingdom he met these same people in battle and now has lost his grim life and his crown. In the year 1485 on the 22nd day of August the tusks of the Boar were blunted and the red rose, the avenger of the white, shines upon us.

The Crowland Chronicle Continuator

1

What's in a Name?

Europe's rulers in the middle ages were generally conservative in their choice of names for their offspring. With a few exceptions, they gave their first-born son their own name. In this way, particular names came to be handed down in dynasties. In France Louis and Charles were used many times over, in Sweden Carl and Gustav (or the two together), in Spain Alfonso, in Habsburg Austria Albert. Naming became an expression of dynastic continuity.

In medieval England the pattern of naming was broadly the same. A handful of royal names predominated. The most common of these were Henry and Edward. In the period between 1100 to 1485 there were no fewer than six Henries and five Edwards. Other names, such as John, Stephen and Richard, only appeared when there was a break in the direct line of descent.

Personal names have always been charged with cultural meaning. Names convey messages and imply associations. Parents choose them with care. We see this in the naming of England's medieval kings. Whenever major cultural change occurred, there was a change of nomenclature. In the late eleventh century, in the wake of the Conquest, there was a switch from Anglo-Scandinavian or Old English names to Frankish ones. Out went Æthelred, Harold and Edgar, and in came William, Henry and Robert. The newcomers brought their own personal names with them.

Henry, the name which was to become commonest over time, actually entered the repertory by accident. It was the name that William the Conqueror gave to the youngest of his three sons. At first, it seemed that there was little prospect of it entering the royal repertory – for the simple reason that there was little prospect of Henry becoming king. William and Robert, Henry's two brothers, were both vigorous and had every expectation of siring heirs. As it turned out, however, fortune was to be on Henry's side. In 1100 William, who had succeeded his father in England, died prematurely, the victim of a notorious hunting accident, and Henry was able to take his crown; while a few years later, after defeating Robert, he was able to annex Normandy too. But no sooner had Henry's name entered the repertory of royal names than it was to leave it again. Henry died without surviving legitimate male issue. His immediate successor was his nephew – his sister's son, a member of the house of Blois called Stephen. The name Henry, however, was certainly not banished for good. On Stephen's death in 1154 the throne was taken by Henry's grandson, another Henry. Henry I's daughter Matilda, that boy's mother, was determined to keep the name alive. For her, it was proof of dynastic right. So Henry entered the repertory of favoured Angevin royal names.

Edward, the other name much favoured by the English royal line in the middle ages, was, by contrast, English in origin. Before the Conquest there had been several Edwards – Edward the Elder, Alfred the Great's son, in the tenth century and Edward the Confessor in the eleventh, to name but two. 'Edward' re-entered the repertory of English royal names relatively late. Henry III christened his first-born son Edward in 1245 in ʻhonour of St Edward the Confessor, to whose cult he was devoted. The choice reflected the reawakening of interest in the country's pre-Conquest past. There was a revival of interest in the cults of the pre-Conquest saints generally. The cult of St Edmund at Bury, for example, enjoyed a new flowering, and Henry called his second son Edmund. At the same time, there was a growing interest in St Æthel-dreda's cult at Ely. Edward became increasingly popular as a royal name in the century or more after 1250. Each of the three kings after Henry III was called Edward, and if Edward, the Black Prince, had lived there would have been a fourth. In the fifteenth century there were two more Edwards. By the end of the middle ages the pattern of naming was beginning to settle into the French pattern. Just two or three names competed. Alongside Louis and Charles in France, can be set Henry and Edward in England.

A couple of centuries earlier, however, the position had looked very different. At that time there was no regular succession of names. In the years after 1066 William looked as if it was going to sweep the field. Between 1066 and 1100 there were the two Williams – the Conqueror

and his son Rufus. But then other names crowded in – Stephen, John
and Richard – before in the thirteenth century things settled down
again. The unusual variety in the twelfth century is to be explained by a
number of factors. In the first place, there was the acute dynastic instability. As we have seen, it was normal for a change of dynasty to bring
a change of personal names. So, with the coming of the Normans came
new names; and with the accession of the house of Blois and then of the
house of Anjou there were changes again. But there was a second factor. Within dynasties there was no regular succession from father to
eldest son and heir. Henry II's eldest surviving son predeceased him,
while in the next generation Richard I had no son at all. The succession,
in other words, passed from father to younger son, or younger son to
younger brother. There were similar complications of descent towards
the end of the fourteenth century, when the crown passed from
Edward III to his grandson and from the latter to his cousin. These periods of irregularity had few parallels in France. In France not only was
there less dynastic change, for just two dynasties ruled between the tenth
century and the sixteenth; within those dynasties there was a more
regular succession from father to eldest son.

Richard was one of the minority names. Like Henry, it entered the
nominal lexicon by one of those accidents of descent. Henry II's first
two sons, William and Henry 'the Young King', had predeceased him.[1]
Thus his heir became his third son Richard. The name was a French
one – to be precise, a Norman French one. Three early medieval dukes
of Normandy had been called Richard – Richard I, who had ruled from
943 to 996, Richard II, his son (996–1026), and Richard III (1026–27).
When Henry II revived the name Richard, therefore, he was acknowl-
edging the Norman inheritance of the Angevin comital line. Through
his mother, Henry I's daughter Matilda, Henry was descended from the
Norman dukes, the descendants of Rollo the Viking. The Normans and
the Angevins had long been enemies and rivals. For generations they
had fought over such border territories as Maine and La Flèche. Yet
now the two dynasties had come together. When Henry II and his wife
called their third son Richard, they were recognising the union – the
consummation – of the two lines.

When later kings and princes chose the name Richard for their
sons, it was quite deliberately to associate them with this first and most

celebrated Richard. Richard I left behind him a powerful historical legacy. He was one of the most celebrated and heroic figures of his age. Through his achievements he had added to the collective fame of the house of Anjou. He generated a new wave of enthusiasm for the crusade. Every later king of ambition aspired to pay acknowledgement to the Ricardian inheritance. In the light of Richard's distinction it is perhaps surprising that there were not more kings named after him. The main reason for the relative lack is that Richard himself produced no legitimate issue; he was succeeded by his brother John, who named his own son after their father – Henry. There were just two later kings named Richard. In the fourteenth century, after the run of Edwards, there was Richard II. Richard was the younger son of Edward, the Black Prince, someone who would be expected to take the first Richard as a role model. Richard's elder brother was another Edward. This Edward – known as Edward of Angoulême – died young, however, and Richard became king as Richard II. But, like the first Richard, he left no son to succeed him. A little under a century later the last Richard, Richard III, came to the throne. Richard was a member of the house of York, which in most generations had shown a preference for the name Edward. Richard was a younger son – and, of course, came to the throne as a usurper. Appropriately he was someone of soldierly ambitions, so his name suited him. It is interesting that both of the most popular Yorkist names – Richard and Edward – reflected the martial, chivalric values which the Yorkist family espoused.

The name Richard, then, was not one of the commonest in the English royal lexicon. It was used more often for younger sons than for the firstborn. In 1306 the elderly Edward I had toyed with the name Richard for the youngest of a large brood.[2] If circumstances had brought more younger sons to the throne, there could have been more kings called Richard. Henry III had an ambitious younger brother in Richard, earl of Cornwall, a couple of years his junior. Earl Richard did in fact become a king, but of Germany, not England, where his nephew succeeded. In the fifteenth century, when the Lancastrians ruled, a collateral called Richard – Richard, duke of York – had designs on the throne. He could have become king since he had been designated Henry VI's heir in parliament in 1460. In the event, however, he was killed in battle at Wakefield before he could realise his claim. A quarter of a century later, yet another Richard stood in the wings. This was Richard of York, Edward IV's second son – the junior of the two princes in the Tower. This promising youth, however, was done to death on the probable orders of yet another Richard, his own uncle.

The three Richards ruled at widely separated times – Richard I at the end of the twelfth century, Richard II a couple of centuries later, and Richard III a century after that. At first sight, the kings do not appear to have had a great deal in common. It is tempting, indeed, to say that they had little if anything beyond the same name. They inhabited very different cultural worlds. Richard I was easily the most cosmopolitan of the three; although English by birth, he belonged spiritually to the elegant, sophisticated world of the aristocracy of France. He was in reality a southerner, an Aquitanian. Richard II, although born in Aquitaine, was far more an Englishman. He had a sense of English identity which his predecessor lacked, and his court was the first at which English was regularly spoken. Richard III a century later was English through and through: he had been born in England; he lived in England; and he died in England. These differences are closely paralleled by differences in the kings' experience of the world. Richard I was the most widely travelled of the three. He went east on crusade and suffered imprisonment in Germany and Austria; he knew the Mediterranean world well. Richard II, although known from birth as Richard of Bordeaux, was actually far less familiar with Europe. He crossed the Channel only twice as king and then never in arms. None the less, he was knowledgeable about the British Isles. Richard III knew very little of either Britain or Europe. He prided himself on his Englishness.[3]

In addition to these differences of background, there were differences of personality and taste. Richard I, the southerner, was a man of culture and sophistication. A considerable musician, he had written troubadour lyrics and he took a keen interest in the music of the liturgy. Richard II, though aesthetically ambitious, lacked his predecessor's natural grace and cultivation. His court was among the most brilliant of his day, yet his own contribution to its achievements is hard to identify. Richard III appears to have shown no particular cultural accomplishment at all. Equally striking is the difference in the kings' engagement with chivalry. Richard I donned the mantle of the chivalric king *par excellence*. A brave knight and a gifted commander, he accorded chivalry a key role in his kingship. Richard II, who by contrast did not excel in arms, treated chivalry differently. While he revelled in chivalric ritual, he strove for peace with France and wanted Christians to unite against the infidel. Richard III's attitude was different again. Richard III, it seems, aspired to a reputation in arms. The signs are, however, that he was lacking the soldierly gifts of his namesake and forebear.

It is clear, then, that there were many differences in the tastes and experiences of the three kings. Yet, at the same time, there are striking parallels. In the first place, all three were younger sons. At birth, not one had an expectation of succeeding to the throne (although Richard II did so from fairly early childhood); each of them took the place of an elder brother. Secondly, as Giovanni Biondi was to note in the 1640s, 'All the [Kings] Richard ... came to violent ends'.[4] The first Richard was killed by a stray arrow shot in the course of a siege in the Limousin, while the other two were done to death by challengers who usurped their thrones. Thirdly, as the Crowland chronicler was to note after Richard III's death, all three lacked issue of their bodies (or surviving issue of their bodies) and had to endure debate among their contemporaries about the succession. Fourthly, all three were men of intense piety, for whom religion and political action were closely connected. And fifthly, and finally, all three were men who aroused strong feelings among their contemporaries – and who continue to arouse such feelings today.

These parallels provide a justification for looking at the three kings together. The kings have far more in common than the mere coincidence of the same name. They shared similarities of background, circumstance and experience. A study of the three kings will admittedly be a somewhat unconventional one. It will not be a continuous history under another name. The three Richards cannot be treated in the same way as, say, the three Edwards or the four Georges – as a convenient coat hook on which to hang a study of an eponymous period. The three Richards have to be treated differently, as the subject of a group study. Narrative history will certainly play a part. A summary overview will be provided of all three reigns. But alongside the overview will be set chapters of a thematic nature. The themes covered will, for the most part, be the obvious ones: how the kings responded to the challenge of their relative kinlessness; how they came to meet violent deaths; and how their piety affected their political actions. But other aspects will be considered too: for example, the way in which the three projected themselves as kings and the uses to which they put chivalry as a weapon of political management. And a theme constantly in the background will be the influence of the first Richard's reputation on the other two.

The three Richards have not been lacking in historians. All three have attracted a great deal of scholarly attention. Richard I, indeed, has a place in historical myth. But attitudes to the kings have not been unchanging over time. In different periods people have seen them in different lights. So how have their reputations fared over the centuries?

Richard I's reputation is the one which has experienced the most dramatic shifts over the centuries. To admiring contemporaries, Richard was quite simply the greatest of kings – a brilliant soldier and a champion of the crusade. According to an anonymous versifier, 'his deeds were so great as to bewilder everyone'.[5] Even his enemies admired him: Ibn al Athir, an Islamic writer on the crusades, said that he was 'the most remarkable man of his age'.[6] There were grumblings in England, particularly in his later years, about the heavy burden of taxation which he imposed. None the less, opinions of Richard were broadly favourable.

Richard's reputation continued to flourish in the years after his death. The St Albans chroniclers, Roger Wendover and Matthew Paris, in the 1220s and 1230s described him as the wisest, most merciful and most victorious of kings, while for Geoffrey of Vinsauf his glory spread afar with his mighty name.[7] For much of the middle ages, indeed, Richard's kingship was held up as a model to his successors. Whenever a new king ascended the throne and made an impression on contemporaries, he was hailed as a new Richard. In the 1270s, for example, the young Edward I was said to 'shine like a new Richard'.[8]

At the turn of the sixteenth and seventeenth centuries, however, a change set in. Samuel Daniel in his major work, *Collection of the Historie of England* (1621), sounded a critical note. Daniel complained, as Richard's contemporaries had, of his avarice: 'he exacted and consumed more of this kingdom than all his predecessors from the Normans'. He also added a new string to the bow of complaint – Richard's neglect of England. Richard, he wrote, 'deserved less than any, having neither lived here, neither left behind him any monument of piety or any other public work, or ever showed love or care to this Commonwealth, but only to get what he could from it'.[9] Daniel's critique struck root. His comments were to be picked up and followed in many later discussions of the king. Sir Winston Churchill, for example, in 1675, described Richard as 'the worst of the Richards', 'an ill son, an ill father, an ill brother and a worse king'; and 'that which renders him most unworthy of the affections of his subjects was not only making himself a stranger to them, but leaving them to be governed by a stranger'.[10] A generation later, Laurence Echard argued much the same. 'Though {Richard} had many noble Qualifications, yet England suffered severely under his Government, through the constant occasions he had for money, and the great rapacity of his Justiciaries during his absence from England, where he never spent above eight months of his whole reign.'[11] The key assumption which underpinned all these criticisms was that Richard's priorities were wrong. Although he was king of England, he neglected England in favour of lands elsewhere. This was not a criticism which had been heard in the middle ages. For many writers, indeed, the fact that Richard had foreign ambitions counted in his favour. By the early modern period, however, attitudes to European empire were changing. As English national identity strengthened under pressure of attack from external foes, so a 'little Englander' mentality set in. Among writers of patriotic hue like Echard and Fuller there was a growing sense that the English were 'an island race'. Against this background of narrowing horizons Richard's reputation was bound to suffer.

By the post-medieval period, a second factor began to count against Richard's reputation: his involvement in the crusade. In the world of pre-Reformation religion Richard's commitment to crusading had counted as one of his strengths; indeed, his success against the infidel was cited in sharp contrast to the French king's failure. In the world of reformed Protestantism, however, attitudes were very different. Crusading was unfashionable. It was associated with bigotry and papalism. It was condemned as a barbaric, savage movement. For the arch-rationalist David Hume, the crusades were 'the most signal and most durable monument of human folly that has yet appeared in any age or nation'.[12] With crusading frowned on, there was little hope for the reputation of the king most closely associated with it. Richard's stock sank to new lows. Not only was he accused of draining his country's wealth through taxation; still worse, he was condemned for spending those taxes on a cause of no worth.

These criticisms of the king held the field until quite recent times. As late as 1951, A. L. Poole in his volume in the Oxford History of England could write censoriously: '[Richard] used England as a bank on which to draw and overdraw in order to finance his ambitious exploits abroad'.[13] In 1955 Frank Barlow could write in a similar vein: '[Richard] had merely exhausted his own empire.'[14] Today, these verdicts strike us as anachronistic. They seem more illuminating about the authors' assumptions than about Richard's failings. In the last generation or two, historians have attempted to be more dispassionate. They have embarked on the valuable exercise of looking at Richard's achievement in the light of contemporary opinion. They have addressed such questions as: what expectations did contemporaries have of a king, and how far did Richard live up to them. Attempting to evaluate Richard's achievement in these terms is not easy. It takes more than an effort of imagination to shake off the heavy burden of received opinion. The knots in which an historian can easily tie himself can be sensed in James Brundage's equivocal judgement of Richard. Richard, Brundage began positively, 'judged by the standards of his times and own class of knightly warriors ... was a fine monarch and a very great man, for he exemplified virtues which they most admired'. But then he added the measured qualification: 'the clergy [however] deplored [his] moral failures; and the bourgeoisie were appalled by the insanity of his fiscal policy'.[15] Brundage conspicuously lacks the courage of his convictions. If Richard 'by the standards of his times' was a great king, then why attach such weight to the views of the clergy and bourgeoisie? The most thoroughgoing reassessment of Richard has been made by John Gillingham in his *Richard the Lionheart* (1978), a book which viewed Richard firmly from a continental perspective. This book was revised, and the process of rehabilitation taken further, in the second edition of *Richard I* (1999). Gillingham's arguments, however, have by no means persuaded all of his fellow scholars. R. V. Turner and R. Heiser, for example, in a jointly written study of the king (2000), while recognising Richard's achievement, offer a more qualified judgement. The king was 'brutal and unrelenting in his financial exactions', they write. Although widely admired as a knightly exemplar, he could be oppressive, and he suffered from 'a prickly personality', given to 'outbursts of anger'.[16] Turner and Heiser's Richard is much less of a paragon of virtue than Gillingham's.

Gillingham's view has also been subjected to criticism by David Carpenter. Using Coggeshall's chronicle as a gauge of opinion, Carpenter argues that there were at least some contemporaries to whom John's accession came as a relief, Richard's rule being seen as oppressive. How Richard is viewed depends on which sources are used and what questions are asked. Doubtless the debate will go on.

The reputations of the two later Richards have also been subject to the vicissitudes of changing opinion. Over the centuries the two kings' stock has either risen or fallen, according to the swing of the historical pendulum. By a coincidence of history, the two kings' reputations have been linked. In the work of the early Tudor historians the two Richards were placed at opposite ends of a definable historical sequence. That sequence was held to begin with the fall of Richard II in 1399 and to end with Richard III's death at Bosworth in 1485. Richard II's fall, the Tudors believed, plunged England into a period of bitter dynastic strife from which it was only to be rescued by Henry VII in 1485. The terminal dates of the sequence – 1399 and 1485 – according to this view, were milestones: staging posts in the course of history. As the event which brought the sequence to an end, Richard III's bloody death was invested with especial significance. It was seen as marking the end of the middle ages. The age of darkness was over. A new era of hope had dawned. England could look forward to renewal under the Tudors.

This view of the past encapsulated more than a little myth-making. At its heart, however, there was just enough conviction for it to win acceptance. It was a view that was to find its classic exposition in the works of Shakespeare. Shakespeare interpreted the fifteenth century as a period of disaster.[17] Henry IV's usurpation in 1399, he believed, brought a curse on the Lancastrian dynasty. Henry himself was condemned to an 'unquiet' reign, punctuated by rebellion, while his successor Henry V suffered an early death. In the third generation, in the reign of Henry VI, the full horror of the curse was to be realised. The kingship of Lancaster fell apart. Henry VI was displaced by his Yorkist cousin Edward IV, but Edward, like Bolingbroke before him, was a perjurer. Accordingly, the Yorkist line, like the Lancastrian, was blighted; it could not survive. Punishment came in the next generation with the murder of the two princes and the usurpation of Richard of

Gloucester. But at Bosworth in 1485 the awful misery was brought to an end. The victory of Henry Tudor and his subsequent marriage to Elizabeth of York reconciled the competing lines and brought peace to a disturbed and troubled land.

Shakespeare popularised and lent authority to this Tudor view of the past. However, he was by no means its original begetter. He relied heavily on the authority of earlier writers. He owed a particular debt to a mid-Tudor compilation, Edward Hall's *Union of the Two Illustre Families of Lancaster and York*, published in 1548 and a work which was itself a recycling of two earlier histories – Polydore Vergil's *Anglica Historia* and Thomas More's *History of King Richard III*. Vergil and More were the real inventors of the Tudor view of the past. Vergil's work was particularly influential. Vergil offered an overarching vision of the fifteenth century. What he did was bring together the fates of the two Richards, demonstrating that the second Richard's fall was the cause of the period of chaos which came to an end at Bosworth. Vergil's view of the past was one that was to hold good for three centuries.

In Tudor historiography Richard II's fate was thus inseparably linked to the story of the fifteenth century. As a result of the king's fall, it was believed, England was plunged into the horror of the Wars of the Roses. This linkage had a distorting effect on later study of the reign. It led to a concentration on the king's final two years – the period from 1397 to his overthrow. What interested the Tudor historians was Richard's quarrel with Henry of Lancaster. Everything before that was irrelevant. It had no bearing on his eventual fate. When Shakespeare began his play in 1398, therefore, he was merely following Hall and the others. He began the story where his audience expected him to begin it.

The Tudor approach to Richard affected interpretations of his reign in a second way. Inevitably, the king was seen as a capricious tyrant. He had to be. Dynastic logic required it. The ruling Tudor dynasty traced its descent from Henry of Lancaster, and Henry of Lancaster had deposed Richard. It followed, then, that Henry must have been in the right and Richard in the wrong. The early literary portrayals of Richard reflected this train of thought. Richard was seen as an immature and irresponsible youngster. No impression was given that he ever grew up. To Vergil he was a weak-willed youth lacking in strength of character, while to Samuel Daniel in the 1590s he was a young effeminate over-influenced by others.[18] In the histories of Hall and Hayward he was made to attribute his downfall to youthful misjudgement. The Tudor typecasting of character was reinforced by reference to his personal appearance. Richard was widely regarded as a man of outstanding good looks. In the Wilton Diptych and in the Westminster Abbey portrait he is shown as elegant and handsome. The very attractiveness of his features now conspired against him. He was condemned as effeminate. His weakness was seen as physical as well as mental. He was considered lacking in strength. Richard was launched on his career as a fop. The looking-glass scene in Shakespeare's play reflected this. As Margaret Aston has so rightly said, the scene is not history, but is linked to the Tudor view of it.[19]

At the other end of the historical sequence stands Richard III. Richard was on the throne for only a little over two years. He was crowned in July 1483 and killed in battle in August 1485. His reign was of little historical importance. It was marked by few legislative or constitutional achievements. And yet it continues to generate interest on a quite disproportionate scale. Many dozens of books have been written about Richard. Since the end of the Second World War there have been at least ten. And the number of articles runs into many thousands. The tide shows no signs of abating.

The popular view of Richard as a villainous schemer owes much to the first and second generations of Tudor historians. For a long time, these men have been dismissed as mere placemen: timeservers or partisan hacks who wrote narratives to order. Their history, it is said, was Tudor official history; it was propagandist. Certainly, a number of them enjoyed the direct patronage of the Tudors. On the whole, however, they were not party hacks. They were writers with minds of their own and, in some cases, were considerable scholars. They sought information as and where they could find it. They drew on contemporary written sources – chronicles and other narratives, for example. But they were also on the look-out for anecdote, reminiscence or gossip. They had a range of informants. There were men still alive who had served Richard in some capacity. But, most of all, there were those senior figures who had grown up under Richard and who were great in the government of his successor – men like Cardinal Morton, Sir Reginald Bray, Bishop Fox and Christopher Urswick. It was these men whose view of the past did so much to determine how that past would be seen in the future.

The first writer to manifest a distinctly 'Tudor' view of the past was an unlikely figure, a Warwickshire chaplain by the name of John Rous.[20] Rous was an amateur antiquary and a minor clerk in the service of the earls of Warwick. If anyone deserves the title of party hack, it is he. In Richard III's lifetime he had written approvingly of the king. In his history of the earls of Warwick, he had paid tribute to Richard, hailing him as a good lord and mighty prince. But with the king's downfall he immediately changed tack. He now preferred to denounce Richard as 'Antichrist'.[21] Some of the stories he told were absurd. Supposing that Richard was born under Scorpio, he said that like a scorpion he displayed a smooth front and a vicious swinging tail. He invented the strange story of the circumstances of his birth: Richard, he said, was born with teeth in his mouth and hair down to his shoulders and lay sullenly in his mother's womb for two years. Some of his more believable yarns entered the Tudor canon: that Richard murdered his nephews, for example; that he was responsible for the death of Henry VI; and that he poisoned his wife and imprisoned her mother for life. His mind was nothing if not inventive.

Rous's work drew on stories circulating in the 1490s. In other works of Henry VII's reign, very little was added to his account. Even Bernard Andre's semi-official *Life of Henry VII* added nothing to the charge sheet. Indeed, in some respects it retreated: Andre's history did not charge Richard with the murder of his wife.

The Tudor tradition proper began with two works from the early years of Henry VIII, both of them famous: Polydore Vergil's *Historia Anglica* of 1513 and More's *History of King Richard III* of a year or two later. Vergil and More were both master technicians – humanistic scholars with a strong sense of the importance of their craft. More's *History* is perhaps the more vivid work. It has been termed 'the first piece of modern English prose'.[22] And certainly it lacks nothing in colour. The opening description of Richard sets the tone. The king, More says, was

little of stature, ill-featured of limbs, crook backed, his left shoulder much higher than his right, hard favoured of visage ... he was malicious, wrathful, envious, and from afore his birth ever froward. It is for truth reported that the Duchess his mother had so much ado in her travail, that she could not be delivered of him uncut: and that he came into the world with the feet forward … and (as the fame runneth) also not untoothed … He was close and secret, a deep dissimuler, lowly of countenance, arrogant of heart, outwardly companionable where he inwardly hated, not letting to kiss whom he hoped to kill, dispiteous and cruel.[23]

More enlivens his narrative by working in many wonderfully described scenes – the entrapment of Hastings in the Tower being the most famous – and the dramatic power of his work is enhanced by the extensive use of dialogue. More's Richard is a terrible monster, evil incarnate – someone entirely removed from human life. More's exaggerations and inaccuracies devalue his work in the eyes of a modern reader. But More's aim was not to produce dispassionate history; it was to turn the spotlight on tyranny. More deliberately set out to write the life of a bad prince: to offer instruction by negative example. Very likely, he saw the works of Tacitus and Suetonius as models. When he over-coloured his narrative, it was always to underpin his moral purpose.

Vergil's *Historia Anglica* is a very different work.[24] It is a complete history of England down to Henry VII's accession. Its aim was to justify the Tudor dynasty to the *litterati* and *glitterati* of Europe. Vergil was an accomplished humanist. The quality of his artistry shows in all sorts of ways – in his stylistic mannerisms, his respect for literary precedent, and his skilful treatment of his sources. He avoided overcolouring his narrative; the crudities of characterisation that appealed to More were not for him. His writing style is moderate and measured. While he vilified Richard, he carefully refrained from wholesale blackening. He created his literary effects by a subtle combination of devices. One of his favourite tricks was to imply that Richard was a dissimulator, saying one thing and doing another – in this way suggesting that he concealed ambition behind a façade of reasonable behaviour. When recounting the events of 1483, he says, for example, that Richard, hearing of his brother's death, burned with ardour for the throne; and yet he swore loyalty to his widow and son. At an earlier point in his narrative, he made use of counterpoint. He recalled that in April Richard summoned all 'the honourable and worshipful' of Yorkshire to swear allegiance to Edward V. Richard, he said, 'was himself the first that took the oath: which soon after he was the first to violate'. Innuendo, smear and guilt by association were never far from Vergil's thoughts as he wrote.

For all his influence on later writers, Vergil said little that was new about Richard. In fact he said remarkably little about Richard at all. Richard's reign formed only a small part of his overall narrative. Vergil's contribution to the development of Richard's reputation is found principally in a different area. His achievement was to give meaning to his reign. He supplied it with a context. Previous writers had treated Richard's reign in isolation. They had seen his evil as unique evil. Vergil saw things differently. He showed Richard's reign to be the final stage in a grand historical sequence. That sequence had begun three-quarters of a century earlier with Henry of Lancaster's seizure of the crown; it had continued with the descent of the Lancastrian monarchy into anarchy; it had been made worse by Edward IV's seizure of the crown; and it had reached its terrifying climax in Richard III's career of infamy. It was Vergil, in other words, who invented the notion of the Wars of the Roses. It was Vergil who was the originator of the Tudor myth. Later in the century Shakespeare transformed these ideas into a dramatic historical cycle. In his characterisation of Richard he created a Macchiavellian, but engaging, stage villain. But the underlying idea was Vergil's.

It was not until the seventeenth century that a challenge was mounted to the picture of Richard as 'England's black legend'. The first to offer a revisionist view was Sir George Buck, an antiquary and courtier who was James I's Master of the Revels. Buck's *History of King Richard III* is a prolix and difficult work, poorly organised and marked by lengthy digressions.[25] None the less, it is a work of seminal importance. Drawing on manuscripts in Sir Robert Cotton's library, it offered one highly significant new insight. Richard had been suspected of pressing a marriage suit on an unwilling Elizabeth of York, Edward IV's daughter. Buck showed that Elizabeth, so far from rejecting a possible match with Richard, positively encouraged one. Buck's *History* drew on a range of contemporary sources – he was the first, for example, to make use of the manuscript of the Crowland Chronicle – and he rebutted the more extreme inaccuracies of Vergil and More. For its date, his book was a remarkable achievement.

In the eighteenth century, the assault on the Tudor orthodoxy was taken up by a vigorous controversialist, Horace Walpole. Walpole's *Historic Doubts*, published in 1768, was a work of dilettantism not scholarly research.[26] Its approach was essentially negative, assaulting the

Tudor tradition but putting little or nothing in its place. Its defence of
Richard was thoroughgoing. Walpole acquitted Richard of all the main
crimes of which he stood accused, from the stabbing of Henry VI's son,
Edward, to the despatching of the princes. Whether he convinced many
of his readers is another matter. In the nineteenth century the tempo of
attack and defence quickened. A number of works maintained the
assault on Richard. The most notable of these were John Lingard's *History of England* (down to the reign of Henry VII) and James Gairdner's
Life and Reign of Richard the Third (1878).[27] Gairdner's was for long to
remain a standard study. Outnumbering these books, however, was a flow
of revisionist works. Sharon Turner's *History of England in the Middle
Ages* (1830) adopted a moderate position, absolving Richard of some of
his crimes, but charging him with the murder of the princes.[28] Caroline
Halsted and A. O. Legge went much further in their championing of the
king, even absolving him of the princes' murders.[29] Halsted's study,
appropriately the work of the wife of a rector of Middleham, where
Richard had lived in the 1470s, was actually of some value. Although
written in an affecting, 'even melting', prose, it embodied solid research
and made pioneering use of the king's letter book.[30]

 In the twentieth century the work of rehabilitating the king's reputation gathered pace. Sir Clements Markham, a one-time sailor and
administrator turned amateur historian, mounted a vigorous defence of
the king in his *Richard III: His Life and Character* (1906). Markham's
intention was to write a book that was both scholarly and authoritative,
and his work on the sources was certainly considerable. He had an
unfortunate tendency, however, to ruin his case by overstatement. By
the middle of the century, writers of fiction were joining in the campaign to clear the king's name. Josephine Tey's *The Daughter of Time*
(1951) and Rosemary Hawley Jarman's *We Speak No Treason* (1971) were
perhaps the two most celebrated examples of the fictional genre, both of
them arousing widespread popular interest. Josephine Tey's book,
couched in the form of a detective story, directly addressed the issue of
the murder of the princes, clearing Richard of blame and pointing the
finger of guilt at Henry VII.[31] In 1955 a milestone in Ricardian studies
was passed with the publication of Paul Murray Kendall's *Richard III*.
This celebrated book, an intelligent if over-imaginative defence of the
king, was for long to remain the standard biography.[32]

Just when Richard appeared to have scored a posthumous triumph over his opponents, the pendulum began to swing back. A reaction set in, and the king's critics found themselves triumphing in argument again. What, more than anything else, precipitated this shift was a new interest in the sources for the reign. Scholars were keen to discover the origins of Richard's early reputation. Since the time of Buck, it had been conventional to say that the Tudor historians had created the picture of Richard as a tyrannical monster. But what were the materials from which they had fashioned that view? And how had they gathered and sifted their information? In a notable study published in 1975, Alison Hanham turned the spotlight on the seminal works of Vergil and More. Searching their texts for evidence of the sources they used, and then analysing the sources themselves, she came to a surprising conclusion: Vergil and his contemporaries did not invent the view of the monster Richard; they found it in the sources they used. While it is true, she says, that they exaggerated the critical emphasis, they were by no means its first begetters.[33]

In the twenty years since she wrote, Hanham's conclusions have been broadly accepted by other scholars in the field. It is now virtually impossible for anyone to maintain that Richard's evil reputation was entirely the fabrication of the Tudor historians. As our understanding of the historiographical development has deepened, so it has become clearer that 'Black Richard' was a perception of some at least of the king's contemporaries.

The point can be illustrated by looking at one of the most familiar of the early sources – the so-called 'Second Continuation of the Crowland Chronicle'.[34] Hanham has shown conclusively that this chronicle was drawn on by Vergil. Its strength is that it is the work of an insider. The author shows a ready familiarity with the workings of government. He talks knowledgeably about defensive measures, royal finance and appointments to local office. It has been suggested that the narrative was written by Richard's chancellor, John Russell, bishop of Lincoln.[35] Russell was someone with long experience of government. However, a rival case has been made for the authorship of Henry Sharp, a councillor of Edward IV and a senior royal clerk.[36] Sharp is in many ways a more plausible candidate than Russell. Against his claims, however, can be set the fact that he was largely retired from administration by the 1480s.[37]

But, whoever the author (and it could have been either man), it is clear that he wrote fairly soon after the battle of Bosworth, perhaps as early as 1486. There are no indications that his thinking was influenced by Tudor propaganda. The date of composition will hardly allow for that. Yet its tone is overwhelmingly hostile to Richard. The message is clear: the criticism of Richard began in his lifetime.

The critical attitude of the Crowland Chronicler is evident right from the beginning. He makes clear his low regard for Richard as a soldier. He says that when, before he became king, Richard invaded Scotland in 1482 he returned to England empty-handed.[38] When he moves onto the events of the usurpation in the following year, his attitude becomes more critical still. Time and again, he stresses Richard's deceitful behaviour. He says that when Richard entered the capital, his expressions of goodwill to the queen and her elder son could not conceal 'a circumstance of growing anxiety' – that is, the detention of the young king's relatives and servants.[39] By mid-June, after Richard and Buckingham had secured the king's younger brother, he says, 'they no longer acted in secret but openly manifested their intentions'.[40] After the news of Rivers's execution, he records his condemnation: 'this was the second innocent blood which was shed on occasion of this sudden change'.[41] When Richard produced a story of the princes' bastardy, the author says this was merely 'the pretext for an act of usurpation'.[42] He continued to be scathing after Richard's seizure of the crown. He was particularly critical of Richard's intrusion of northerners into administrative positions in the south – the southern people, he said, longed for the return of their old lords in place of the 'tyranny' of the northern men.[43] He condemned the king's levying of 'forced loans' or benevolences, a form of taxation which, he says, Richard had previously condemned in parliament. He reports, with obvious disgust, that Richard's unscrupulous agents extracted immense sums from the king's subjects.[44] But then he apostrophises, implying that he knew far more than he could tell: 'Oh God, why should we dwell on this subject, multiplying our recital of things so distasteful, and so pernicious in their example that we ought not so much as to suggest them to the minds of the perfidious.'[45] The author of the Crowland Continuation, although probably one of Richard's ministers or clerks, was not to be numbered among his admirers.

A similar note of criticism was struck in a second major narrative of the time, Domenico Mancini's account of the usurpation. Mancini's narrative was only brought to widespread public notice in the last century. The text of it was found by C. A. J. Armstrong in the municipal archives at Lille in 1934. The discovery represented a major breakthrough in Ricardian studies. Mancini was an eyewitness to the usurpation. He was staying in London in the crucial weeks of the summer of 1483 and watched events unfolding before him. His style was that of the classical humanist. He wrote a rounded rather than a sharply focused account. He generally refrained from expressing his own opinions. He weighed one factor against another and considered alternatives. He was above all judicious. And yet, for all this, his attitude is clear. He did not like Richard. He believed that Richard was aiming for the throne all along. He regarded his motives as essentially selfish. He says that Richard's explanations for arresting Edward V and for executing Hastings were all untrue. For most of his account he is content to speak through the opinions of others. He says (typically) that one person said this and another said that. But his indictment of the king is all the more damning for that reason. It provides evidence of the deep popular distrust to which Richard's ambition gave rise.

Mancini's is by far the most important contemporary narrative to have come down to us. It provides us with a more authoritative account of Richard's *coup d'état* than any other. As Michael Hicks has written, discovery of the text should have revolutionised Ricardian studies.[46] Yet strangely, as he also observes, it did not. The main reason for this is that it confirmed opinions rather than challenged them. It did not undermine the Tudor account; it actually lent it support. The fact that Mancini was consistent with More was awkward, even strange; but it did not upset anything. Today the position is very different. We can appreciate the full significance of Mancini's witness. The Tudors did not invent the character of black Richard. The blackening of Richard was begun by his contemporaries.

In the last few years the battle for Richard's reputation has accordingly gone full circle. After a period when Richard's defenders were firmly in the ascendant, opinion has swung back to roughly where it was. The argument is generally accepted that Richard was accused of unscrupulous behaviour by at least some of his contemporaries. The counter-argument that these contemporaries were mainly southerners may or may not convince. The controversies surrounding Richard have done much to illuminate his character and motives. There are many things about him on which we are now far better informed than we were. But a partisan approach can only take us so far. For this reason, the terms of the debate about Richard are now shifting. Instead of yet again going over whether or not Richard was a good king, or whether or not he killed the princes, historians are now asking different questions. They are asking, in particular, what the norms of political behaviour were. They want to know, for example, what expectations contemporaries had of their kings. What did the job of a king consist of? In other words, they are exploring the mentalities of the age. These are issues which are germane to the careers of all three Richards. Accordingly, it is to the matter of political society and its assumptions that we now turn.

The tomb of Richard I, and his mother Eleanor of Aquitaine, at Fontevrault. (*A. F. Kersting*)

2

Kingship in Medieval England

When in the 1590s William Shakespeare embarked on his epic history cycle, he constructed his story around kings and dynasties. Beginning with Richard II's deposition in 1399, he traced the rise and fall of the house of Lancaster, the replacement of Lancaster by York, Richard III's grisly death at Bosworth, and the triumphant establishment on the throne of the Tudors. Constructing his story around kings seemed natural to him. His epic tale of national degeneracy and rebirth centred on kings. Kings gave bodily expression to the polities they ruled. Kingship was the most vital, the most significant social and political institution of the age. In his own queen, the Gloriana Elizabeth, Shakespeare could see monarchical power exercised with the charismatic force that it had been in the middle ages.

The English had been familiar with the institution of monarchy from time immemorial. In the form in which it was later to develop, kingship had arrived with the Saxons in the fifth and sixth centuries. By the twelfth century, the English were learning something of the shadowy pre-Saxon kings from Geoffrey of Monmouth's *History of the Kings of Britain*, written in the 1130s and quickly a best seller. Geoffrey's world, a fabulous yet seductive creation, was a world full of kings – kings with such exotic names as Belindus and Lud, Cadwallo and Cadwallader, Arthur and Uther Pendragon. Geoffrey satisfied his readers' longing for a compelling origins myth – a re-creation of the past which provided a romantic backcloth to the more prosaic present. He concocted the story of misguided old King Lear. He conjured up the legends of King Arthur and the Knights of the Round Table. He even launched Old King Cole on his career as a merry old soul. Geoffrey's account was regarded with scepticism by the more sober-minded historians of the day. Even Bede's solidly rooted *Ecclesiastical History*, however, had attested a world in which kings were ever-present. 'Kings', 'sub kings' and 'princes' abound in Bede's pages. No wonder that, centuries later, John of Gaunt was to think of England as 'this royal throne of kings'.

The multiplication of kings in early England resulted from the process of dislocation which followed the Romans' withdrawal. Between the fifth century and the seventh a network of tribal kingdoms was established, much as Bede had recorded in his *History*. There were kingdoms in Kent, Wessex, Mercia, Northumbria, East Anglia, to name but the most important, and all of them had their kings and their kingly stock. Only gradually was the number of kingdoms whittled down. In the eighth and ninth centuries there was a process of amalgamation and merger, by which the smaller kingdoms were absorbed into the larger, leaving only one substantial polity after the Viking onslaught – that of Wessex. In the tenth century Wessex, through its conquest of the former Danelaw, became England. By the last century before the Conquest England assumed the character of a unitary monarchy. However, centralisation preserved within it old habits and assumptions. Right into the Angevin period people thought in terms of a kingly stock – a widely defined family from whom kings could be chosen.

From the early medieval period English kingship – European kingship, indeed – acquired one of its most distinctive characteristics. This was the merging of the public and the private spheres. What this meant was that the king combined in his person capacities which would later be regarded as separate. In one capacity, he was a public figure, a ruler, a crowned head: someone who was set apart from his subjects. In the other, he was a private lord, a proprietor, the owner of land, his rule having something of the character of lordship. This second capacity found expression in the term used to describe the land attached to the royal office. This was known as the demesne – from the Latin *dominicus*, one's own; it was the king's own estate. In the unsettled early middle ages, when institutionally kingship was weaker, the exercise of lordship had greatly strengthened royal power. In the ninth century, for example, Alfred had used the exercise of lordship to powerful effect to create a following in his wars against the Danes. After the Conquest, when England was feudalised, this lordly or territorial aspect of royal power took on a new form. This was the doctrine that the entire land of England was held from the king. In other words, the great men of the

realm were legally the king's tenants or 'vassals'. By virtue of this relationship, they had to perform homage to him and they risked forfeiture
if they betrayed him. In this way the public and the personal aspects of
kingship were bound ever more closely together. Before the twelfth century there was a powerful sense of the king as a lord, with the realm his
estate. However, there was also a recognition of rulership as something
greater, an office with responsibilities attached. The 'public' was never
lost sight of alongside the 'private'.

The obligations imposed on the king were conventionally expressed
in the oath which he swore at his coronation. Largely a creation of the
tenth century, the English oath comprised three main parts. The king
was required to swear, first, to protect the Church; secondly, to maintain the peace; and, thirdly, to administer proper justice to his subjects.
At Edward II's coronation in 1308, a fourth clause was added: the king
was to swear to uphold the laws which the realm should choose. In
this fourfold form the oath was administered to all kings down to the
seventeenth century. The oath embodied the conventional medieval
expectations of a king. In the advice literature of the time the king
was enjoined to keep his subjects in peace and to be merciful in his
judgements.

At the heart of the institution of kingship was an assumption inherited from biblical times: that kings were set over men by God. The king
exercised governance *dei gratia*, by the grace of God; he was God's vicar,
a deputy for God himself. In the twelfth century this lofty-sounding
doctrine was challenged by the pope's claim to be a mediator between
man and God. Papal pretensions to such a role were fiercely resisted by
the kings of the day. Kings saw themselves as directly legitimated by
God, and much of the ceremonial and imagery that surrounded them
gave expression to this view. Visually, the notion of the sacred was most
clearly articulated in the anointing ceremony at the heart of the coronation. As the great ritual reached its climax, after the singing of the
psalms, the king was touched on the head and the shoulders with
chrism, the holy oil used in baptism and confirmation. In this way, it
was believed, the king was given something of the character of a priest,
invested with sacral powers, and set apart from other mortals. Earlier in
the service, the oath would have been administered to him. The purpose
of the oath was to remind him that, while he was above men, he was

also under obligation to men. The impact of the oath, however, was in practice somewhat limited. For the way in which he behaved in office, the king was answerable only to God. Towards his subjects, in contrast, he was free. As John Gower was to say in the 1380s, 'his estate should be free towards all other than God'.[1]

On the Continent exalted notions of kingship received support from the nostrums of Roman law. At the heart of the Roman tradition was a view of the prince as supreme lawgiver. The king created the law; and, because of this, he could not be bound by the law. As the legists put, 'the will of the king has the force of law'; or 'the king is free of the law'. In France, a land in which the Roman legal tradition flourished, the king's power was greatly reinforced by the view of his position as both the maker and upholder of the law. In England, however, despite the partial assimilation of continental legal ideas after the Conquest, the Roman system of law never properly took root. A ruler of high kingly ambition, like Richard II, might mouth the Roman adage that 'the laws were in the king's breast or in his mouth'.[2] In practice, however, in medieval England the realisation of such a vision was impossible. The law of England was, and was to remain, the unwritten common law – in other words, that body of custom and legislation created by the increasingly regular rhythms of royal government. As enforcer and upholder of the common law the king was embedded within that law. In a sense, by the twelfth and thirteenth centuries he was a victim of the successes of his own government. For the greater his achievement in familiarising his subjects with regular legal routines, the stronger the expectation from his subjects that he too respect those routines. The outcome of the changing climate of expectation was the constitutional revolution represented by Magna Carta (1215). Magna Carta changed for ever the relationship between the king and the law in England. Its achievement was to bring the institution of kingship under the law. In the Charter's most famous clause (clause 39) King John swore to arrest or disseise no one except by the law of the land. No later king was to question or challenge this principle. In 1225 Magna Carta was confirmed by John's son Henry III, and in many subsequent reigns it was confirmed again. The body of rights that the king was left with was known as the prerogative. This is best regarded as the assortment of powers that he was free to exercise at will – for example, appointing officials and

summoning and dissolving parliaments. Outside these limited areas he
was bound by the law. As 'Bracton' was to put it in the 1230s, 'the king
is below God and below the law'.[3] The king of England stood in a position roughly between a medieval French monarch and a modern
constitutional monarch. In Fortescue's elegant formulation, the kingdom of England was a *dominium regale et politicum* – a dominion regal
and political. It had a 'mixed' constitution, something that distinguished
it from its neighbours.[4]

What Fortescue was articulating in his dictum was an old idea,
although his conceptualisation of it was new. As the authors of advice
literature regularly pointed out, the king ruled for the 'common good'.
He did not rule solely in accordance with his own interests. Only a
tyrant did that. And a tyrant, by definition, was a ruler who was above
the law. A ruler like the king of England protected or advanced the
'common weal', as it was called, the common interest. He cherished the
wellbeing of his subjects. The doing of justice was the true measure of
his rule. 'Do law always; that is a king', John Gower was to remark
around 1400. To work for the common good was a Christian principle,
it was believed, and tyranny an offence against God. As the English
envoys said to the French king in 1439, 'God made not his people ... for
the princes; he made the princes for his service and the weal ... of his
people'.[5]

Central to the exercise of kingship was the taking of counsel. The king
was in need of wise counsel, for in wisdom he discovered the will of
God. The more widely he took counsel, the better would be the quality
of his government. As Fortescue put it, many heads are better than one.[6]
Counsellors advised the king; they informed him and debated with him.
Their task was to speak disinterestedly for the common good. Kings
searched out wise counsel wherever and whenever they could. All English late medieval kings had formal conciliar bodies, composed of
'councillors', men who were sometimes appointed and paid as such.
However, most of the advice, or 'counsel' as it was known, which kings
received was given to them informally, by magnates or attendants as
much as by ministers and councillors. Informal 'counsel' very likely
played a more important role in determining issues of policy than formal 'council'. Often formal councils dealt only with routine, day-to-day,
administrative matters.

A great responsibility rested on the shoulders of those charged with giving advice to the king. They had to be committed to maintaining the king's rights – in the words of their oath, 'to counsel, prefer, increase and advance the welfare and prosperity of his lord and most especially of his sovereign lord'. Furthermore, they had to advise honestly and without partiality, and to accept whatever decision resulted even if they were overruled. Giving counsel was a difficult and a demanding task. Counsellors risked the king's enmity if they gave him critical advice. But equally they could profit from the opportunities for personal gain made available to them. Michael de la Pole, earl of Suffolk, Richard II's chancellor and leading councillor, was driven from office in 1386 following allegations that he used his office to secure personal advantage.

Much political debate in the middle ages centred on who the king's counsellors should be and how they should be chosen. In theory, the king was free to choose his own counsellors: this was an aspect of the prerogative. But in practice there was an expectation that he would choose men 'of wisdom, cunning and experience ... whom he could trust'. When the affairs of the realm were going badly, it was his counsellors who were singled out for blame, for there was a convention that the king himself was above reproach. Reform in these circumstances could only be achieved by replacing one set of counsellors by another. In 1386, for example, after de la Pole's dismissal, a new 'continual' council was appointed for twelve months at the Commons' behest. Councils imposed on the king against his will, however, rarely lasted for long. In medieval theory the king was entirely free in his estate; he could not be constrained. It followed from this that he should choose his own counsellors – which, except at times of momentary weakness, he generally did. And most of his subjects appear to have been happy with that.

Kingship in late medieval England was sustained by an impressive apparatus of bureaucracy and administration.[7] In the palace of Westminster, cheek by jowl with the king's own apartments, were the offices of the central government. These can be said to have comprised two main categories, the secretarial and the financial. The main secretarial office was the chancery, whose head, the chancellor, had custody of the great seal. Great seal letters could be issued on orders from the king under the privy seal (a lesser seal) or, later, under the signet, or simply by royal word of mouth: the letters would then be dispatched 'patent'

(open) or 'close', as appropriate. On the financial side the main office
was the exchequer, which audited the sheriffs' accounts and collected
the greater part of royal income. Periodically, other financial agencies
aspired to challenge exchequer supremacy. In the reigns of the first two
Edwards, for example, the wardrobe established for itself a position as
the office principally responsible for the payment of the wages of war.
After Edward II's deposition, however, the exchequer succeeded in re-
establishing its pre-eminence over all other bodies. The king's needs for
a private income were met by the chamber, which annually received a
subvention from the exchequer.

A link between the Westminster-based bureaucracy and the wider
realm was provided by the local administration in the shires. The key
official at county level was the sheriff, whose duties included serving and
returning writs, collecting the county farms (revenues) and apprehend-
ing malefactors. In the thirteenth century, in recognition of his growing
workload, the sheriff was joined by a group of new officials. Chief
among these were the escheator, who collected the crown's feudal revenues; the coroner, who recorded the pleas of the crown; and the
keepers, later the justices, of the peace. Unlike the clerks in the central
offices at Westminster, these local officials were not full-time employ-
ees. They were members of the country gentry who served largely out of
self-interest and received allowances to cover their expenses.

By the standards of the day, medieval England was a much governed
country. A carefully articulated chain of command linked the king,
through the sheriff, to his lesser officials and his subjects. Yet there were
limits to the king's capacity to secure obedience. In particular, the king
was lacking in instruments of coercive power. For example, he had no
local police force or standing army at his disposal. He had in his service
no equivalents of the French *intendants*. Although he had a paid bureaucracy on his doorstep at Westminster, this was more concerned with
recording and disseminating information than with enforcing his
wishes. In a sense, the impressive-looking edifice of royal power was
embarrassingly hollow. The king, should he be confronted with opposition from his own subjects, had only his corps of household troops to
turn to.

To translate his commands into action, therefore, the king had
to engage the goodwill and cooperation of his greater subjects. He

had to show them that it was worth their while to serve him. He had to give them a stake in his rule. Generally, he did not find the task particularly difficult. There were a variety of ways in which both he and they needed each other. The great men of the realm – the nobility and lords – looked to the king as the ultimate guarantor of the law which upheld their title to property. Without effective kingship, they were in no position to enjoy their revenues in peace. They looked to the king for the resolution of major disputes – less because they stood in awe of him than because submission to him entailed no loss of face. At a more basic level they also looked to him for the regular flow of patronage. They relied on the small change of patronage – grants, money, offices – to recruit retainers and to maintain their position locally. A noble without access to the king's ear was a noble without power in his locality. Yet at the same time, just as the nobility stood in need of the king, so the king stood in need of the nobility. The nobility were his leading counsellors, the commanders of his forces in war, and the main agents of his rule in the localities. The king and the nobility needed each other. The relationship between the two was rarely confrontational; rather, it was one of mutual cooperation and dependence. The king and the nobles were not so much enemies as allies. If trouble broke out between them, it was less because of an inherent clash of interests than because of genuine disagreements over personnel and policy.

The kings of England in this period may all be considered, in a broad sense, members of one royal line – the Angevins. The Angevin family took their name from Anjou, the area of western France in the Loire valley centring on Chinon and Angers. The Angevins had been established on the throne of England in 1154, as a result of Henry of Anjou's marriage to Henry I's daughter, Matilda. Although the direct line of descent came to an end in 1399, with the deposition of the childless Richard II, the two cadet branches that followed were both sprung from the same stem – the Lancastrians being descended from the third son of Edward III and the Yorkists, by female descent, from the second. The Angevins were later to be known as the Plantagenets. This was a name coined by Duke Richard of York in 1460 to stress the legitimacy of his descent from Count Geoffrey of Anjou, Henry II's father. One of the Angevins' symbols had been the broom pod or *planta genista*.

The Angevin origins of the dynasty led to a strengthening of England's long-standing ties with the continental mainland. Throughout the period before the Conquest England had enjoyed close links with continental Europe. By the tenth century a nexus of cultural, social and political ties joined England to the Frankish lands and even to the Rhineland and Italy. Several Anglo-Saxon monarchs, notably Æthelred II, had taken foreign-born spouses. A turning-point, however, was represented by the Conquest in 1066. By virtue of this aggressive act, England was drawn into a dynastic union with the duchy of Normandy. A new political structure was created. From this time, the English kingdom and the duchy were ruled by a single person (or, at least, a single family), journeying backwards and forwards across the Channel. In the 1140s the link was temporarily broken by the separation of England and Normandy in the civil war of King Stephen's reign. However, it was reconstituted in 1154 on the accession of Henry I's grandson, Henry, count of Anjou. The new Angevin structure, for all its similarities, was different in both scale and nature from the Norman 'empire' which had preceded it. Not only was it very much bigger, for to England and Normandy were now joined Anjou itself – Henry II's inheritance – and Aquitaine further south, the inheritance of Henry's wife Eleanor; it was also more loosely structured. Each land was governed in accordance with its own customs. No attempts were made at political harmonisation. The only attribute that the lands had in common was a shared allegiance to the same ruler.

The effect of the creation of the new Angevin 'confederation' was to involve England in near-continuous war. The sheer scale of the Angevins' territories aroused the enmity of the kings of France. The Angevins' lands were not just very much larger than the French kingdom (which comprised little more than the Ile de France), the revenues they yielded were much greater. Already, in the years following the Conquest the French kings had made several attempts to sever the link between England and Normandy. In the Angevin period they renewed and intensified these efforts. Philip Augustus of France (1180–1223) took advantage of Richard's absence on crusade and subsequent captivity in Germany to annex parts of Normandy. The gains which he made at that time were quickly reversed on Richard's release. But on the latter's death in 1199 and John's subsequent accession he renewed the assault.

In 1204, after a brief burst of campaigning, he conquered Anjou and, shortly after it, Normandy. From that time on, the Angevin kings were to be resident largely in England. The link between England and Aquitaine, down in the south, was to survive for very much longer. Aquitaine, although a long way from England, was also a long way from Paris and resisted the Capetian urge to expand. Aquitaine remained a dominion of the English crown down to the final English defeat in 1453. The economies of England and Aquitaine neatly complemented each other, Bordeaux sending wine to England, and the latter cloth or grain in return. The two lands were, however, separately governed. No attempts were made at administrative assimilation.

In the fourteenth century fresh Anglo-French tensions were generated by the dispute over the succession to the French crown. In 1328 Charles IV, the last in the direct line of the Capetians, died without issue. The two candidates with the best claim to succeed were his cousin, Philip of Valois, and his nephew, Edward III of England (the son of his sister Isabella). Unsurprisingly, the French nobility and judges awarded the crown to Philip, and Edward, a minor at the time, accepted their decision. Only some twelve years later, by which time he had revealed himself a ruler of ambition, did he formally lodge his claim. The war which resulted, known as the Hundred Years' War, is usually regarded as a war for the French crown. But its immediate origins were actually feudal. What precipitated hostilities was a dispute over Aquitaine. In 1259 Henry III had agreed to hold the duchy from the French king by liege homage. Liege homage was the tightest and most exacting form of feudal homage, giving the French king extensive rights over his vassal. He could demand service from him; he could interfere in his lands; and receive appeals from his courts. As a result of these impositions, the position of the king-duke by the fourteenth century had became intolerable. In the summer of 1337, in the wake of Edward III's defiance of a summons from his overlord, the latter confiscated the duchy, in this way provoking hostilities. When Edward shortly assumed the title and arms of king of France, he did so as a direct response to the problems that he faced in Aquitaine.

The war, once begun, proved difficult to end. Edward's celebrated victories in the field, at Crécy, Poitiers and elsewhere, greatly strengthened him in his dealings with the French ministers. Yet the knock-out blow which alone could have delivered final victory eluded him. Contrary to expectation, after the French king's capture at Poitiers in 1356 the French government did not collapse or capitulate. From time to time, English negotiators offered to renounce the English claim in return for concessions in Aquitaine – for example, a grant of the duchy in full sovereignty or the recognition of greatly enlarged boundaries. But a compromise deal was never struck. In the end, the dispute was resolved not by negotiation but by the total victory of one side over the other. In the summer of 1453 the last English force, under the command of the earl of Shrewsbury, was defeated at Castillon, and the English expelled from Aquitaine once and for all. The dominions of the English crown were henceforth confined almost entirely to north of the Channel. To the south, only the port of Calais was left.

Just as the fortunes of the English monarchy in France ebbed and flowed, so too did its fortunes in the British Isles. Although after the Conquest the Norman or Angevin kings were mainly preoccupied on the Continent, periodically they aspired to a lordship over their neighbours in Britain. In the eleventh and twelfth centuries, English ambitions to ascendancy had been achieved mainly by colonisation and armed infiltration. After Hastings, for example, the Anglo-Normans had established settlements in Wales and the Scottish borders, and in the 1170s they founded a colony and administrative centre in Dublin. In the thirteenth century, however, the assault on the non-English peoples, and particularly the Welsh, became sharper and more direct. Obligations of lordship were more commonly committed to writing, in this way becoming easier to enforce. The definition of military obligations became more precise. And, most lethally of all, political power was expressed in legal and jurisdictional terms, which tended to reinforce English ascendancy. All of these developments bred resistance among the native Welsh, and resistance in turn provoked English intervention. In 1282 a rebellion by David ap Gruffydd, Prince Llewellyn's brother, provoked a brisk but devastating invasion by Edward I, in which he overran Gwynedd, Llewellyn's principality, ending its independence and absorbing it into the English state. The days of Welsh independence were effectively ended, although there was to be a major rebellion against English rule in the early 1400s.

Scotland, a stronger and more united polity, proved better equipped to withstand Edward's expansionist ambitions. In the 1290s the Scots suffered terrible defeats, notably at Falkirk in 1298, but their government was able to mobilise resources and put armies into the field. The decisive battle between the two sides was fought at Bannockburn in 1314, when the English were heavily defeated. Bannockburn was to assure the Scots their independence for the rest of the middle ages. In Ireland, while these struggles were going on, the position was different again. In the course of the twelfth and thirteenth centuries the English had found that they were strong enough to establish a colony in eastern Ireland, yet not strong enough to subdue the country as a whole. Consequently, in the late middle ages their policy was to concentrate on consolidating what they had got. Richard II's two expeditions to the province in 1394 and 1399 represented the last significant attempt by a medieval English ruler to go on the offensive against the native Irish. Richard's achievement was transient, however. There was no gain to the English colony in the long term. In the fifteenth century, English governments, facing mounting difficulties in France, were content to leave the Anglo-Irish largely to their own devices.

The traditions and the changing ambitions of the English monarchy provide the context within which the careers of the three Richards were played out. All three kings were highly conscious of the burden of the past on their shoulders; and all three, in their different ways, were sensitive to the obligations of their office. Yet in background and outlook they differed sharply. They differed most obviously in the circumstances of their accession: Richard I and Richard II came to the throne by lawful descent, but Richard III by usurpation. They differed too in temperament and taste. The second Richard was something of an aesthete, the first rather less so, and the third hardly at all. They differed, finally, in the extent of their dominions. Richard I ruled a vast empire stretching from Hadrian's Wall to the Pyrenees, Richard II a diminished version of that empire, and Richard III only the kingdom of England, with Wales. These differences were magnified by the long intervals between their reigns. Richard I ruled in the later twelfth century, Richard II in the fourteenth and Richard III in the fifteenth. Such diversity of experience might seem to challenge the viability of a comparative study of their reigns. But, as we have seen, there were characteristics which they had in common. All three kings were lacking in adult male issue. All three were intensely pious. And all three met violent deaths. In the course of examining these similarities we will discover much about the nature and exercise of kingship in medieval England. And along the way, we will also discover something of the influence which the first Richard's fame exerted on the other two.

The choir of the church of St Thomas Becket, Portsmouth (now Portsmouth Cathedral). (*A. F. Kersting*)

The English Royal Line
William I to Edward III

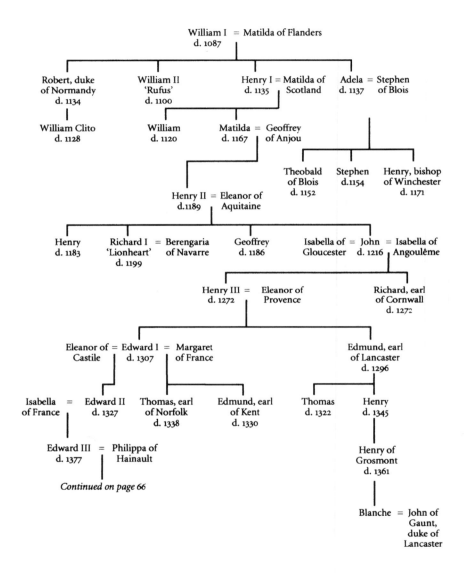

William I = Matilda of Flanders
d. 1087

Robert, duke of Normandy d. 1134

William II 'Rufus' d. 1100

Henry I = Matilda of Scotland
d. 1135

Adela = Stephen of Blois
d. 1137

William Clito d. 1128

William d. 1120

Matilda = Geoffrey of Anjou
d. 1167

Theobald of Blois d. 1152

Stephen d.1154

Henry, bishop of Winchester d. 1171

Henry II = Eleanor of Aquitaine
d.1189

Henry d. 1183

Richard I 'Lionheart' d. 1199 = Berengaria of Navarre

Geoffrey d. 1186

Isabella of Gloucester = John d. 1216 = Isabella of Angoulême

Henry III = Eleanor of Provence
d. 1272

Richard, earl of Cornwall d. 1272

Eleanor of Castile = Edward I d. 1307 = Margaret of France

Edmund, earl of Lancaster d. 1296

Isabella of France = Edward II d. 1327

Thomas, earl of Norfolk d. 1338

Edmund, earl of Kent d. 1330

Thomas d. 1322

Henry d. 1345

Edward III d. 1377 = Philippa of Hainault

Henry of Grosmont d. 1361

Continued on page 66

Blanche = John of Gaunt, duke of Lancaster

3

Richard I

Richard the Lionheart's career was the stuff of which legends are made. This greatest of the Richards was one of the most charismatic rulers of his day.[1] As a warrior he was more than a match for the renowned Saladin. He conquered a whole kingdom – the kingdom of Cyprus – in a matter of weeks. In the Holy Land, his siegecraft at Acre drew the admiration of the other crusading commanders. His achievements in politics and war were larger than life. Yet the setbacks which he suffered were also on a heroic scale. Not only was he humiliatingly shipwrecked on the Adriatic coast on his return from crusade; he had to endure the rigours of imprisonment at the hands of a jealous rival. His tribulations at sea read like those of Odysseus on his return from Troy. Not surprisingly, Richard's life quickly became surrounded by myth. The scale of his achievements was greatly magnified. Every army that he faced was doubled or quadrupled in size to exaggerate the scale of his victories. With passing time, romantic lure was added to the heady brew of invention. The story was concocted of his discovery in prison by his minstrel Blondel. To this background, it is hardly surprising that Richard should have been believed to have died searching for a hoard of buried treasure.

Richard was born into one of the richest and most successful families of his day. His father, Henry of Anjou, was king of England, duke of Normandy and count of Anjou. His mother Eleanor was heiress to the great duchy of Aquitaine in south-west France. Richard was the third-born of a sizeable brood. His eldest surviving brother Henry, the 'Young King', had been born in 1155, while his younger brothers, Geoffrey and John, were born in 1158 and 1167.[2] He himself was born at Oxford in September 1157. Richard was to be his mother's favourite. With his father his relations were always testy: Richard suspected him of favouring his brothers. In 1173 Richard was one of the ringleaders of a major rebellion against his father in which the king of France was involved. In 1184 he was drawn into rebellion again – this time over a proposal for a reapportionment of the Angevin lands to the advantage of his brother John. He was again estranged from his father, and in alliance with the French king, at the time of the former's death in 1189.

Richard's close identification with his mother meant that it was virtually certain that when he grew to manhood he would be given responsibility for assisting her in the government of Aquitaine.[3] Ruling Aquitaine was no easy task. Although the duchy was rich and prosperous, its nobility were quarrelsome and jealous of their independence. Along the borders there were nobles who habitually played the Angevins off against the Capetians. Richard entered into his responsibilities with relish. His first major challenge came in 1176. In that year he was faced by a rebel coalition which included the sons of the count of Angoulême, their half-brother Viscount Aimar of Limoges, Viscount Raymond of Turenne, and the lords of Chabenais and Mastac. The lordly rebels objected to Richard's control of the city of Limoges. Richard crossed the Channel to seek his father's help. The younger Henry, his brother, immediately promised aid, and Richard was everywhere triumphant. He crushed the mercenary Brabantines in May, captured Limoges, Aimar's stronghold, and linked up with his brother at Poitiers. He forced the leading rebels to surrender in Angoulême and, after holding his Christmas feast at Bordeaux, headed south towards Dax and Bayonne, almost reaching the Spanish border. The speed of his movements, always a characteristic of his warfare, caught his opponents entirely unawares.

In 1179 Richard faced a fresh challenge in the Angoumois. Vulgrin, son and heir of the count of Angoulême, had refused to do homage to him, being stiffened in his resistance by his ally, Geoffrey de Rancon. The Rancons appear to have felt threatened by the advance of Angevin power in the valley of the Charente. Richard launched an attack against a major Rancon fortresses – Pons – but the campaign went badly, and he had to retreat. A few months later, he launched a new offensive, this time against the citadel of Taillebourg, on the Charente. The operation proved a spectacular success. Richard surrounded the place so effectively that the starving defenders had to break out in search of food. Turning on them, Richard counter-attacked and took the town by storm. The capture of Taillebourg established his reputation as a master of siege warfare. When news of his triumph reached his father, he was accorded a hero's welcome.

Richard's achievements in Aquitaine aroused the jealousy of his elder brother Henry, known as the Young King. The Young King was courteous, generous and chivalric, but he lacked the ability and determination of his sibling. In the early 1180s he began plotting against him. Richard's imposition of royal authority on Aquitaine had provoked considerable disaffection among the more fickle of the duchy's lords. The Young King now encouraged these dissidents to rebel. At the same time, he launched a diplomatic offensive: he set about persuading his father to make Richard and Geoffrey recognise him as heir. Henry II said that he would back the idea. Geoffrey then agreed to do homage to his brother, but Richard refused. To Richard, such a move would have led to Aquitaine's subordination within the Angevin empire. The Old King was now faced with open feuding between his sons. At Angers he attempted a reconciliation between them. Geoffrey, however, defected and launched an invasion of Aquitaine. The Young King made a base for himself in the city of Limoges. When his father appeared with a force before the city walls, he found himself fired upon by his son's archers. The situation threatened to spiral out of control. The Young King was running short of money for his troops and his mercenaries were causing havoc in the countryside. Then, on 26 May, the Young King fell ill. Three weeks later, he died. Richard was now heir to his father's crown.

The question still remained of how the brothers' respective responsibilities were to be defined. In Michaelmas 1183 their father put a proposal to them. Richard should succeed to the position of his deceased brother: in other words, he should become his father's heir apparent, while John should take over as viceroy in Aquitaine. The proposal had much to be said for it. Richard, however, was adamant in opposition. He was not prepared to throw away eight years' hard work in Aquitaine. Withdrawing from his father's court, he headed south. The Old King authorised John to take possession of the duchy by force, but his forces, which were insubstantial, were driven back. In 1185 the Old King made a fresh attempt to address the issue. It was now proposed that Richard resign his duchy to his mother, the two of them acting as joint rulers.[4] This was a proposal to which the son could raise no objection. Rather grudgingly, he accepted it. For the moment, peace between the brothers was restored.

The ructions in the Angevin 'empire' were by now attracting the attention of the French king, Philip II. Philip – known to history as the 'Augustus' – was a clever man. Fox-like, he played on the Angevins' divisions to his own, and to his kingdom's, advantage. In 1188 he decided to risk an armed throw. He launched an invasion of Berry, besieging Richard and John at Châteauroux. It is possible that he was hoping to achieve an easy triumph, but, if so, he was disappointed. The Old King rallied to his sons' assistance. With armies massing, a battle seemed imminent. But then a strange thing happened. Richard paid a visit to the French king, 'who held him in such high honour that each day they ate at one table and slept in one room'. Philip evidently plied his adversary with charm: he was always resourceful with words. Battle was averted and the two armies backed off. But in the following year the struggle was renewed. This time the *casus belli* was a dispute over the southern county of Toulouse. In 1187 Raymond, the ruler of Toulouse, urged on by his minister Peter Seilun, had seized a group of Aquitainian merchants, and Richard had retaliated by overrunning the county and seizing Seilun himself. Seeing Richard's attack on Toulouse as breaching their accord, Philip invaded Berry again. Richard moved quickly northwards to confront him, and the invasion was halted. The Old King now took the initiative to secure a deal. In November a meeting was arranged between the two Angevins and Philip at Châtillon-sur-Indre. Philip offered attractive terms: he would renounce his conquests in Berry if Richard would renounce his in Toulouse. This clever offer played on the differences between the two men. Henry was disposed to accept. Richard, however, was not: he did not want to surrender his hard-won gains. Believing that he could win more favourable terms by dealing with Philip in person, he entered into direct negotiations with him, and Philip once more deployed his charm. The two men agreed on a settlement, and this was offered to Henry at Bonsmoulins. Henry promptly rejected it. Richard then turned to Philip and performed homage to him for Normandy, Anjou and Aquitaine. The breach between father and son was final. Early in 1189 the war between Henry and Philip was renewed, with Richard taking the latter's side. In May and June the great Loire valley cities of Le Mans and Tours were taken by the French. On 6 July, however, Henry died at Chinon. Richard succeeded unchallenged to his place.

Richard's reaction to his father's death was muted. After paying a brief visit to his lying-in-state at Fontevrault, he crossed to England.[5] On 13 September he was crowned king in Westminster Abbey. A few days later, at a council at Pipewell, he appointed new ministers to govern England, Hugh Puiset and William de Mandeville being appointed co-justiciars and William Longchamp chancellor.[6] Then in early December he left England for the Continent again. On 30 December he had a meeting with Philip at Nonancourt. By this time he was turning his attention with some urgency to the great project on which he had settled: a mighty crusade to the East.

The crisis which precipitated the launching of the crusade had erupted in July 1187. At the Horns of Hattin in Galilee an army under the command of King Guy de Lusignan had been cut to pieces by the Moslem leader Saladin. A few months later, on 2 October, Jerusalem itself had fallen. The very existence of the Latin kingdom seemed threatened. Towards the end of the year Pope Gregory VIII issued an appeal for a new crusade. Richard (not yet king) had responded by taking the cross immediately: he felt a personal commitment to the cause because Jerusalem was ruled by a branch of the house of Anjou. Later, both Henry II and King Philip of France took the cross. In the dominions of both kings preparations were set in motion for a crusade.

Richard's own preparations were on an appropriately massive scale. Richard looked to England to supply the bulk of his logistical needs, as England was by far the richest of his dominions. A massive fleet was assembled at Dartmouth to take his force east. No fewer than thirty-three ships were supplied by the Cinque Ports alone. According to Richard of Devizes, the fleet as a whole carried 9000 soldiers and sailors. Richard's ministers paid the closest attention to provisioning and supplies. As many as 50,000 horseshoes, for example, were ordered from the Forest of Dean. The cost of the expedition was enormous. Expenditure on men and equipment, disregarding repairs, totalled some £14,000.[7] The cost was met by exploiting every possible source of revenue. Officials were despatched to all the royal treasuries to take possession of the late king's silver hoard. There was a huge auction of royal assets –

offices, lordships, castles, towns: everything, Howden says, was put up for sale.[8] England was drained almost to the last penny.[9] But Richard's other dominions were tapped too: Normandy, Anjou and Aquitaine also contributed their share.

Richard's intention was to send his fleet ahead of him, effecting a rendezvous with it at Marseille. Before he could set out, however, various matters had to be settled: order had to be brought to his continental dominions and an agreement of sorts reached with the French king on border security. It was mid April before he was able to embark on the slow journey across France to the Mediterranean.[10] After he had linked up with the French king at Vézelay, he arrived at Marseille at the end of July. Contrary to his expectation, his fleet was not there to meet him. Its arrival had been delayed by a mutiny among the sailors at Lisbon. Anxious to be on his way, he accordingly arranged for commercial shipping to take him instead. At the beginning of September 1190, accompanied by his great retinue, he finally set sail. Moving slowly down the Italian coast, and putting in at Genoa and Naples, he arrived at Messina on 23 September. Here he decided to over-winter, for poor weather conditions in the eastern Mediterranean made any passage later in the year too risky. As it happened, he had important family business in Sicily to sort out.[11] His brother-in-law, King William, had died in the previous November without issue. William's nearest relative was his aunt Constance, who was married to a German, but the crown was seized by his illegitimate cousin Tancred. Tancred was anxious to lay his hands on William's widow's dower: he was badly in need of money. Accordingly, he threw the lady (Richard's sister) into prison. Richard naturally insisted that she immediately be released, and under protest Tancred granted his request. But Richard also made other demands which Tancred refused. Then one day in October, a brawl broke out between his men and Tancred's, and Richard ended up taking possession of the city. To secure a peace with Richard, Tancred had to hand over 40,000 ounces of gold. Richard had scored his first significant victory.

It was while Richard was at Messina that his bride-to-be, Berengaria of Navarre, accompanied by her future mother-in-law, was brought to him. The match between Richard and Berengaria had been arranged long before his departure.[12] The couple could not be married at Messina, however, because it was still Lent. Richard accordingly decided on a postponement of formalities till later in his journey. On 10 April 1191 he took to the high seas again. The situation in the Holy Land was growing ever more serious. Three days out from Messina, disaster struck. A fierce storm blew up and his fleet was scattered. Richard ended up at Rhodes, but the vessels carrying Berengaria and her retinue were driven to Cyprus, where they were plundered.[13] Richard's reaction, on hearing of his fiancée's misfortune, was to seek appropriate recompense from the Cypriot ruler, Isaac Comnenus. When Isaac denied him satisfaction, he undertook the lightning conquest of the island. The whole operation took less than a month. Isaac himself was captured and shackled in chains. To raise money for the campaign, Richard sold the kingdom to the crusading order of the Templars, who two years later, finding it too costly to maintain, sold it to Guy de Lusignan, the king of Jerusalem. By this roundabout route Cyprus became a crusader staging post: a vital link in the communications chain between the crusader kingdom and the West.

It was at the Cypriot port of Limassol on 12 May 1191 that Richard and Berengaria were finally married. The ceremony, in the castle chapel, was performed by John, bishop of Evreux. Four weeks after his marriage, Richard set out on the last stage of his epic voyage east. His destination was the Holy Land city of Acre.[14] After successfully engaging an enemy galley en route, he dropped anchor at Acre on 8 June. The ancient crusader city was a centre of great economic and strategic importance. It was not only one of the leading trading emporia of the Middle East; it was also an important military centre and the port through which supplies were brought in from the West. In 1187, after the débâcle at Hattin, the city had fallen to Saladin's men. For well over a year, the army of Jerusalem had been struggling to get it back. But, weak and disunited, they had enjoyed little success. Indeed, eventually they were in their turn enveloped by a great Moslem army, which denied them victuals. The arrival of Richard and his mighty force gave the Latins new heart. Richard's reputation was already awesome; news of his conquests had travelled far ahead of him. More to the point, he brought with him well equipped soldiers and supplies. On arrival, he immediately assumed control of all military operations. Massive new siege engines and mighty new battering rams were brought up. By stages, breaches were made in the city's walls, and on 12 July, just a month after his arrival, the city surrendered. The capture of Acre was a signal triumph. The crusaders were understandably exultant. But the atmosphere of excitement was marred by an unfortunate episode. A quarrel broke out between Richard and King Philip of France. Jealous of Richard's success, and annoyed by the latter's repudiation of his sister, Philip stormed off, never to return.[15] Richard was to pay a heavy price for this breakdown of relations later, on his way back to Europe.

From this moment on, Richard was the single most influential commander on the crusade. It was his views which were decisive in determining strategy, and his judgments which settled disputes between rival captains. His goal was never in doubt: it was the liberation of Jerusalem. But before he could advance on the Holy City, he needed to secure control of the Mediterranean coastline, the conduit through which supplies would be brought in from the West. On 22 August he left Acre to head south for Jaffa. All the way, a distance of some seventy miles, he stuck closely to the coast. The advance across the barren, sun-scorched countryside was slow. Day after day, the left flank of his force was harassed by Saladin's cavalry. Richard was insistent that his men resist all provocations, for to break ranks would be fatal. As the crusaders pressed doggedly on, Saladin realised that his only hope of halting them lay in forcing an engagement. On a plain to the north of the town of Arsuf he ranged his men across his enemy's path. Richard had no alternative but to give battle. The engagement which followed (7 September 1191) was bloody and bitterly fought, but Richard emerged the victor.[16] Saladin and his forces were thrown aside. With the way to the south now open, Richard could resume his march. Three days later, he entered Jaffa.

Richard had achieved his first objective, that of securing the Mediterranean coastline. He next had to think about the recovery of Jerusalem. The city lay some eighty miles inland, due east of Jaffa, in the bleak Judean hills. In October, when he was still buoyed up with success, Richard was confident that he could take the city. But, as the time passed and he pondered the difficulties, he became less sanguine. To surround the city and invest it, he would need extra resources, of both manpower and money. To be confident of holding the city after he left, he would need further resources still. He was acutely aware that his supply lines were overstretched. To ensure their security he needed to establish settlers along the route. Yet he had too few men with him to be able to accomplish this on any scale. Reluctantly he came to the conclusion that conquering Jerusalem was impossible. He marched his men inland to Beit Nuba, only twelve miles from the city and within sight of its walls, only to fall back again. In the following year he marched to Beit Nuba a second time, but again had to fall back. Conscious of the logistical problems he faced, he resigned himself to the fact that he would never enter the city in triumph. From Beit Nuba he gazed longingly at its skyline of domes and battlements. But he knew that the task of entering the city was beyond him.

In early 1192 a council of war was held in the crusader camp to decide an alternative strategy. Richard had long been attracted by the idea of attacking Egypt, because that way, he believed, he could drive a wedge between the two halves of Saladin's empire. There was opposition to the idea, however, from the French and the Burgundians, for whom the goal was Jerusalem or nowhere. It was while these debates were going on that news was received that Saladin was bringing reinforcements in from Egypt. Richard realised that, even if he could not take Jerusalem, Richard might still spring a surprise on his opponents. The reinforcements were said to be crossing the Negev desert. Advancing deep into the wasteland, Richard launched a bold attack on the caravan at al-Hasi (23 June 1192) and scattered it. Contemporaries regarded the victory as one of the greatest of his career. It is possible that had he advanced on Jerusalem at this point he could have taken the city, for his opponents were fatally weakened. But ever conscious of the danger to his supply lines he held back. Instead, he entered into negotiations with Saladin. Early in the talks agreement was reached on giving pilgrims access to the Holy Places. Saladin's insistence, however, on the dismantling of a castle built by the crusaders at Ascalon led to deadlock. Shortly afterwards, hostilities between the two sides were resumed. The final showdown between Richard and Saladin took place at Jaffa.[17] In the summer of 1191 Saladin had seized control of the town in a lightning attack. Richard ordered a two-pronged operation to relieve it, Henry of Champagne leading an attack from the landward side and he himself from the seaward. Richard showed himself at his rumbustious best. Forcing his way up the beach, he pushed the strong Moslem forces back and established Christian control again. He then set up an encampment outside the town. A few days later Saladin, struggling to regain the initiative, counter-attacked. Anticipating an easy triumph, he instead went down to humiliating defeat. Richard's forces, hastily deployed behind a shield wall, cut their opponents to pieces. By the time of the battle of Jaffa, after nearly two years of war, the two sides had fought themselves to a standstill. Neither had the power to gain a decisive advantage over the other. In September 1192 negotiations were reopened and this time they were quickly concluded. Richard and Saladin assented to a three years' truce with a guarantee of access for pilgrims to the Holy Places. On 9 October 1192, Richard and his fellow crusaders set sail for home.

If the story of Richard's crusade reads like an epic, that of his journey home has something of the character of farce. In the course of the crusade, Richard, a vain man, had given gratuitous offence to a good many of his fellow commanders. The most embittered of these was Leopold, duke of Austria. Leopold had been among the crusaders present at the taking of Acre. When the crusading force had gone in, he had held his banner aloft before him; the banner, however, had been trodden down by a knight and insulted. Leopold remembered this incident and held Richard responsible. It seemed to him a symbol of the Angevin ruler's intolerable pride. A couple of years later, fortune delivered his adversary into his hands. Richard had had a difficult sea passage back from the East. The weather was stormy and the waters choppy. Deciding against sailing through the Straits of Gibraltar, he put ashore in Istria, near Venice. He then crossed the Julian Alps and reached the neighbourhood of Vienna. At the village of Erdburg he had the misfortune to fall into the hands of none other than Leopold himself (21 December 1192). To the Austrian his capture was nothing less than a godsend: proof that the Holy Spirit was on his side; and he determined to capitalise on his advantage. Initially he imprisoned his captive at the castle of Durnstein, high above the Danube, where, according to later legend, he was found by his faithful minstrel Blondel. But in February the next year he surrendered him to the emperor, Henry VI, another of Richard's rivals, who realised the bargaining power that possession of his person could offer. For over a year Richard's fate was haggled over by an assortment of kings and princes, each of whom sought personal advantage from his misfortune. What the emperor was looking for was Richard's cooperation in dissuading relatives of his in Germany from opposing imperial rule.[18] Richard had little choice but to negotiate with his captor for fear of being turned over to Philip of France.

In March 1193 the two sides agreed on a deal whereby Richard would pay Henry 100,000 marks and supply him with fifty galleys and two hundred knights for a year. The French king and his ally, Richard's brother the slippery John, did all they could to obstruct the deal: the last thing they wanted was to see Richard at large again. And once they thought Richard's release imminent they frustrated his ministers' attempts to raise the money. Philip himself invaded Normandy and captured the castle of Gisors. By the summer of 1193 the long delays were leading to a renegotiation of the terms. At the end of June, at Worms, a final deal was struck: the emperor would release Richard in return for a ransom of 150,000 marks and the contracting of a marriage between Richard's niece Eleanor and Duke Leopold's son.[19] Immediately, in England, Normandy and the other Angevin dominions the machinery was set in motion for collection of the money. On 2 March 1194 Richard was finally released.

During the year that Richard was imprisoned the French king had done his utmost to weaken his rival's position in his continental dominions. In addition to capturing Gisors, he had overrun the Vexin and much of the Seine valley and had laid siege to Rouen. But now that Richard was back in the field, the tables were turned. Philip was thrown onto the defensive again. Not only was Richard's generalship far superior to his adversary's; he had the greater resources of money and manpower to dispose of. For the remaining five years of his life Richard devoted himself to re-establishing his family's position on the Continent.

As soon as he left Germany, Richard embarked on a brief visit to England. At the ancient Wessex capital of Winchester on 17 April he had himself crowned again.[20] This was a ceremony which he deemed necessary to wipe away the stain of imprisonment. A few weeks earlier, at a council at Nottingham, he had taken punitive action against John and his fellow conspirators. While John himself escaped lightly, a number of his allies had their lands seized. Then in early May he left England for the Cotentin peninsula. England could look after itself: it was a stable and well-governed realm. It was in Normandy that his presence was urgently needed.

The position in Normandy by this time was desperate.[21] In the months since his capture of Gisors, Philip had seized most of the upper part of the duchy, east of the Seine, while westwards he was advancing on Beaumont-le-Roger. In the central Angevin dominions, in Touraine and Poitou, the situation was just as alarming. Philip had seized the castles of Loches and Châtillon-sur-Indre, while in Aquitaine he was urging the local nobility to rebel. Characteristically, Richard threw himself energetically into recovering the initiative. In May he quickly broke Philip's siege of Verneuil, thus relieving the pressure on Rouen, and he stabilised the position in the Seine valley. From Normandy he marched south into Touraine. In June he relieved Loches and two other castles and entered the city of Tours. By July he was patrolling Saintonge and the Angoumois. But the rapid pace of his advance could not be sustained for long. He was in danger of running out of money and supplies. In late July, at Tillières, he made a truce with Philip, relinquishing the Vexin in return for lands in the east of the duchy. The two sides had fought themselves to a standstill.

Richard knew that the truce would bring only a breathing-space in the long struggle with the French. Accordingly, he was not surprised when in the following year hostilities were resumed. In late July Philip launched a surprise attack on Richard's castle at Vaudreuil, south of Rouen. Richard retaliated by attacking Philip's lands further south. He had territorial claims in the county of Berry and he launched a campaign there, which took him deep into the Auvergne. Philip launched a counter-attack in Berry, laying siege to the castle of Issoudun but failing to take it. In January 1196, when hostilities were beginning to wind down, a peace conference was convened at Louviers. Richard secured terms altogether more favourable to him than those offered in the previous year: he recovered virtually all the lands that he had lost, except the Norman Vexin and the border castles of Nonancourt and Vernon.

In the breathing-space afforded him by the treaty Richard concentrated on strengthening the defences of Normandy. At the town of Les Andelys on the Seine near its entry into Normandy he built his great castle of Château Gaillard – literally the 'saucy castle'. Towering high above the river, Château Gaillard was so strong that Richard boasted that he could defend it even if its walls were made of butter. The castle was as much a symbol of his authority as a strongpoint in his border defences.

At the same time, Richard engaged in a search for allies. Concentrating his efforts particularly on the princes of the Low Countries, he found partners in the counts of Boulogne and Flanders and the dukes of Limburg and Brabant. In 1198, therefore, when hostilities with the French were resumed, he was well prepared. The new round of fighting began with an incursion by Count Baldwin of Flanders into Artois, aimed at taking the town of St-Omer. Philip was powerless to resist this attack because he was already engaged in Normandy, in the Vexin. St-Omer fell to the Flemings after a siege of some six weeks. Further west, Richard launched an attack of his own on the trading town of Abbeville, on the River Somme. The fighting on both sides was fierce. In the course of one engagement, at Gisors, Richard scored an unexpected triumph at the expense of his rival: the French king was unhorsed and tossed into the River Epte. Richard made the most of his enemy's discomfiture in his newsletters home. His charismatic leadership, combined with the loyalty to him of the Norman aristocracy, were giving him a definite edge in the struggle.[22]

Richard's final campaign was fought much further south, in the central area of the Limousin. Early in 1199 a long standing enemy of his, Viscount Aimar of Limoges, rose in rebellion and entered into an alliance with the French. The Limousin was a strategically vital area for Richard: its loss would effectively sever the Angevin dominions in two. Richard accordingly marched south as soon as he heard of the revolt. In early March he laid siege to the viscount's castle of Chalus-Chabrol. The operations proceeded swiftly, and within a week the garrison were close to surrender. But one evening, as the king was patrolling near his tent, an archer on the ramparts took a chance shot at him. The bolt struck him on the shoulder. He was not wearing his armour. Quickly, the wound turned gangrenous and the infection spread. The efforts of Richard's surgeons to save him proved unavailing. On the evening of 6 April the king died. He was forty-two. Contemporaries were conscious of the passing of a great man. In the words of Giraut de Borneil, 'in many trials he proved himself more virtuous and valiant than all other mortals'.[23]

As was the custom in France at the time, the king's body was divided up for burial. His brain and entrails were interred at the abbey of Charroux, on the border between Poitou and the Limousin. His heart was taken to Rouen, where it was buried in the cathedral alongside the body of his elder brother. The rest of his remains, together with the crown and regalia which he had worn at Winchester, were taken to Fontevrault, the Angevin family mausoleum in Anjou. The purpose of the macabre distribution of parts was probably to elicit prayers for his soul in as many churches as possible.[24] At Fontevrault, a generation later, an effigy was placed over his grave, showing him crowned and holding the sceptre. Alongside the effigy lies that of his mother, and next to that again his father's. In death the three Angevins appear in closer harmony than they ever had been in life. For years, Queen Eleanor and her husband Henry II, and Richard and his father, had been quarrelling. In the surroundings of their resting place at Fontevrault they found a peace which had eluded them while they lived.

Anne of Bohemia interceding with her husband, Richard II, on behalf of the citizens of Shrewsbury, from Shrewsbury Charter. (*Shrewsbury Museums Service*)

4

Richard II

Richard II reigned almost two hundred years after his predecessor and namesake. He came to the throne in 1377 and was deposed twenty-two years later. The shape and configuration of his dominions differed sharply from his predecessor's. Much of the Lionheart's Angevin 'empire' had been lost by the fourteenth century. Maine, Normandy and Anjou, the very heartland of the Angevin inheritance, had all gone – seized by King Philip of France in 1204. Only Aquitaine, down in the far south west, was left: a largely self-governing dominion which waxed and waned in size in proportion to the military fortunes of the English crown. Since the twelfth century an important piece of north-eastern France had been gained – the town and hinterland of Calais, which had been captured by Edward III in 1347. At the same time there had been a shift in the geographical focus of royal power within the British Isles. In Ireland English rule, which had been expanding in the late twelfth century, was in retreat again, barely reaching beyond the 'pale' around Dublin. In Wales, however, English territorial strength had markedly increased. Gwynedd, the last of the independent Welsh principalities, had been extinguished, absorbed, like other parts of north Wales, into the English state. By the late fourteenth century there was a distinct sense in which a 'British' dimension to the ambitions of the English crown balanced the continental.

Yet the continental ambitions of the English crown lived on. The king of England, as duke of Aquitaine, still counted as one of the great princes of France. Indeed, it was the continuing English involvement in French affairs that formed the background to the struggle we know as the Hundred Years' War. The dynastic origins of the conflict went back to the early fourteenth century. In 1328 the last of the Capetian kings, Charles IV, had died. Ten years later Edward III claimed the crown by right of descent from his mother Isabella, Charles's sister. The struggle between the two monarchies dragged on for over a century. Although the English were ultimately to be expelled from France, in the course of the long struggle they were to enjoy periods of remarkable success. In the mid fourteenth century they scored signal triumphs at Crécy (1346), Calais (1347) and Poitiers (1356). A major reason for English success in the field was the disunity of their French opponents. There were moments when the French seemed keener to fight each other than to fight the enemy. But the English were also blessed with the advantage of superior military leadership. In the generation from 1340 they produced some outstanding military commanders. First among these in repute and achievement was Edward, the Black Prince, eldest son of Edward III. The Black Prince was the father of King Richard II.

The future Richard II was born on 6 January 1367 at the Aquitainian capital, Bordeaux. His father held sway over Aquitaine, a dominion with which he had been invested in 1362. His mother, Joan of Kent, a noted beauty, claimed descent from Edward I. In early childhood the key influences on Richard were as much French as English. His wet nurses were French, and it is likely that he spoke French before he spoke English.[1] His tutors, or *magistri*, were men with wide knowledge of France. One of them, Guichard d'Angle, earl of Huntingdon, was actually a French lord. The formalities of his father's court, in which he grew up, were heavily French-influenced. The cosmopolitanism of his upbringing was highlighted by the company which came together at his baptism. No fewer than three European kings attended – Jaime of Majorca and the exiled kings of Castile and Armenia. French influences were to be a major influence on the development of his kingly style as he grew to manhood.

Richard was brought to England at the age of four, when his father, stricken with dysentery, surrendered his principality to the king. His remaining boyhood years were spent chiefly at his father's residences of Kennington and Berkhamsted. In June 1376, at the age of nine, he became heir to the throne on his father's death. Five months later he was invested with his father's titles, and five months after that made a knight of the Garter. Popular expectations of the young prince were high. In parliament in January 1377 the chancellor captured the national mood when he said that the prince had been sent to England by God in the same way that God had sent His own Son into the world, to redeem

His people. As everyone listening was aware, the prince would soon be entering into his inheritance. His grandfather, the elderly Edward III, was nearing his end. In June 1377, at Sheen, he died – with just a priest at his side, according to Walsingham.[2] Richard was now king.

Richard's coronation on 16 July in Westminster Abbey was notable for its symbolism.[3] The ceremony was carefully choreographed by his councillors. At one point the order of proceedings was reversed in order to emphasise Richard's succession by hereditary right. In the past the king had taken his oath only after he had been presented to the congregation for approval, but this time he took it first – a rearrangement which reinforced the people's allegiance to a king who was already their ruler *de jure*. The rearrangement was probably engineered by the king's uncle John of Gaunt, duke of Lancaster, who was a consistent supporter of the prerogative. It was probably Gaunt, too, who was responsible for having the order of proceedings written down afterwards. The ceremony would almost certainly have made a powerful impression on the mind of the young king. Much later, in 1388, he was to recall its most solemn moment – that point in the ceremony when he was touched on the chest with holy oil.[4] At the time, however, it was probably less a specific moment that influenced him than the memory of the liturgical splendour as a whole. Richard was always to be a lover of ceremony. The development of ceremony, and of the liturgical splendour of monarchy, was to be a major characteristic of his reign.

With Richard's accession a boy king was brought to the throne for the first time for nearly two hundred years. Only once before since the Conquest had a boy succeeded – in October 1216, when Henry III had become king aged nine. On that occasion, a regency government had been instituted. William Marshal, earl of Pembroke, a man widely respected by his contemporaries, had been appointed 'rector' until such time as the boy was competent to govern. When Richard succeeded, however, no regency was instituted, the fiction being maintained that the king was of full age. The reason for the seemingly strange decision was that there was no agreement on a suitable candidate to be regent. The obvious candidate was John of Gaunt, but Gaunt was a controversial figure and too unpopular to command wide acceptance. No other person, however, had Gaunt's ability or stature. In default, then, the king was given possession of the great seal, day-to-day responsibility for government being entrusted to a series of councils acting on his behalf. These councils held office until January 1380, when they were dismissed following the dispersal and loss of a naval force in the Channel, for which they were held responsible. After 1380, the king had the right to choose his advisers himself.

These opening years of the reign were dominated by the continuing but inconclusive struggle with France.[5] After the breakdown of the treaty of Brétigny, the war had been renewed by the French king, Charles V, and the lands which the English had conquered in France were gradually whittled away. In the mid 1370s the French and their Castilian allies stepped up their joint operations at sea. At the very moment of Richard's accession, a series of devastating raids were launched on the English south coast for which the English were unprepared. After the coronation, a fleet was put to sea under the command of Thomas of Woodstock, the king's uncle, which brought relief to the English garrison at Brest but which otherwise achieved little. The main problem on the English side was a lack of proper military co-ordination. The council organised a number of expeditions against the enemy. In 1378, for example, John of Gaunt launched a major assault on St-Malo. In the following year Sir Thomas Trivet led an expedition further south to Navarre. In 1380 Thomas of Woodstock led a chevauchée, a mounted raid, all the way across France from Calais to Bordeaux. These activities, however, were conceived largely in isolation from one another. There was a lack of overall strategic vision. In the most successful periods of engagement the king himself had provided the necessary coordination. But when the king was a minor that was impossible. The military activity thus added up to a total considerably less than the sum of its parts. Yet all this activity had to be paid for. Nearly £500,000 was spent on warfare between 1376 and 1381 – an almost unprecedented sum. The greater part of this money came from the wool customs and the levy on moveable property. But in an effort to increase the yield from lay taxation and, at the same time, to broaden its incidence the idea of the poll tax had been introduced. In 1380 a third poll tax, the highest in the series, had been granted by parliament to keep Buckingham's army going in Brittany. Widespread evasion was encountered in the process of its collection. By March 1381, when it was clear that yields would be very low, commissions were appointed to clamp down on the defaulters. In Essex the commissioners set about their task with exceptional thoroughness. At the end of March at Brentwood a group of them were set upon by the local villagers. Over the next few weeks acts of resistance occurred elsewhere. By the end of May the whole of south-eastern England was ablaze.

The Great Revolt of 1381 was the most remarkable popular rising of the English middle ages.[6] The rebel leaders acted decisively and with speed. Within weeks of the initial scuffle at Brentwood, rebel bands from Essex and Kent had pushed their way into the capital. The government and the ruling classes were seized by panic and paralysis. Richard and his ministers retreated to the comparative safety of the Tower. The elites of town and country looked to them for a response, and yet they were uncertain what to do. The chroniclers saw Richard himself as principally responsible for the eventual restoration of order. In their view it was the courage which he showed in his meeting with Wat Tyler, the rebel leader, at Smithfield that broke the rebels' resolve and ended the rising in London. But their knowledge of events was partial, and their interpretation coloured by hindsight. In reality, the position was more complex. The signs are that there was a vigorous debate in the Tower about how to respond to the crisis. According to the chronicler Froissart, who gives the most helpful account, the king's advisers divided into the hawks and the doves. The former, favouring vigorous counter-measures, urged the deployment of troops to dispel the rebels by force. Their rivals, however, led by the earl of Salisbury, favoured conciliation, arguing that by negotiation the rebels could be persuaded to depart in peace. It was the advocates of the latter approach who won the day. Arrangements were made for a meeting between Richard and the rebels the next day at Mile End.

Richard arrived for the Mile End encounter (14 June) with a small escort of household staff. He promised the rebels their main demands – in particular, the coveted prize of freedom: the ending of villeinage. But his concessions failed to persuade them to disperse. If anything, indeed, they made the situation worse by feeding their appetite. A splinter group of the rebels broke into the Tower, murdering the archbishop of Canterbury and other important officials there. The conciliatory strategy, it was clear, would have to be rethought. Later in the day, arrangements were made for the king to meet the rebels a second time, on this occasion at Smithfield. For this encounter, however, a cunning plan was hatched. It was decided to pick a quarrel with Wat Tyler, and when he threatened danger to the king a signal would be given to the levies to come out from the city. The plan worked perfectly. Tyler behaved boorishly. He rode up to Richard demanding a drink (it was a blisteringly hot day). William Walworth, the mayor, seeing his opportunity, plunged a dagger into him. Immediately, the levies rode out from the city, enveloping the rebels, as one chronicler said, like sheep in a pen. The bubble of rebel success had been burst. By Saturday evening the worst of the crisis was over. The commons of Essex and Kent were being driven back out of the capital.

It can hardly be denied that Richard had behaved with courage when he met the rebels at Smithfield. Equally, however, it is apparent that those rebels were the victims of a carefully staged trap. Not only was Tyler, their most charismatic leader, killed before their eyes; they themselves were surrounded and outmanoeuvred. The authorities had succeeded in regaining the initiative. Within days, Richard and his ministers were co-ordinating tough measures of coercion. On 23 June a series of commissions was issued to arrest and to try the rebels. Richard himself led a judicial visitation to Essex. What amounted to a series of bloody assizes had begun.

The Peasants' Revolt marked a turning point in the politics of Richard II's reign. Not only was there an immediate end to attempts at tinkering with the tax system; more important than that, a new mood of conservatism was ushered in. The Peasants' Revolt had given the government and the upper classes a shock. They had been long aware of the ambition and assertiveness of the lower orders – after all, the labouring classes had been pressing wage demands for years; but never before had they felt their power. Faced with the raw evidence of peasant violence and aggression, they recoiled in horror. In parliament there were calls for the better performance of obedience. Chancellor de la Pole in 1383 told the Commons that 'true obedience to the king is the foundation of all peace and quiet in the realm'.[7] Alongside these calls for obedience, there was a greater emphasis on religious orthodoxy. To contemporaries, orthodoxy went hand in hand with obedience, for it rested on a similar acceptance of authority. In May 1382 letters were issued for the arrest of unorthodox preachers, while six years later orders were given for the seizure of heretical writings.[8] Gradually, noblemen like Gaunt who had earlier lent their support to Wycliffite ideas returned to the orthodox fold. In general, there was a concern to reinforce hierarchy and authority in society. The later development of Richard's kingship needs to be seen in this context.

In the years immediately after the Revolt, relatively little is heard of Richard. The most significant event at this time was his marriage to Anne of Bohemia, the emperor's daughter, which took place in 1382. Immediately after the marriage, in Westminster Abbey, king and queen went on two lengthy itineraries, one to the west country and the other to East Anglia. It is only from 1383 that Richard's role in politics begins to emerge with any clarity. From the turn of 1383–4 it is evident that a new court party was forming around the king. The leading members of the group were former retainers of Edward, the Black Prince, chief among them the vice-chamberlain, Sir Simon Burley, and the new chancellor, Sir Michael de la Pole. Burley was one of the most significant early influences on Richard and probably the chief source of his exalted conception of regality. His associate Michael de la Pole had enjoyed close connections not only with the prince but also with Gaunt and, like himself, had absorbed something of the prince's taste for strong government. Alongside these two senior men was a group of younger courtiers. Two of the most prominent of them were Thomas Mowbray, earl of Nottingham, and Sir Ralph Stafford. Mowbray was a courtier both by instinct and family tradition – royal blood flowed in his veins – while Stafford was the heir to a wealthy and distinguished comital dynasty. More controversial was a man of inferior standing, Robert de Vere, earl of Oxford. De Vere sprang from one of the least amply endowed of the comital lines. Yet Richard loaded him with grants, and in 1386 awarded him the novel title of duke of Ireland. He was a man of little promise or ability. He even dishonoured himself by abandoning his wife, a granddaughter of Edward III, in favour of one of the queen's lady in waiting. The fact that he rose so rapidly at the king's court made him unpopular with royal magnates like Thomas of Woodstock who received far fewer rewards.

A feature of the political life of these years was the growing enmity between the king's younger favourites and the most senior of his uncles, John of Gaunt, duke of Lancaster. Lancaster aroused the distrust that he did because of his great influence and wealth. It was widely suspected that he wanted to manipulate foreign policy to serve his own ends: he had a claim to the crown of Spain by right of his wife Constance, daughter of Pedro the Cruel, king of Castile. Yet, as the Westminster chronicler recognised, he was a man of great brilliance. He was the outstanding figure of his day.[9] In April 1384 de Vere and some of the younger courtiers tried to procure Lancaster's political destruction by bringing trumped-up charges against him of plotting against the king. According to the Westminster writer, a peculiarly hare-brained plan to assassinate him was concocted at a tournament in February 1385.[10] The factionalism and sleaze that pervaded Richard's entourage attracted the critical notice of contemporaries. Richard's court was compared unfavourably with that of his predecessor. Where Edward III's court had been a centre of companionship and honour, Richard's was a hotbed of intrigue and dishonour.

If Richard's unhappy choice of counsellors aroused concern, so too did his failure to respond vigorously to the diplomatic and military recovery of France. In the 1380s the French continued their already considerable drive to re-establish an ascendancy in Europe. In January 1384 they had won a major diplomatic triumph by securing the succession to the county of Flanders of their king's uncle John, duke of Burgundy. In England it was widely believed that a military response to the growing French challenge should be mounted, for in the city of Ghent the English had a powerful ally. Yet, despite the entreaties of the Commons, Richard refused to cross the Channel with an army. The weakness of English power before the French advance became clear in 1386 when the French proposed mounting an invasion of England. By an unfortunate coincidence of timing, at just this time Lancaster sailed for Spain, taking with him a large force. The government was left with few resources to mount an adequate response. Money was needed in large quantities and urgently. Accordingly, it was resolved to summon a parliament. The assembly was to be one of the most momentous of the reign.

Chancellor de la Pole opened the session (1 October 1386) by asking the Commons for a grant of taxation. His request produced gasps of astonishment – he asked for no fewer than four fifteenths and tenths. The Commons, according to an eyewitness account, reacted angrily.[11] They said they could not consider the proposal because they had their own business to deal with first. They demanded that Chancellor de la Pole be removed from office and put on trial ('impeached') on charges of malfeasance. Richard reacted to their response brusquely. He said that he would not remove a scullion from his kitchen at the Commons' request. But when Thomas of Woodstock and Bishop Arundel, visiting him at Eltham, reminded him of the fate of earlier kings who had defied the popular will (a veiled reference to Edward II), he gave way. De la Pole was removed from office and, shortly afterwards, put on trial and found guilty. He was sentenced to the forfeiture of his estates. But worse was to come for Richard. A 'great and continual council' was appointed for twelve months to survey the estate and condition of the household, to look into the cost of defending the realm, and to enquire into all gifts of fees and offices that the king had made; and, once its enquiries were completed, it was authorised to ordain what reforms it saw fit and to ensure the officers' compliance with them. The composition of the council was by no means extremist, and there were many moderate figures in its ranks. But Richard still resented its intrusions. He regarded the mere fact of its appointment as an assault on his prerogative. Accordingly, he avoided its prying attentions by undertaking a lengthy itinerary of his realm. Leaving the capital in early February, he made his way north to Nottingham and Lincoln and then swung west to Lichfield and Shrewsbury. In the summer, as the expiry date of the council's term approached, he sought a clarification of his legal powers in two meetings with the judges.

The decision to consult the judges was an altogether novel one. It turned what had hitherto been a political crisis into a legal and constitutional one. The judges had long been used to answering questions from the king or his councillors on technical aspects of legal procedure. But never before had they been asked for an opinion on a matter of burning political importance. On every point put to them they backed the king. When asked if the statute appointing the council had derogated from the king's prerogative, they said that it had, and that those who had compelled the king to assent to it should be punished 'as traitors'. When asked whether the king was free to dissolve parliament, they again replied affirmatively, adding, in two further replies, that ministers could not be impeached without the king's assent and, consequently, that the trial of de la Pole had been illegal.[12] The judges' replies were a powerful weapon in Richard's political armoury. Very likely he intended using them as evidence in an anticipated prosecution of the sponsors of the continual council. But by October 1387 word of the judges' answers, which to this time had been kept secret, had leaked out. Those against whom they were aimed took fright. They knew that a showdown could hardly be far off. On the principle that attack was the best form of defence, they took the initiative themselves. At a meeting at Waltham Cross (Hertfordshire) a group of them – the duke of Gloucester (Thomas of Woodstock), and the earls of Arundel and Warwick – formally 'appealed', or prosecuted, the king's leading allies – Robert de Vere, Michael de la Pole, Robert Tresilian, the chief justice, Alexander Neville, the archbishop of York, and Nicholas Brembre, the king's chief associate in London. Later these three senior Appellants, as they were known, were joined by two others, the earl of Nottingham and Gaunt's son, the earl of Derby. Richard reacted by authorising the despatch of a force against them. Commanded by de Vere, this was quickly outmanoeuvred by the Appellants and defeated on the banks of the Thames at Radcot Bridge, near Burford. At Christmas the Appellants entered London. At their insistence, a parliament was summoned to meet on 3 February 1388.

The 'Merciless Parliament', as it was to become known, was to prove a pivotal event in the history of Richard's reign.[13] Not only did it witness the destruction of the inner court circle of the previous five years, it generated tensions and animosities which were to last right down to Richard's final moments as king. Richard never forgot the humiliation that he suffered at the hands of the Appellants in this parliament. Even when he was outwardly conciliatory, as he was in the early 1390s, he was seeking to reassert his shattered authority. Much of what happened in the second half of the reign can be seen as a reaction to the Appellant coup and its sequel.

The chief aim of the Appellant lords was to cleanse what they saw as the Augean stables of the court. Those whom they found most objectionable – principally, de Vere, de la Pole and Neville – had already fled. The most significant of the defendants left behind were Brembre, a onetime mayor of London, Judge Tresilian and Burley. Brembre and Tresilian were pronounced guilty of treason and executed in the first session of the parliament in February, and Burley, after much arguing, in May. It was then arranged for the estates of the condemned to be sold in a giant auction to provide the Appellants with the means to pursue their foreign policy objective – the renewal of the war with France. At the close of the parliament in June, all those attending took oaths to uphold its Acts, and a comprehensive system of oath-taking was put in motion in the shires. The Appellants left nothing to chance.

So long as the Appellants rode high in public opinion, as they did in the spring and summer of 1388, Richard could only watch and wait. He made a vain intervention in April to save the life of Sir Simon Burley. But, that apart, he did little. In the autumn, however, his patience reaped its reward. The alliance between the Appellants and the parliamentary Commons began to break down. In parliament in September the Appellants requested a grant of taxation to pay for the war at sea, despite promising respite from taxation in the spring. The Commons reacted coolly.[14] The Appellants' military record had been distinctly unimpressive. In mid August an English force had been badly mauled by the Scots at Otterburn (Northumberland). At the same time, the solidarity of the Appellants themselves began to weaken. The two junior Appellants – Derby and Nottingham – had always been less committed to the cause than their seniors, and Richard played on their sense of disaffection. From late summer he was winning them over to his side with inducements and douceurs. By the spring of 1389 he felt sufficiently confident of his position to seize the initiative. At a meeting held in the Marcolf Chamber at Westminster he dismissed the Appellants' councillors and appointed his own. No one challenged his authority to do so. The Appellants were a spent force.

The five or six years that followed were characterised by a marked relaxation of earlier tensions. The making of a long truce with France in May 1389 assisted in the process. No longer were recurrent requests put to the Commons for grants of taxation. But Richard was also sensible enough to learn from his past errors. In particular, he took care to distribute patronage more evenly. Instead of confining his goodwill to a favoured few, he rewarded a much larger circle. John Holand, earl of Huntingdon, Edward, earl of Rutland and Sir William Scrope were all among those who benefited from his largesse. John of Gaunt's return from Spain in November 1389 also contributed to the process of healing. John of Gaunt was from this time to be a major source of

reassurance and support to the king. With his Spanish ambitions abandoned, he fitted more easily into the world of English politics. He now
brought stability and strength where earlier he had brought discord.

Richard, while being careful to give less offence than before, was none
the less firm in his resolve to rebuild the power of the crown. From 1389
he took a number of measures to this end. In a novel initiative, he
launched a baronial-style affinity (its members identified by the white
hart badge), so that never again would he find himself as powerless in
the face of his enemies as he had been in 1387; from 1389 he took nearly
a hundred knights into his pay. At the same time, in a search for greater
financial security, he promoted the extension of public taxation to
peacetime. Hitherto, the levying of taxes had been undertaken principally to pay for war. Richard, however, now broke that link, saying, as
he did in 1393, that he wanted taxes 'for the trust which his subjects had
in his government and the love which they had for his person'.[15] In this
way, he made the flow of taxation meet some of the peacetime costs of
government.

Richard also took measures to project a grander and more exalted
image of his monarchy. He knew that the kingly office had to be raised
in dignity if it was if he was to promote the better performance of obedience. So he sought to exalt his person, to surround himself in
semi-religious mystique, and to stress the sacral roots of his authority.
To this end, he encouraged the use of lofty new forms of address. From
1389, his subjects were encouraged to address him as 'your majesty'
rather than – as they had generally addressed kings before – in the
simpler language of lordship.[16] At the same time, there was a lengthening of the hierarchy of degree. New titles were introduced into the
peerage – for example, that of marquess for Richard's friend Robert de
Vere – while magnates of royal stock such as John Holand and Edward
of Rutland were raised in dignity to the rank of duke. The ritual of court
life became richer and more elaborate. According to the *Eulogium*
chronicler of Canterbury, Richard would sometimes 'have a throne prepared for him in his chamber, on which he would sit ostentatiously
from dinner till vespers, talking to no one but watching everyone; and
when his eye fell on anyone, regardless of rank, that person had to bend
his knee to the king'.[17] By such measures Richard cultivated an image
of 'distance'. He raised himself above his subjects. The image he had of

himself was captured in the great Westminster Abbey portrait – a king who was iconic, god-like, and all-powerful.

By the summer of 1397 it seemed clear that Richard had largely succeeded in his object of restoring and rebuilding royal power. The former Appellants were now marginalised. A powerful new courtier nobility had been established. The country could be considered in a state of 'obedience'. But in the summer of 1397 this calm was shattered. Without warning, Richard struck out at his opponents. On the night of 10 July he had Arundel, Gloucester and Warwick, the three senior Appellants, arrested. In a proclamation issued shortly afterwards he said that he had uncovered evidence of a plot by them against him. When the lords were brought to trial in parliament in September, however, no evidence to support such claims was put forward. The charges all related to past events. Arundel and Warwick were both found guilty. Arundel was sentenced to death and Warwick to exile on the Isle of Man. Gloucester, Richard's most dangerous enemy, was found dead in prison at Calais before he could be brought to trial. Almost certainly he was murdered on the king's orders.

The background to the coup is probably to be found in the king's growing sense of insecurity. In the parliament of January 1397 the Commons had renewed their earlier criticism of the size and cost of the royal household. Richard reacted to their criticisms angrily, saying that these matters pertained to the prerogative and that it was not within the Commons' competence to discuss them. He was probably reminded of the Commons' earlier stinging criticisms of his extravagance in the 1380s. At the same time, there were signs that the former Appellants might be stirring against him again. Two years previously in parliament Arundel had loudly denounced Richard's friendship with Gaunt and had been obliged to apologise. In the first half of 1397, Warwick, another former Appellant, had suffered judicial reverses which left him with a powerful sense of grievance against the court. In January the earl was fined for occupying the estates of Richard's former confessor, John Burghill, now bishop of Llandaff, while six month later he was condemned by king's bench to surrender the lordship of Gower to Thomas Mowbray, with whose family he had long disputed it – and, worse still, to hand over to Mowbray arrears of the profits and issues. If no plot against the king was in prospect, it was easy for him to suppose that there might be one.

To chroniclers at the time it seemed that Richard's government had suddenly turned burdensome and oppressive. Walsingham, in a famous comment, said that Richard 'began to tyrannise his people'.[18] What Walsingham meant was that he had begun to afflict them with bonds and taxes. It is easy to see how Richard's coup could be interpreted as marking a sudden change in his kingly style, a change to unbridled authoritarianism. But, contrary to appearances, there was an underlying consistency in the king's actions. Richard saw himself as simply intensifying his campaign for obedience. In a speech to parliament in 1397 his chancellor said that in a well-governed realm 'every subject should be obedient to the king and his laws'.[19] The language here is strikingly reminiscent of that employed in the submissions which Richard had exacted from the Irish chieftains on his visit to Dublin three years before. Donnchadh O'Byrne, for example, swore 'faithfully to serve and obey the king as his liege lord against all men ... with every kind of submission, obedience and fealty'.[20] The Irish settlement in many ways anticipated the central features of the later settlement in England. In each case Richard sought to unite his subjects in obedience to his rule. In a letter he sent in 1398 to Albert, count of Holland to justify his actions he deployed arguments of a slightly different kind.[21] Here he said that by punishing the Appellants as rebels he had brought 'peace' to his realm. By 'peace' in this context, he meant something closely related to obedience; he meant unity, or the absence of discord. This was the sense in which the word was understood in contemporary academic circles. Jean Gerson, the chancellor of Paris, a few years later was to enjoin peace on the rival factions at the French court. He argued that peace – that is, unity – was essential if the realm was to regain strength. Richard interpreted 'peace' in this way as the expression of a realm at ease with kingly authority.

In the wake of his remarkable triumph Richard embarked on a major remodelling of the nobility. Those who had lent him their support duly received their reward. Three of his most reliable allies – William Scrope, Thomas Percy and Thomas Despenser – were raised to earldoms, while others already ennobled were raised to higher dignities in the peerage, five becoming dukes. Walsingham disparagingly referred to this last group as the 'duketti'. To outsiders, the court presented a powerful image of strength.

The reality, however, was very different. The court was actually riven with faction. There were differences between the two former junior Appellants and those who were closer to Richard. There were also differences between those who were content with the status quo and those who wanted to carry the counter-revolution further. The event which brought these tensions into the open was the quarrel between Gaunt's son, Bolingbroke, now duke of Hereford, and Thomas Mowbray, now duke of Norfolk.

The story, as Hereford was to tell it, was that Norfolk stopped him one day on the road near Brentford, maintaining that the two of them were to be 'undone' by the king for their part in the events of 1387–88. Hereford expressed disbelief, saying that they had both received pardons. Norfolk nonetheless persisted, saying that the pardons were worthless and adding that the king and his friends intended to go further, reversing the judgement of 1327 and encompassing the destruction of the duke of Lancaster's inheritance.[22] The story which Norfolk unfolded was in all likelihood true. John of Gaunt aroused intense jealousy among the younger courtiers because of his enormous power and wealth. The Lancastrian inheritance was the most extensive in England, and there were many who coveted a share in it. What worried the king most, however, was the problem of what would happen after Gaunt's death. Gaunt was by now ageing and his heir was a former Appellant and a man whom he distrusted. The Lancastrian inheritance, presently a bulwark of royal power, could become a challenge and a focus for opposition. There was good reason for seeking its removal.

Hereford, on hearing Norfolk's words, was understandably alarmed. His immediate reaction was to report the events to the king. The latter found himself in a difficult position, for he scarcely wanted the royal dirty linen washed in public. Accordingly, he ordered the two men to appear before a parliamentary subcommittee in April. At this session Norfolk strongly denied Hereford's account of what had transpired between them, while Hereford stood by his word. In the absence of any means of establishing either man's guilt or innocence, it was resolved that the dispute between them be resolved by the law of arms. Richard ordered the two men to appear in the lists against each other at Coventry on 19 September. As the day approached, however, he was faced with a further dilemma: how to deal with the outcome. If Norfolk won, the crowds would suppose that he had fixed the matter in his favour, while if Hereford did, the latter would immediately become a popular hero. Richard resolved the matter by taking the dispute into his own hands. At the last moment he called the duel off, sentencing Hereford to exile for ten years and Norfolk to exile for life. Four months later, Gaunt died. Richard now faced the most difficult dilemma of all. Should he allow Hereford to succeed to his father's inheritance? Or should he, rather, extend his exile to life? On 18 March he published his decision. He seized the inheritance, extending Hereford's exile to life. Three months later he set out for Ireland, where his earlier settlement was unravelling.

Richard departed for Ireland believing that his kingdom was safe. Hereford was in Paris, under the watchful eye of the duke of Burgundy, who valued his good relations with Richard in the interests of Anglo-Burgundian trade. The duke of York, his uncle, was keeping an eye on the realm's defences. But in June Hereford slipped the leash. Learning that Richard was in Ireland, he fitted out a small expedition and landed at Ravenspur on the Yorkshire coast.[23] He immediately attracted wide-spread support locally. At Doncaster he won over the Percies, the main power-brokers in northern England. From Doncaster in early July he marched south west across the midlands and then north along the Marches to Chester. A message was sent to Richard in Ireland, but it was another two weeks before he made the journey back. By that time support for his cause was ebbing away. Many of his leading subjects had given him up as lost. In Conway Castle on about 16 August he surrendered to Northumberland, his adversary's representative. Hereford ordered a parliament to be summoned in the king's name in September and articles of deposition were drawn up. When the Lords and Commons assembled, Richard was formally deposed, and Hereford took his place as Henry IV. Richard's reign was deemed to have ended on 29 September 1399

Henry next had the problem of deciding what to do with his predecessor. The deposed Richard, so long as he lived, would be a constant challenge to the legitimacy of the new Lancastrian regime. His former allies and retainers, and possibly too those disaffected with the new government, might seek his restoration. The new king's answer was to remove his predecessor as far from sight as possible. In December he sent him northwards to the great Lancastrian fortress of Pontefract.

However, the strategy of concealment did not work. In January 1400 a
rebellion led by the ex-king's former courtiers sought his restoration.
The rebellion, as it happened, failed dismally: the ringleaders were
soon rounded up and executed. But the fact that the rising took place
at all sealed Richard's fate. In the middle of February the former
king was done to death in his cell at Pontefract. His body was brought
southwards for burial in the obscurity of King's Langley friary (Hertfordshire). Henry was insistent that Richard should not be buried in the
traditional royal mausoleum of Westminster, for interment there would
draw attention to his kingliness. However, he did want all of his subjects
to know that their ex-king was dead. So when the cortège made its slow
way south, the body was put on display at each overnight stop. Another
generation was to pass before Richard's body was finally moved to
Westminster. In 1414 Henry V, who as a boy had been knighted by
Richard, had the ex-king's remains honourably reinterred in the abbey
before setting out for Agincourt. It was a useful symbolic way of healing the wounds that had been opened up by his father's usurpation. A
decade and a half after his death, Richard's body was finally laid alongside that of his first wife, Anne, in the tomb which he had commissioned
for them both in the 1390s. The likenesses of the two on their effigies are
almost certainly attempts at portraiture.

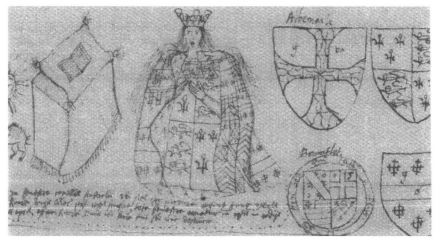

Portrait of Anne Neville, the queen of Richard III, in a window in Skipton
church (Yorkshire) (now lost). (*British Library*)

The English Royal Line
Edward III to Richard III

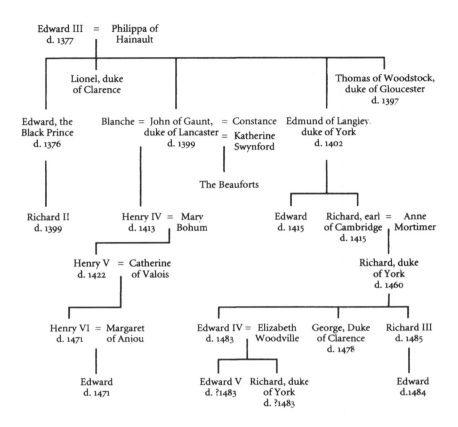

5

Richard III

Richard II's deposition was to inaugurate nearly a century of dynastic instability in England. For some fifty years to the middle of the fifteenth century the Lancastrians' position had looked secure. Henry IV had enjoyed remarkable success in establishing his dynasty on the throne. Once the threat from the Percies had been removed, as it had by 1405, Henry faced no serious challenge to his kingly title. In the next generation the heroically able Henry V had strengthened the dynasty's legitimacy by the successful prosecution of war in France. It was in the next generation again, that of Henry VI, that the Lancastrians ran into difficulties. Henry VI's inanity changed everything. The king's sheer incapacity for government called into question his own, and his dynasty's, entitlement to rule. In 1461, after six years of intermittent civil war, Henry was deposed. Richard, duke of York's son, Edward of March, took the crown as Edward IV. Richard of Gloucester – the future Richard III – was the new king's younger brother.

Richard of Gloucester was born at Fotheringhay (Northamptonshire) on 2 October 1452. The boy's lineage was exalted. His father, Duke Richard, could claim descent from Edward III through two lines. In the direct male line he was descended from Edward's fourth surviving son, Edmund of Langley, duke of York, his father being the younger of Edmund's two sons, while on the female side, still more impressively, he could trace a direct line of descent from Edward's second son, Lionel of Antwerp, through his mother Anne (née Mortimer), Lionel's grand-daughter. His distinguished lineage, not to mention his wide kin connections, ensured for the duke a leading role in the politics of the day. In the 1440s, as the king's lieutenant general, he performed distinguished service in the closing stages of the war in France. In the summer of 1441 he successfully defended Pontoise, in Normandy, against a major assault by the French king and his forces. His strong chivalric sense was a major influence on his ethical code and his political conduct. When after 1450 he quarrelled with Henry's favourite, Edmund, duke of Somerset, it was because he felt that Somerset had dishonoured him by surrendering Rouen to the French.[1] York's rather old-fashioned, traditional sense of chivalry was to be inherited by the youngest of his three sons.

Richard of Gloucester was no more than a boy when, in the summer of 1460, the kingship of Lancaster entered its death throes. By the mid to late 1450s his father had emerged as the regime's most persistent and implacable critic. Queen Margaret, Henry VI's feisty consort and the effective champion of the court, was desperate to secure his political elimination. At a stand-off at Ludford, near Ludlow, in October 1459 she very nearly succeeded. A smallish Yorkist force under the command of York himself was drawn up on the banks of the River Teme opposite a larger Lancastrian one. It seemed that the long-delayed showdown between the two sides had finally come. Yet at the last moment the Yorkists backed off. Word spread among the Yorkist soldiery that the king was present with his troops on the other side, and their resolve broke. York fled to Ireland, and Warwick and the other Yorkist lords to Calais. Margaret, fatally for her cause, was unable to press home her advantage. Her enemies had fled beyond her grasp. In the following year the Yorkists stormed back in force. In June 1460 Warwick, leading the Calais garrison of which he held the captaincy, landed at Sandwich, marched through London and defeated the Lancastrians at Northampton, even capturing Henry himself. The initiative now lay firmly with the Yorkist challengers. In early autumn Duke Richard returned from Ireland and in the October parliament formally claimed the throne. The duke's bid was ill-received by his peers. While many of the nobility sympathised with his cause, the majority were still committed to the Lancastrian royal title. York had to settle for a compromise which allowed Henry to reign for his lifetime but provided for his own succession on his death. In Queen Margaret's eyes, however, any settlement which threatened the right to the crown of her son was unacceptable. In the winter of 1460 she embarked on a new campaign against her enemies. By late December she was heading south from her northern headquarters, and in a dizzying reversal of fortune defeated and killed Duke Richard at Wakefield. Two months later at St Albans she regained possession of her husband. Paradoxically, however, it was her very success that proved her undoing. The Yorkists, now deprived of a ruler through whom they could govern, had to create one of their own. On 4 March 1461, York's son Edward was installed on the throne as Edward IV. Just over three weeks later, the new king gave substance to his title by crushing the Lancastrians at Towton.

The young Richard of Gloucester was barely nine when his brother became king. In his early childhood he had been brought up by his mother, the Duchess Cecily, a member of the Neville family and a lady renowned for her piety. In the final whirlwind of Lancastrian misrule he lived for a while under the protective roof of a London widow.[2] After his brother became king, he was given a small establishment of his own in the royal palace at Greenwich. In 1465, however, he was entrusted to the upbringing of his Neville kinsman, Richard, earl of Warwick, at Middleham (Yorkshire). Here he was given his first introduction to northern society, to the world of the clannish gentry of Yorkshire and the Borders, the men who were to prove his political mainstay later.

Policy differences with Edward and a festering resentment at the influence of his wife's Woodville kin led Warwick and George of Clarence, the king's brother, to rise in rebellion in 1469. For a few uneasy months that autumn Warwick attempted to rule England using the king as his puppet. Such a bizarre governmental arrangement was hardly calculated to inspire political society with confidence. In the spring of 1470 Edward forcefully reasserted his authority, driving Warwick and Clarence into exile. The two malcontents fled to Angers in France, where they were reconciled on Louis XI's initiative to Queen Margaret and her husband. Six months later, with French backing, Warwick launched a fresh invasion of England. Henry VI was restored to his throne, while Edward fled to his sister's court in Flanders, with Richard following him.[3] Henry's government, entirely dependent on Warwick's sponsorship, failed to win popular approval, and in March 1471, with Burgundian support, Edward counter-attacked. Edward landed on the Yorkshire coast at Ravenspur, marched down the length of England and defeated the Lancastrian at Barnet and Tewkesbury. On 21 May 1471 he entered London. Within a day or two, the hapless Henry had been put to death in the Tower.

In this period of dizzying instability Richard had been his brother's

most trusty ally. Where his sibling Clarence had been fickle and unreliable, Richard had been unswervingly loyal. In his brother's second reign
Richard was to reap his reward handsomely. Edward loaded him with
estates and offices forfeited by the rebels. On 14 July 1471 he granted him
in tail all Warwick's estates north of the River Trent, including the
major lordships of Middleham and Sheriff Hutton in Yorkshire, and
Penrith in Cumberland. A few months later, in December, he went further, giving him the forfeited estates of the hard-line Lancastrian, the
earl of Oxford. Along with these grants of land, the king awarded him
a series of offices which had been held by Warwick. The most important of these were the chamberlainship of England and the chief
stewardship of the duchy of Lancaster.[4] More grants were to come
Richard's way later. In June 1475 the king granted him the major lordship of Skipton in Craven (Yorkshire), forfeited by the Cliffords, and
three years later, in an exchange of properties, the lordship and castle of
Richmond. Finally, in January 1483 Edward created for him a mighty
palatinate comprising the counties of Cumberland and Westmorland.

As a result of these grants, Richard became almost the equal of his
brother Clarence in wealth. His estates and offices brought him an
income in the region of £3500-£4000 a year. And to the lands which he
received by grant were shortly to be added those which he acquired by
marriage. In April 1472 Richard, stealing a march on Clarence, secured
the hand of Anne Neville, one of the Kingmaker's daughters and co-
heiresses. By virtue of this match he acquired a claim to Warwick's
estates, some of which he already held, and, as well, to the estates of his
widow, Anne. He did not, however, succeed in gaining possession of the
lands immediately. His claim, and his determination to pursue it, set
him at odds with Clarence, who was married to the other coheiress.[5] In
the spring of 1472 a series of hearings was held to carry out a division
between the two claimants. At the end of the sessions in April Clarence
was confirmed in possession of the estates which he already held, while
Richard was assigned lands of equivalent value in Yorkshire (including
Middleham and Sheriff Hutton), County Durham and the Welsh
Marches.

Implementation of the award, however, was frustrated by a second
difficulty. Neither party was prepared to receive his share of the lands
by royal grant, since such grants could be revoked by act of resumption.

Each insisted on holding by inheritance. But if the two brothers were to enter into their estates as heirs of the deceased earl, the claims of the dowager countess of Warwick would have to be extinguished; and that would by no means be easy. The countess, a feisty lady, insisted on standing by her rights and fled into sanctuary at Beaulieu Abbey. Eventually Richard succeeded in whisking her away northwards, provoking rumours that he was browbeating her into signing away her lands. As the row dragged on, and with no end to it in sight, the king eventually imposed his own settlement. In May 1474 he pushed through an act of parliament settling all the Warwick estates on Clarence and Gloucester in right of their respective wives. The dowager countess's claims were extinguished by the device of declaring her legally dead. Richard had shown how high-handed he could be in pursuit of his claims: a portent of things to come. But the king had hardly behaved any better. In using statute law to manipulate title, he had provided a model of how might could triumph over right which his brother would shortly follow.

There is further evidence from this time of Richard's acquisitiveness – in particular, of his territorial acquisitiveness. In 1471, as we have seen, his brother had granted him the estates, scattered across eastern England, of John de Vere, earl of Oxford, a Lancastrian die-hard. The earl's mother, who was by now an elderly and infirm widow, had her customary dower interest in these estates; but she also had an estate of her own, since she was an heiress. In 1473, almost certainly with the king's backing, Richard forced her to surrender her entire estate to him. The countess's son and his friends later complained that this had been achieved 'by heinous menace of loss of life and imprisonment' and that the duke had acted out of 'inordinate covetise and ungodly disposition'. Only after Richard's death was restitution obtained.

Equally questionable in character was Richard's involvement in the judicial destruction of his brother Clarence. Clarence was executed for treason in February 1478. It is true that the prime responsibility for the removal of the duke lay with the king himself, who had grown increasingly irritated with his brother's behaviour; the notion, familiar from Shakespeare, that Richard was involved in murdering him was dreamt up by Tudor propagandists. None the less, Richard was an accomplice to an act of judicial murder and the prime beneficiary of his brother's death. One of the grants made to him – that of the earldom of Salisbury, a subsidiary title held by Clarence – was actually made to him three days before Clarence's death. The various other grants in his favour were presumably the price that he exacted for giving the king his support. The first such grant was an act allowing him to alienate portions of the Warwick inheritance which he had been forbidden to alienate by the act of 1474, and the second an exchange of lands with the king by which he acquired the valuable lordship of Ogmore in South Wales. In the light of the generosity with which the king treated him, it is hard not to conclude that he was a willing accomplice in what amounted to an act of fratricide.

Richard's behaviour in these years showed a number of disagreeable traits which, over time, were to become more pronounced. His ruthlessness, for example, and his intolerance of restraint, both already evident in the 1470s, were traits which were to be more blatantly displayed on his climb to the throne. In some ways, the young Richard can be seen as a not untypical late medieval aristocrat. His insatiable appetite for land and his willingness to take advantage of elderly dowagers are characteristics found in others of the baronial class. But there was one aspect of Richard's behaviour which may be regarded as exceptional. This was the remarkable freedom that he showed in reorganising and altering the shape of his estates. Other landowners tended to cling onto the lands which they had inherited. Richard did not. He was constantly purchasing or leasing land, seeking out grants, or exchanging one piece of land for another.[6] The reason for this was that, as a younger son, he had inherited very few estates from his parents. He felt none of the mystical attachment to land which the longer established lineages felt. This made for a remarkable independence of outlook on his part. Relatively free of restraint, he was more prepared to act independently and unilaterally. How these habits of thought might be translated into political action would, in course of time, become clear. But for the moment Richard was his brother's most loyal and committed supporter, one of the pillars of the Yorkist establishment. As he said in his motto, 'loyalty binds me'. This record of loyalty would change in the course of 1483.

Edward IV's death on 9 April 1483 appears to have taken his subjects by surprise. Edward was still only forty-one, and his illness had been brief. His heir was his eldest son, the twelve-year-old Prince Edward. In

a conventional tribute the Italian visitor Domenico complimented the
young man as highly promising, and 'scholarly in advance of his years'.[7]
But, whatever his accomplishments, it was clear that he was not mature
enough to govern. Accordingly, arrangements would have to be set in
place for a minority. Opinion was divided on what form the minority
government should take. One view was that a protectorate should be
inaugurated, with Duke Richard acting as protector, on roughly the
lines of Gloucester's protectorate in Henry VI's minority in the 1420s.[8]
The contrary view was that there should be no protectorate at all: the
young prince should be crowned king as soon as possible, and government be carried on in his name by a conciliar body, much as in the
minority of Richard II.[9] This latter view appears to have been espoused
by the Woodvilles, the queen's relatives, and their allies, and it may have
been the view of the late king too. Richard himself was not involved in
the discussions. He was at Middleham Castle in Yorkshire in April, but
Lord Hastings, the chamberlain of the household, kept him in touch. It
appears that at this stage no firm conclusions were reached on the form
that government should take. However, all the council were agreed that
the new king should be the focus of popular loyalty.

At the time that his father died the new king was at Ludlow, with his
Woodville uncle, Anthony, Earl Rivers. Rivers and his young charge and
their respective retinues set out for the capital on 24 April. They were
reassured by conciliatory greetings from Richard, offering the queen his
condolences and the council his loyalty. Richard suggested to Rivers that
the two of them meet at Northampton to accompany the king to London together. When he arrived at Northampton, Richard met the earl,
although his young charge had already gone on to Stony Stratford.
Richard, his close ally Buckingham, and Rivers then enjoyed a convivial
dinner. Rivers had no sense that anything was amiss.

Then the next morning Richard launched his coup. Rivers and two
others of the king's attendants, Grey and Vaughan, were arrested and
despatched to prison in Pontefract. A few days later Richard put a cart-
load of Woodville weapons on display in the capital, claiming that the
Woodvilles had been hatching a plot against him. The story put about
by Richard of a Woodville plot was picked up by Mancini, the Italian
who wrote an account of the usurpation, and was subsequently
repeated. But the notion that the Woodvilles were plotting against the

duke is almost entirely fictitious.[10] There was no earlier history of tension between the Woodvilles and Richard. The Woodvilles had hardly ever operated as a discrete group. Rivers himself entertained no suspicions of Richard when the two met at Northampton; he certainly would not have dined with him if he had. So far from the Woodvilles plotting against Richard, it was actually Richard who was plotting against the Woodvilles. Richard was taking the first steps to a possible seizure of power.

When news reached the capital of Lord Rivers's arrest, the reaction was one of consternation and dismay. The queen, taking her younger son Richard and her daughters with her, withdrew to sanctuary in Westminster Abbey. The Woodvilles now found themselves thrown onto the defensive. At a council meeting on 10 May, the new king's coronation was postponed – initially to 24 June, and then to Sunday, 22 June.[11] A day or two earlier, Duke Richard had been confirmed in office as protector. Recognition of his position gave him the powers of appointment and patronage vested in the crown. Immediately, he granted generous rewards to his ally Buckingham. He made the duke chief justice and chamberlain of both North and South Wales for life, and appointed him constable of all the castles and lordships in Wales and the Marches at the disposal of the crown, some fifty-three in all. This was a grant of quite unprecedented range. Buckingham was in effect made a viceroy in Wales. Nothing illustrates more clearly Duke Richard's need for magnate support at this time. And nothing perhaps more strongly suggests that he had in mind further moves to come.

For the next four to five weeks an uneasy calm reigned in the capital. Slowly but surely, Gloucester tightened his grip on the royal administration. On 10 May Edward IV's chancellor Thomas Rotherham was replaced by the keeper of the privy seal, Bishop Russell. In the shires Richard replaced Woodville men by men whom he considered more committed to his own person. In Kent, for example, William Haute was replaced as sheriff by Sir Henry Ferrers, Lord Hastings's nephew. Richard had to be careful, however, not to give undue offence. He quickly encountered opposition when he made a demand in the council that Rivers and his friends be condemned as traitors. His fellow councillors insisted that the alleged ambushes prepared for him at Stony Stratford were not directed against someone who was then protector.

Given this resistance, he withdrew his demand. So long as he acted within his rights, however, and upheld the princes' interests, he enjoyed some measure of support.

The period of uneasy calm was ended on Friday, 13 June. It was on this day that Richard suddenly and without prior indication executed Lord Hastings. The story of Hastings's arrest and execution is familiar from Shakespeare. Richard accused Hastings, the most honest and upright of Yorkists, of plotting against him with the queen. Before Hastings could offer a reply, he was dragged from the chamber and beheaded.[12] Two senior bishops were arrested at the same time; and so too was Lord Stanley. Richard justified his attack by alleging a Woodville coup – the same ploy as he had used in April. In a letter to the city of York he appealed for help

> Against the queen, her blood, adherents and affinity, which have intended and daily do intend to murder and utterly destroy us and our cousin, the duke of Buckingham, and the old royal blood of this realm and, as is now openly known, by their subtle and damnable ways forecasted the same ...[13]

The idea of a plot against the duke was picked up by the Tudor historian Polydore Vergil. According to his account, Gloucester suddenly announced to the meeting that the Woodvilles were using sorcery against him and that Lord Hastings was involved in their machinations. But the only evidence ever produced of a Woodville plot comes from Richard himself. No other source so much as hints at it. In reality, Richard appears to have been launching a pre-emptive strike. He was removing a powerful and respected figure who, so he thought, would be likely to obstruct his path to the throne. Richard was conscious that in a matter of weeks, when Edward was crowned, his protectorate would be ended. The Woodvilles would then be able to organise a counter-coup. If he was safeguard everything that he had gained, it was essential that he make a bid for the throne. Very likely he had sounded out Hastings about such an initiative and had received no favourable answer. Hastings's removal would in this event be a prerequisite for the next and most dangerous stage of his plan.

On Sunday, 22 June, in a sermon at Paul's Cross, the fashionable London preacher Ralph Shaw set out Duke Richard's claim to the crown.

Two days later, on Tuesday, the 24th, Richard's ally Buckingham presented a similar case to the mayor and aldermen of London at the Guildhall. The argument which the two spokesmen proposed was embodied in the following January in the *Titulus Regius*, Richard's title to the throne. It was alleged that Edward IV's two sons were bastards and for that reason were unfit to rule. Their father's marriage to Elizabeth Woodville had been brought about solely by sorcery. Worse still, the marriage was legally invalid, since the king was already under precontract to Lady Eleanor Butler. And because the offspring of Richard's brother Clarence were disqualified by their father's attainder, Richard was Edward's true heir.[14] A moral case for Richard's kingship was put forward too. Richard's succession was conducive both to good government and to the common weal. Edward IV's government had been corrupted by the malign influence of the Woodvilles. The laws of the Church had been broken, justice set aside, and the prosperity of the realm diminished. Richard would restore the blessings of good government. His 'wit, prudence, justice and princely courage' were already known to all. He had both the will and the qualifications to rule. For these reasons he was 'the very inheritor of the Crown and the Dignity Royal'.

How far people were taken in by Richard's barrage of propaganda is hard to say. The chroniclers suggest that reactions to it in London were muted. By now, most people in the capital appear to have accepted that Richard's usurpation was inevitable. They felt that there was almost nothing they could do to stop it. The final stage in Richard's ascent to the throne was shortly engineered by Buckingham. On 26 June the duke presented a petition to Richard asking him to assume the crown. After an outward show of hesitation the duke accepted. On 6 July 1483 he was crowned king in Westminster Abbey.[15]

Richard's seizure of the crown had been carefully prepared and well thought out. Throughout the three months from April 1483 his actions had been informed by a degree of consistency which points to remarkable clarity of purpose. The argument sometimes advanced that he was merely reacting to events fails to convince. At every stage he dictated events; he commanded the initiative. Time and again, he caught his opponents unawares. Even the wily and worldly wise Hastings was surprised. The signs are that the spur to Richard's actions was naked ambition. No other explanation comes close to fitting the facts. Yet Richard clothed his moves in the language of self-righteousness. In letters and pamphlets he emphasised his unique fitness to govern and his mission to cleanse the offices of government. Increasingly convinced of his own destiny, he overrode everyone and everything in his way.

Richard had gained the throne with remarkable ease. None the less his regime was distinctly lacking in legitimacy. There was widespread popular sympathy for Edward's deposed sons. Mancini says that people wept openly in the streets of London when they thought of them. Richard's position was actually a good deal less secure than it looked. By dint of his usurpation he had split the hitherto strong Yorkist establishment. Those who had been closest to Edward IV and his household felt alienated. Richard had justified his course by claiming to uphold his brother's inheritance against the avaricious Woodvilles; yet what he had done was to besmirch his brother's name and depose and imprison his sons. There was no logic or consistency in his arguments. By the way he become king, Richard ensured that he would not for long remain king.[16]

By the summer of 1483 rumours appear to have been circulating of the deaths of the two princes. Entries were made in contemporary chronicles or calendars recording that Edward V was killed on 22 June or 26 June, or some similar date.[17] Certainly there can be little doubt that Richard planned to dispose of the princes sooner rather than later. Proof of this is found in a grant that he made to Lord Berkeley barely two months after his accession of a share in the Mowbray inheritance, which the younger of the two princes held.[18] Rumours of the princes' deaths around midsummer proved the trigger to resistance to Richard. In the autumn of 1483 a series of risings broke out across southern and south-western England. The risings have long gone by the name of 'Buckingham's Rebellion'. However, they were planned well before Buckingham became involved in them, and few if any of the rebels had any connection with the duke. The majority of the rebels were former servants of Edward IV, and the more important of them had held senior positions in his household.

There were three main centres of rebellion.[19] The first of these and the earliest to erupt, was Kent and the south east, where virtually all of the rebels were former servants of Edward IV. Further west there was an outbreak in Hampshire, Wiltshire and Berkshire, where some of

Clarence's former retainers were involved. To the west again, there were eruptions in Somerset and Devon, where the ringleaders were Thomas Grey, marquess of Dorset, Elizabeth Woodville's son, and Sir Thomas St Leger, a retainer of Edward IV. In all of these areas the opposition was quickly crushed. But Richard's victory was a Pyrrhic one. To reimpose his authority on southern England, he had to bring in servants and retainers of his from the North. Yorkshiremen and Cumbrians were appointed sheriffs and JPs in Kent, Hampshire, Cornwall and other southern counties.[20] The intrusion of these men caused deep resentment. There was a widely held belief that local government should be exercised by local men. For outsiders to be appointed to office constituted 'tyranny'.[21] Richard's reliance on outsiders cost him the goodwill of the gentry of southern England. His rule was perceived as factional. Much as he tried to present himself as a national figure, he failed. After 1483 his power base, which had never been wide, narrowed still further.

In the year following the rebellion, one misfortune after another afflicted the king. At the beginning of April his only son, Edward of Middleham, died. This left him without an heir of his body. There seemed little prospect that his wife Anne would be able to give him another son: Anne was sprung from a stock that over three generations had produced only daughters and not sons. Rumours began to circulate that Richard intended to divorce Anne and marry his niece Elizabeth of York. When in 1485 Anne fell seriously ill, it was rumoured that he was trying to dispose of her. Anne's subsequent death, in March, merely added to his problems. It seemed to many that Richard's cause was morally blighted. God was inflicting a curse on the king and his line. The series of deaths was Richard's punishment for his crime in usurping the crown.[22]

Opposition to Richard now began to centre on the obscure exile Henry Tudor.[23] Henry had inherited the Lancastrian claim through his mother Lady Margaret Beaufort, a descendant of John of Gaunt. By as early as the autumn of 1483 dissident Yorkists involved in Buckingham's rebellion were transferring their support to Henry because of fears that the two princes were dead. The failure of Buckingham's rebellion drove many of these Yorkists to seek exile at Henry's court at Rennes. In Rennes Cathedral on Christmas Day 1483, in the company of witnesses who included both Yorkists and Lancastrians, Henry swore to marry

Elizabeth of York as soon as he had won the throne of England. So long as he remained an obscure exile at Rennes, Henry posed little threat to Richard. But in the autumn of 1484 the French government, in a sudden switch of policy, decided to give him their backing. The marshal of France, Philippe de Crèvecoeur, was keen to stir up trouble for Richard and thus to weaken the English position in the Channel. The French government generously provided Henry with shipping, troops and finance. On 31 July 1485 the pretender set sail from Harfleur. A week later he disembarked at Milford Haven in the south west of Wales. French support was as crucial in launching him on his way as it had been for Bolingbroke in 1399.

Richard, it seems, was informed of Henry's landing on 11 August: his intelligence network had served him well. Although firmly on the defensive, he relished the prospect of engaging with his enemy. A victory in battle would validate his kingship and provide him with the supreme authentication of his title. On the day that he received the news he directed his supporters to muster at Nottingham. Henry had been forced to take a highly circuitous route across Wales. Because his direct path through Glamorgan was blocked by magnates loyal to Richard, he struck north eastwards across central Wales into the midlands. On 15 August he reached Shrewsbury. From there he continued across Staffordshire and into north Warwickshire. Richard meanwhile was marching south to head him off. There is disagreement about where exactly the two sides met in battle. Although the engagement between them has always been known as the 'battle of Bosworth', it was not necessarily fought at Bosworth. The traditional battle site of Ambion Hill, to the south of the town, is now regarded as the least likely: it is too small. In 1985 Colin Richmond suggested that the fighting took place at Dadlington, further south, where some of the fallen were buried and where a chantry was established for their souls.[24] The site is certainly a possibility. But the most plausible location is probably the one suggested by Michael Jones – the area of flat land to the east of Atherstone (Warwickshire) drained by the River Anker. There are place names in the locality which preserve the memory of a battle, among them Bloody Bank and King Dick's Hole. More significantly, there are records of a couple of payments by Henry VII reimbursing landowners at Atherstone and nearby Merevale for damage suffered in the course of the battle.[25] The arguments for the battle being fought in the Atherstone area seem strong.

Bosworth is an ill-documented battle, as the dispute over where it was fought shows. Indeed, it is the worst documented important battle in English history. Only one account of the engagement by an eyewitness survives, and all the later accounts are brief and contradictory. One point, however, is clear. Richard's army was far smaller than it could have been. In his haste to engage with Henry, Richard had not allowed his northern retainers enough time to move south to link up with him. He was thus lacking the services of some of his most committed supporters. It is very difficult to say exactly how many men were engaged on either side. Henry may have had some 5000 men, and Richard perhaps 7–8000, but these can only be inspired guesses. Richard inaugurated the hostilities by leading a big cavalry charge. To encourage his men, he donned his crown and displayed the royal arms, in traditional chivalric fashion. His charge, however, failed to break Henry's strong defensive position. If the account of a French eyewitness is to be believed, Henry had a force of French pikemen with him.[26] These men, who were practised in defensive warfare, would break cavalry attacks by pulling into square formations which cavalry could not penetrate. From this point in the battle, the two sides became locked in close hand-to-hand fighting. At some stage Richard lost his horse: this part of the Shakespearean version is probably right. He was by now in serious personal danger. Although he fought doggedly on, he was separated from his supporters and surrounded by enemy formations. Northumberland's men held back. Eventually the king was overwhelmed and cut down. When he fell, the battle was effectively over. At Bosworth, as at Hastings, the death of the king proved decisive.

Richard's body was stripped and carried naked on horseback to nearby Leicester for burial. At first, it seems, it was interred in the great collegiate church of Our Lady in the Newarke, founded in the fourteenth century by Duke Henry of Lancaster. Perhaps because the Newarke was a church with such strong Lancastrian associations, however, it was later moved to the Greyfriars. Eventually its resting place was marked by a monument of some sort, now lost.[27]

Richard's death at Bosworth marked a turning-point in English history. The brief tenure of the crown by the house of York was brought to a premature end, and a new dynasty took over. Undoubtedly the out-come of Bosworth was a surprise: by all accounts, Richard should have won against Henry. He himself expected to win. Not since 1066 had an English king been killed in battle on his own soil. So what had gone wrong? A number of relatively minor tactical errors by Richard con-tributed to his defeat. The most obvious of these is that he went into battle with too few men. He should have waited for his retinues from Yorkshire to reach him. Moreover, his reliance on a cavalry charge was probably misguided. In seeking to break the pikemen formations, he should have made more use of his infantry. In his tactics against the pikemen, Richard made the same mistake as another contemporary ruler, Charles the Bold, duke of Burgundy. Charles was worsted by groups of Swiss pikemen at Grandson, Murat and fatally at Nancy. More generally, the point could be made that Richard never overcame the cir-cumstances of his accession: his power base was too narrow, and he had fractured the Yorkist establishment. Moreover, he relied excessively on northerners, and northerners were never popular in southern England.

But was there some larger historical process at work? Some years ago, Colin Richmond offered a persuasive interpretation of Bosworth which set it in the broader pattern of English medieval history.[28] Polit-ical cohesion in late medieval England, Richmond argued, depended on the successful pursuit of foreign war. The reigns of Edward III in the fourteenth century and of Henry V in the early fifteenth had both shown this. In the summer of 1475 Edward IV had been given the chance to emulate Henry V's achievement by reopening the war with France. When confronted by Louis XI's army near Agincourt, however, his nerve failed him; he allowed himself to be bought off at Picquigny with a large French pension. So Edward had failed to channel the English nobility's aggressive instincts into a foreign war. Because of this, the healing of the social and political tensions in the nobility in Edward's later years was only superficial. When the king died in 1483 the York-ist regime collapsed in feuding and faction-fighting. How different Edward V's accession turned out to be from that of Henry VI half a century earlier. When the Lancastrian elite were fighting the French, they stood together. When the Yorkist elite were not, they tore at each other's throats.

Professor Richmond's argument is a persuasive one, which it is tempting to accept. But it begs an important question: how was it that Henry VII was able to achieve cohesion and stability where the Yorkists had failed? Or, more precisely, how was it that Henry VII was able to achieve those ends while himself refraining from foreign war? It could be argued that Henry was the beneficiary of his predecessor's unhappy legacy of faction. In other words, the memory of the Yorkist bloodletting was so vivid that Henry's subjects accepted his rule, whether they liked it or not. And there may well be some truth in this argument. Equally, it could be maintained that Henry kept his nobility in check by offering them the late medieval equivalent of bread and circuses – lavish tournaments. And there may be something in this argument too. Henry's tournaments were certainly lavish spectacles. But perhaps we should consider a different explanation altogether – namely, that there was a change in the political culture of the nobility. By the late fifteenth century the signs are that the traditional chivalric ethic was losing some of its function and purpose. It did not completely wither away: as political theatre it was to enjoy a later flowering in Elizabeth's reign. But no longer did it provide the sole justification for the status and privileges of the nobility. In its place, rather, a new ethic was gradually developing, one which dressed the old chivalric honour code in rich humanistic clothing. True nobility, it was now believed, was found less in the traditional practice of arms than in civilised and peaceable pursuits – in learning and good manners, and in service to the state. It was this new body of ideas which the Tudors were to turn successfully to their political advantage. Service to the crown was increasingly privileged as a source of honour and legitimation for the nobility over service in war.

It is doubtful if Richard III would have found much to identify with in this new definition of nobility. Richard's ideas, it has been maintained, belonged more to the world of old-fashioned militarism.[29] To a greater extent than his brother, he believed in national renewal through war. Paradoxically, had he lived, he might have succeeded in achieving that goal where his brother had so signally failed. In many ways, Richard can be seen as standing in a distinguished tradition of chivalric kingship that stretched back to Richard the Lionheart. If we are to understand the values and beliefs of the third Richard we need properly to understand those of the first. For in the history of chivalry, the example of the first Richard stood supreme.

6

Kingship, Chivalry and Warfare

With his strategic flair, gift for leadership and talent for organisation, Richard I showed that he was much more than a brilliant knight errant. He was an able as well as an heroic king.[1] Richard possessed many of the qualities which were later to be associated with Henry V. He exhibited the Lancastrian ruler's mastery of military organisation: he appreciated, as Henry did, that armies had to be fed, shipping mustered, supply lines secured, and alliances negotiated. Richard also showed Henry V's ability to select loyal and efficient servants. Hubert Walter, his chief minister in England, was one of the outstanding royal servants of the age. It is possible to detect in Richard something of Henry's relentless mental and physical energy. He rarely relaxed, rested or did nothing. On his famously brief visits to England he was busy settling the nation's affairs. He showed himself a statesman and politician as much as a soldier.

Yet, again like Henry V, it was by his prowess in arms, for the most part, that Richard was judged by his subjects. Contemporaries admired him for his chivalrous behaviour, his bravery in combat and his skill in siegecraft. He set standards of kingly conduct by which all other rulers of his day were themselves judged. Rulers as powerful as Philip Augustus of France were compared to him and found wanting. The quality of Richard's kingship was likewise the measure against which all his successors on the throne of England were judged. In 1313 the Malmesbury chronicler, venturing to criticise Edward II, compared him unfavourably to the Lionheart.[2] From the Lionheart's time on, kings of England were expected to be kings in the Lionheart's mould.

The warrior traditions of the English (or Angevin) monarchy went back a long way; they certainly did not begin with Richard. If their origins lay anywhere, they were to be found in the circumstances in which the English state had come into being centuries before. Unlike some medieval regnal states, England had not been created by dynastic

alliance or extension of jurisdiction; it had been forged in the crucible
of war. The most significant period in the story of England's emergence
had come in the tenth century. Until the later 800s the English people
had been organised in the loosely structured kingdoms of the 'Hep-
tarchy' – Northumbria, Mercia, East Anglia, Wessex, Essex, Kent. In the
chaotic period of the Viking onslaught, however, this network had been
broken. One by one, the kingdoms of midland and northern England
had collapsed before the Viking assault; by 880 only Wessex (and on the
Scottish borders, Bernicia) was left. The programme of aggressive
expansion by which Wessex was transmuted into England was the Wessex kings' response to the crisis. Taking advantage of the slowing of the
Viking advance, the rulers of Wessex seized the initiative, launched a
series of strikes into the midlands and north and absorbed the lands of
the former kingdoms into their own. This was a policy of expansion
through brute force; it was deliberate imperialism.[3] It is true that the
skilful use of propaganda and diplomacy played a key role in the Wessex kings' success. However, their main instrument had been victory in
war. Egbert, Æthelred, Alfred and their successors were fighting kings.
They modelled themselves on Old Testament descriptions of the kings
of ancient Israel. Alfred saw himself as a second King David. He encouraged his people to think of themselves as a new chosen race. By drawing
on familiar Old Testament models he legitimised his own rule as leader
of militant England.

The warrior traditions of the Old English monarchy were reinforced
by the warrior traditions of their aristocracy. The great lords of Anglo-
Saxon England, the thegns and gesiths, were the king's companions in
arms, the leaders of the fyrd (the militia), and the men on whom the
burden of military service principally fell. Their values were heroic.
Glory, for them, lay in honour, sacrifice and endurance. Among the
poems they listened to were *Beowulf* and the song on the battle of
Maldon – poems which told of struggle and sacrifice, and which stressed
loyalty to one's lord, even unto death. To men of this sort, fighting
was more than an employment, or even a profession; it was a source of
fulfilment and exhilaration. It justified their exalted position in society.

The values and traditions of the Old English monarchy were further
reinforced by the Conquest of 1066. The triumphant Normans were a
keen warrior race. Of Viking descent, and retaining something of the

Viking outlook, they gloried in fighting and made a cult of their valour. Duke William himself had been engaged in the practice of arms since boyhood. The knights in the forefront of the Norman armies were pioneers in the use of new tactics. They made novel use of the massed charge and the feigned flight – tactics which had to be practised in campaign after campaign if they were not to fail in the field. The Normans were hardened professionals – and all the more devastating for having developed a camaraderie that arose from the shared experience of frequent war.

The distinctive character of the new Anglo-Norman state also lent weight to the militarism of its aristocracy. From the first, there was a strong expansionist dynamic to the Normans' takeover of England. The victory at Hastings did not mark an end to Norman ambitions. Hastings was merely one stage in a continuing process. From their base in England the Normans went on to settle in Wales, southern Scotland and eventually, in the twelfth century, Ireland. In part, the advance was the work of opportunistic individuals, such as Robert FitzHamon and John de Courcy, who planted castles and, beside them, monasteries and sometimes small towns. In some areas, however, such as north-east Wales, piecemeal infiltration was accompanied by a solid military advance. Tensions between the Anglo-Normans and local populations might provoke raiding and harrying and, in due course, full-scale invasion. In many places along the Welsh border colonialism was accompanied by fierce fighting.

In the same period, the Normans were faced with increasing warfare and conflict in their own homeland. As a result of their conquest of England the Normans inevitably made an enemy of the king of France, who resented the rise on his northern frontier of a major expansionist power. From the end of the eleventh century it was to be a cardinal principle of French policy to undermine the Norman (and, later, the Angevin) position in France – indeed, ultimately to sever the link between Normandy and England altogether. The struggle between the Normans and the French was a long one, and it was conducted by both fair means and foul. Whenever a disobedient vassal of the duke appealed to the French king for aid, the latter would respond to his call; and whenever there was rivalry between the duke and his sons, or between the sons themselves, he added fuel to the family fire. On more than a few occasions the French assembled a force to invade Normandy, but each time the Normans were saved by the disunity of their opponents. In 1119, when a full-scale assault on the duchy was finally mounted, Henry I and the Normans were saved by a signal victory in the field, at Brémule. Nor should it be supposed that the French king was the Normans' only mortal foe. To the south of Normandy, beyond the border territory of Maine, lay the county of Anjou, whose rulers were the long-standing rivals of the Normans. Time and again the counts of Anjou took advantage of the king-dukes' problems to nibble away at their borders and undermine their influence. In the 1140s, during the civil war between Stephen and Matilda, while Stephen was engaged in England, the Angevins took over Normandy completely.

A consequence of this constant warfare was that the people of England were repeatedly called on to provide their king with manpower and resources. Not only were knights resident in England summoned to fight in other parts of their ruler's dominions; English taxpayers were charged with bearing their costs. Fighting war in the twelfth century was expensive – and, with wages rising, becoming ever more so. The means had to be found to pay mercenaries, feed infantrymen and bribe allies. The greater proportion of these resources were found in England. This was partly because England was, by contemporary standards, rich but also because it had an administrative infrastructure which could provide for the speedy collection of taxes. Gelds were regularly levied on lands in England to the 1160s and tallages thereafter; gifts and aids were collected from English towns; and a variety of feudal incidents, such as relief and scutage, from English tenants in chief. This system of financial exploitation has been likened to a system of plunder.[4] But, while it was predatory and erratic, it was also effective; it worked. As has been observed, administratively the English state grew as a war state.[5] Under pressure of the demands for money its structures became deeper and more complex. The financial demands which Richard was to make in the 1190s had long been anticipated in those of his predecessors.

In the same way, Richard's lengthy absences from his realm had also in part been anticipated by his predecessors. No post-Conquest ruler had spent quite so much time away from England as Richard, for none had been absent on crusade. None the less, each of the four rulers who had governed both England and Normandy since 1066 had spent long periods of time in the latter dominion. Henry II, in fact, had spent as much as twenty-one of his thirty-five years south of the Channel. The tendency on these rulers' part to accord more attention to their continental possessions was founded on a realistic assessment of where the main challenge to their interests lay. England, it was rightly believed, could look after itself. The continental dominions, on the other hand, could not. With their long land frontiers with the Capetian kingdom, the Angevins' continental dominions lay wide open to French attack. In the north, the southern border of Normandy was particularly vulnerable, the exposed territory of the Vexin jutting deep into Capetian France. Further south, the territories of Anjou, Poitou, Angoulême and the Limousin were constantly being subjected to incursions by French castellans. The fact that the southern territories lay a long way from Paris afforded them little or no protection. Throughout Richard's adult career the heartland of the Angevin 'empire' was to be found in the Loire valley. England might well be Richard's wealthiest dominion, and, true, it provided him with his kingly title; however, it had no special claim on his affections. By descent he was an Angevin and by upbringing an Aquitanian. His homeland, insofar as he had one, was western France. His life's task was the defence of his ancestral possessions there.

By the time that Richard became king, the Angevin monarchy – the English monarchy as it would become – had thus already established itself as an institution of aggressive and expansionist character. As a means to the end of state-building, military takeover was practised far more by the Anglo-Norman and Angevin rulers than it was by the contemporary Capetian rulers of France. When the Capetians extended their dominions, as they did rapidly in the twelfth and thirteenth centuries, it was generally (and certainly before 1204) by the extension of jurisdiction – legal imperialism – rather than by military aggression. Perhaps this difference of dynastic attitude and circumstance added something to the tensions between Richard and Philip on crusade.

Richard's kingly career, by dint of its sheer distinction, greatly strengthened the Angevin monarchy's identification with successful war. The fostering of this link with warfare was to be one of the principal legacies of his reign. From this time, not only did leadership in war figure more prominently in the expectations that people of England had of their king; success or otherwise in war was accorded a higher importance as a test by which a king's discharge of his duties was judged. For Richard's successors, his was the career against which their own would be measured.

Richard's magic was to work its effect in various ways. In the first place, the enormous fame of his achievements in arms was to live on after him. His struggle in the East with his rival Saladin was to become the stuff of legend. Poems and tales were soon written in celebration of it. Moreover, as if his genuine achievements were not enough, new ones were soon added. A story of wide circulation concerned a legendary personal encounter with the great Saladin. According to the story, which is attested from the 1200s, Richard accepted a challenge from Saladin to ride a horse which had been given to him by his opponent. Unknown to Richard, the gift was a trick: the horse was a colt born to the mare which Saladin was going to ride and the plan was that when the mare whinnied the colt would kneel down, leaving Richard at his opponent's mercy. Richard was forewarned of the danger by an angel. Preparing for the duel by stuffing his colt's ears with wax he entered the lists. When Saladin's mare whinnied, and the colt did not react, Richard, taking advantage of his opponent's discomfiture, unhorsed him and chased him from the field.[6] In 1251 Henry III was to commission a wall painting of the story to decorate a chamber of his palace at Clarendon (Wiltshire), and a series of floor tiles depicting the duel were laid at Clarendon, the Tower of London and elsewhere.[7] The episode became sufficiently popular to enjoy a wide literary and artistic circulation.

Another story that enjoyed wide popularity told of the king's captivity in Germany. Its origins concerned his nickname – Coeur de Lion – which was a contemporary one. The story tells how the king of Germany's daughter fell in love with Richard and spent some agreeable nights with him. When the girl's father learned of the liaison he planned to murder Richard by having a hungry lion introduced to his cell. But Richard, armed only with forty silk handkerchiefs, was able to kill the lion by thrusting an arm down the beast's throat and pulling out its heart – which he then proceeded to sprinkle with salt and eat in front of the astonished gaze of the king and his court.[8] To the time of Richard's captivity also belongs the famous story of Blondel, the fictitious minstrel who is said to have discovered the king's whereabouts by singing songs outside castle after castle until at last he heard the king's voice answering back. This romantic tale was another one that enjoyed early popularity. What all of these stories show is that within decades of the king's death his career was being invested with legendary gloss. Even the strange tale of how he met his death added to the aura. Richard was supposed to have died searching for hidden treasure. According to the most common version, he had been drawn to the castle of Chalus-Chabrol in the Limousin by reports that a hoard of gold was buried there. In the ensuing encounter he received an arrow wound which proved fatal. In reality, Richard was drawn to Chalus-Chabrol not by hidden treasure but by news of a rebellion by its lord. The fiction of buried treasure, however, fitted in with his romantic image better.[9]

Legend grew up around Richard's name, it seems, almost spontaneously. But the growth of the subsequent cult owed more than a little to his own efforts. Richard was a master of self-promotion. He was keenly aware that his image needed crafting and cultivating. And he contributed to the process of crafting himself. Thus he took care to keep his subjects informed of his diplomatic coups and victories in the field. He was one of the first English kings regularly to use newsletters. Whenever he scored a major triumph, he made sure to publicise it. On his way to the East in 1191 he wrote to his justiciar William Longchamp justifying his seizure of the kingdom of Cyprus. Seven years later, when he was back in Normandy, he described his victory over King Philip and the French on the bridge at Gisors.[10] These semi-official newsletters were circulated and copied into the chronicles. Richard also ensured that his victories and achievements were sympathetically reported. In the work of Ambroise, the minstrel who accompanied him on the Third Crusade, he secured full and approving coverage of his exploits in the East. Ambroise was an eyewitness to the events that he described. None the less, he was far from immune to Richard's 'spin'. We can take, for example, his story of Richard's capture of the emperor of Cyprus. According to Ambroise, the captive Emperor Isaac had asked to be spared being fettered in irons; Richard, in response, fettered him in silver chains.[11] The story, which was presumably fed to Ambroise, was one calculated to emphasise Richard's power, and to make him appear a new Caesar. It was easy for a chronicler to present him in this light, for Richard knew the importance of the grand gesture. When he set off for the East, he took the sword Excalibur with him. By assiduous self-promotion he ensured for himself widespread support in his dominions. In England, in course of time, he became a popular hero: the first ruler since the Conquest to achieve that status. In the romance of Fulk Fitzwarin, as later in the Robin Hood ballads, he was held above reproach. In Richard Coeur de Lion, the English monarchy had at last acquired its own Charlemagne.

By one very practical measure Richard strengthened the identification of the knightly class with his system of values. He authorised the introduction of tournaments into England. Tournaments had been viewed disapprovingly by his predecessors. Henry II, like his grandfather, had banned them: he believed that they encouraged disorder. Accordingly, knights who wanted tourneying experience had to go abroad. In 1194, according to William of Newburgh, Richard reversed this policy. A system of licensing was introduced. Five places in England were designated official tournament sites: the fields between Salisbury and Wilton (Wiltshire), between Warwick and Kenilworth (Warwickshire), between Brackley and Mixbury (Northamptonshire), between Stamford and Warinford (probably Suffolk) and between Blyth and Tickhill (Nottinghamshire). A fee was charged for a licence to hold a tournament, and each participant was charged a sum according to his rank, from earl down to landless knight. William, earl of Salisbury, was appointed 'director of tournaments', and Hubert Walter deputed his own brother to collect the fees. According to Newburgh, Richard's purpose in encouraging tournaments was to improve the quality of English knighthood.[12] Noticing the superior expertise of the French knights, he reports, the king wanted his own knights to have a training which would make them their adversaries' equal in skill. So successful was the measure that, a decade or two later, in the well-informed opinion of William Marshal thirty English knights were worth forty French. Over the centuries the character and purpose of the tournament in England gradually changed, as it did elsewhere. In the thirteenth century tournaments were essentially clashes between massed bands of knights fought over a wide area. In the late middle ages they were transmuted into one-to-one 'jousts' – combats fought in the lists with blunted weapons before admiring lords and ladies. But even though they tended to become theatrical they never entirely lost their value as training for war. And kings were often keen to sponsor or promote them.

Through the enduring power of his reputation and through his efforts to promote the wider dissemination of his values, Richard became the agent of a major change in English monarchical style. In the years following his death the values of the English monarchy increasingly became the values that Richard had championed. Richard's fame and prestige were such that his successors were bound to live under his shadow. The sheer scale of his achievements, across so wide a field, brought lustre to his line. But it also placed his successors under a heavy burden of obligation. Richard's style of kingship was now considered the style to which his successors should aspire. Young kings, or kings-to-be, from this time were judged by how far they lived up to his exacting standards. In the 1270s the youthful Edward I was greeted approvingly: he was said to 'shine like a new Richard'.[13] When, in the next generation, Edward II was held up for reproach, it was said that, had he practised arms, he would have excelled Richard I in prowess.[14] When in funerary eulogies tributes were paid to deceased kings, as for example to Edward I in 1307, it was conventional for the deceased ruler, providing he deserved it, to be compared to the Lionheart in bravery.[15] Richard had succeeded in raising the prestige of the Angevin royal line, and he had achieved this through his prowess in arms. War was from now on seen as the way to bring fame and distinction to the dynasty. By virtue of Richard's influence, the English monarchy was transformed into a chivalric monarchy. Chivalric values were to be the hallmark of its style and political character. Both the second and the third Richards would have to live with this aspect of their predecessor's legacy.

The gradual working-out of Richard's posthumous influence, however, was by no means a simple or a straightforward process. In the course of the thirteenth century the Angevin monarchy suffered some major reverses. In 1203–4, in John's reign, the French overran Normandy, Anjou and Maine. By the 1220s, of the great string of continental dominions which Richard had ruled, only part of the duchy of Aquitaine, in the south west, was left. The effect of these massive losses was to turn the Angevin monarchy into a more purely English monarchy. Something of the cultural cosmopolitanism which had characterised Richard's court ebbed away. By the mid thirteenth century a definite streak of xenophobia can be detected in English political language. Hostility to the French and to aliens generally became a theme in English royal rhetoric.

In the 1290s Edward I accused Philip IV of France of wanting to extirpate the English tongue. Yet, surprisingly perhaps, the effect on Richard's posthumous reputation was slight. Richard, although an Angevin, was treated as an honorary Englishman. He was invested with a new English identity. He was accommodated to the English mythic tradition. By the end of the thirteenth century, at the latest, his career was being celebrated in English romances. In a seven thousand word poem copied in the Auchinleck manuscript, and based on an Anglo-Norman original, Richard's achievements in arms were evoked in lively and imaginative detail.[16] Among a range of semi-miraculous feats, the king was credited with putting Saladin to flight and tearing out the heart of a lion.[17] Later, allusions to his career were worked into the ever-growing corpus of Arthurian literature. In the alliterative *Morte Arthure* of about 1400 Sir Ferrer's warning to King Arthur not to approach the besieged castle's walls without armour is a clear reference to Richard's death at Chalus.[18] At the same time, aspects of Richard's career were represented on tiles and roof bosses in churches, and on tapestries and wall hangings in England's grander residences. Richard's duel with Saladin was depicted on Chertsey tiles, in wall paintings at the royal palace of Clarendon and on a folio of the Luttrell Psalter, while the king's fight with the lion was represented (again) on tiles and on a boss of the cloister of Norwich Cathedral.[19] Episodes from Richard's career were depicted on Arras tapestries in the English royal tapestry collection.[20] Books celebrating the Lionheart's deeds were found in gentry book collections.[21] Gentlemen, like the Cheshire knight Sir William Carrington, seeking to burnish their lineages, invented ties between remote ancestors and the Lionheart, particularly the Lionheart on crusade.[22] Richard the Lionheart was still the role model to whom England's late medieval kings and noblemen were enjoined to look up. The fourteenth-century chronicler Langtoft portrayed him as the ideal Christian king whom his successors should aspire to follow.[23] Higden writing in the 1330s, recalling the heroes of the past, said the Greeks had lauded Alexander, the French Charlemagne and the English Richard the Lionheart.[24]

Richard's memory was thus still actively cherished in the fourteenth century, when another warrior king, Edward III, was winning his spurs. Edward, who became king in 1327 on his father's deposition, would have been familiar with his predecessor's career from early adolescence. Not only would he have gazed at the depictions of his feats in paintings and cloths in royal palaces; he would have listened to romances about him read by his tutors. The signs are that a heavy burden of chivalric expectation rested on his shoulders. A distinguished biographer of his father wished the young Edward 'the bravery of Richard I, the longevity of Henry III and the wisdom of Edward I'.[25] As events were to show, these hopes would not be disappointed. Edward carefully fashioned himself as the century's new Lionheart. He acquired tapestries for the royal collection depicting the Lionheart's encounters with Saladin.[26] Like his distinguished forebear, he was exceptionally gifted in the exercise of arms. Not only did he live up to contemporary expectations of chivalric knighthood, he also showed a shrewd tactical sense as a field commander. Over a thirty-year career he raised the English monarchy to unparalleled heights of fame. Through his run of victories – at Sluys, Crécy and Calais – he wiped away the stain of earlier defeats in Scotland. He made English arms respected again. He further glamorised the practice of war. He brought a touch of charisma to a monarchy which in his father's time had come to look jaded.

How did Edward achieve these successes? Like the Lionheart, he was a past master at turning chivalry to political advantage. Just as the Lionheart had earlier done, he encouraged the staging of tournaments. He and his captains convened tournaments and Round Tables both before campaigns, to provide training for the knights, and after them, to celebrate victories. Frequently, the king participated himself, on some occasions, as at Lichfield in 1348, incognito. Tourneying brought the king and his nobles and knights together as comrades in arms. The experience which they shared developed in them an *esprit de corps*, a spirit of brotherhood. Through the process of bonding, Edward established a new consensus, a consensus based on shared chivalric values. In this way, the warrior ethic of Richard I was strengthened and reaffirmed.

However, Edward III also went further than his predecessor. In 1348 he established an Order of chivalry – the Order of the Garter. The Order was an exclusive brotherhood of twenty-six knights including the king himself and the prince of Wales. The patron of the Order was a saint long associated with crusading – the heroic St George. Perhaps the legend was already circulating that Richard had placed himself and his knights under St George's protection at the siege of Acre.[27] The new

Order, with its strong associations with tourneying, provided a more formal and hierarchical model of chivalry than any previously seen. In the earliest statutes of the Garter, a strong emphasis was placed on loyalty to the king as superior of the Order. In this way, the horizontal ties of chivalry were carefully overlain by the vertical. Chivalry – in origin an international ethic binding knights of all loyalties – was now given a national veneer and subordinated to the demands of English kingship.

Taken together, the legacies of Richard and Edward ensured that chivalric monarchy was a phenomenon with which all English late medieval kings would have to come to terms.[28] Chivalry defined the English regal style, just as sacramentalism did the French. John of Gaunt acknowledged as much in the speech put into his mouth by Shakespeare in *Richard II*:

> This nurse, this teeming womb of royal kings
> Feared by their breed and famous by their birth,
> Renowned for their deeds as far from home
> For Christian service and true chivalry.[29]

'For Christian service and true chivalry' for Shakespeare (through Gaunt) meant fighting on crusade.

The first of the two later Richards to have to engage with this political legacy was Richard II. Richard was neither by instinct nor taste warlike: after 1389 it was his consistent policy to seek peace with France. Yet the burden of chivalric expectation which rested on him was heavy. Not only was he the son of Edward, the Black Prince – the heir, biological and political, of the most highly regarded soldier of his day; he also bore the Christian name Richard, which prompted people to think of him as a second Lionheart. There is evidence of sorts that he took an interest in the Lionheart's career. He had a fondness for reading of his ancestors' achievements in the chronicles and he commissioned a series of statues of England's kings to go in Westminster Hall.[30] In his main residences he could find a visual record of the Lionheart's career. The Lionheart's exploits were represented on decorative tiles and in wall paintings in such residences as the palaces of Westminster and Clarendon. In his will the Black Prince had actually left his son a set of wall hangings of the 'Pas Saladin', to add to a collection already rich in historical subjects.[31] In the light of his family's early history, Richard is likely to have reflected on the significance of his birth in Aquitaine. Aquitaine was, after all, the Lionheart's stamping ground; it was where he had grown up and shown his mettle. Potentially, a wealth of ideas would have occurred to him connecting the Lionheart's career to his own father's. It would be an exaggeration to say that Richard II saw himself as consciously living under the Lionheart's long shadow. But, at the very least, he would have been aware of the cultural significance of his name, and he may well have taken delight in playing on that name. His choice of the white hart badge as an emblem probably owed something to a pun on the 'hart' of 'Richart': Philippe de Mézières alluded to both the 'hart' and rich' in his *Epistre* to the king. Richard was thus in no doubt of the expectations aroused by his name. As he was constantly reminded, his subjects looked to a revival of earlier royal feats of arms – but not just his father's: those of his Angevin forebear too.

Richard, while not instinctively a soldier, thus nurtured his chivalric inheritance. He realised its value to his kingship. The most obvious way in which he revealed his chivalric colours was in his promotion of tournaments.[32] Between the mid 1380s and his downfall in 1390 he sponsored a whole series of such events – at Westminster in 1385, at Smithfield in 1386, May and October 1390 and 1397, and at Windsor in 1399. In addition to these grander gatherings, there were regular Christmas jousts wherever the court was held, and jousting elsewhere each April as part of the annual Garter festivities. Richard was particularly adept at using tournaments as an accompaniment to the launching of diplomatic initiatives. In October 1390 he sponsored a spectacular event at Smithfield to tempt a potential ally, William, count of Ostrevant, into an English alliance. Count William was invited to participate in the event – which he did – and, at the end, he went away so impressed by the cordiality of his reception, the brilliance of the jousting and the splendour of the balls and banquets that, while not formally entering into an alliance, he became a consistent upholder of the English cause. William, duke of Guelders, was another prince with Low Countries interests who was drawn into the English fold by such means. Yet Richard was aware not only of the diplomatic, but also of the wider political uses to which his sponsorship of tournaments could be put. He was particularly alert to their value in providing opportunities for the ceremonial display of his kingship. Unlike his father and grandfather, he did not take part in them himself (or rarely did so). He preferred to keep his distance. As Henry VII was to do later, he sat on a high dais and looked down. He elevated himself. He used tournaments to stress hierarchy. In this way, he reconciled their martial character with his emphasis on sovereignty.

Richard also used another chivalric ritual – ceremonial knightings – to beneficial effect. The knighting ceremony was a central institution of chivalry; it marked the formal admission of the aspirant tiro to the elite. Richard realised that knightings could be used to stress hierarchy and order, in the same way that tournaments could. In the summer of 1385, when he invaded Scotland, he carried out a mass knighting on the Anglo-Scottish border, in this way drawing attention to the royal capacity to honour and elevate men. Nine years later, when he led his first expedition to Ireland, he again used a mass knighting to a similar effect. As Froissart records, when he admitted the Irish provincial lords, or 'high kings', to his obedience, he demonstrated his ascendancy over them by dubbing them knights – indeed, reinforcing the point, according to one account, by making them serve on him at dinner.[33] Chivalry, in Richard's hands, became an instrument in the pacification of the Irish, a means to the establishment of English lordship.

Chivalry was to remain a crucial element in the practice of English kingship well into the fifteenth century. Henry V's mighty achievements in arms against the French virtually guaranteed that this would be so. As a result of the king's victory at Agincourt, his conquest of Normandy, and the securing of the succession to the French crown in the treaty of Troyes, the prestige of the English monarchy was raised to new heights. Under Henry's inadequate son and successor, Henry VI, the tide was to turn and the English were eventually to be driven from France, with Calais alone left to them. But not even this dismal ending led to a loss of confidence in traditional values. When the sixth Henry's critics denounced him, it was not for an excess of chivalric zeal; it was rather for his lack of it. Henry V's conquests had breathed new life into the traditional paradigm.

The point was not lost on the Yorkist Edward IV in 1461 when he seized the crown from the hapless Henry VI. A key element in the new king's campaign to restore confidence in royal authority was the reopening of the war with France. In the 1470s Edward sponsored a reinvigoration of the English knightly class as a means to that end. At lavish knighting ceremonies at court large numbers of aspirant tiros were dubbed, and pressure was put on those deemed knightworthy to take up the rank. If there was a manifesto for the new Yorkist monarchy, it was William Worcester's *Boke of Noblesse*, a tract written (or rewritten) in the 1470s, which advocated national renewal through war. Richard the Lionheart figured prominently in Worcester's list of kingly heroes on whom Edward should model himself. Worcester praised Richard for his commitment to the crusade, his conquest of Cyprus, and his success in defending his inheritance against the king of France. Arguing that every good knight should be a lion, he may consciously have been engaging in wordplay on the king's nickname.[34]

Richard III, as one born to a noble line and nurtured in a chivalric tradition, was determined to live up to the ideals that Worcester had set out. His father, Richard, duke of York, had played a major role in the defence of Lancastrian Normandy. In 1440 he stabilised the English position in the Pays de Caux and in the following year he successfully resisted a French assault on the town of Pontoise.[35] Richard was devoted to his father's memory and no less determined to follow in his footsteps. As a youth, he played a not inconsiderable role in the struggles of 1470–71. At Barnet, the battle at which his brother had won back his throne, he had been in the thick of the fight.[36] A few weeks later at the crucial battle of Tewkesbury, at which Queen Margaret was defeated, he was given command of the vanguard of the royal army. Through his valour he successfully associated himself with the traditions of his line.

The first significant chance for the young duke to win a reputation for himself came with his appointment as Lieutenant of the North in 1480. In this office he was given overall responsibility for the defence of northern England against the Scots. The main challenge facing the English at this time was the recovery of the border town of Berwick, which had been ceded to the Scottish king in 1461. In 1482 Richard saw a possible means by which successful recovery could be effected. In the spring of 1482 a leading Scottish magnate, the duke of Albany, the warden of the West March, had defected to the English. Richard now had a Scottish ally – and an ally, moreover, who could bring others from his own side with him. In July, therefore, Richard marched north with a force of some 20,000 men to lay siege to Berwick. The townsmen, judging it pointless to resist so massive a force, quickly gave in, but the garrison in the castle held out. Leaving some of his men to reduce the fortress, Richard decided to advance on Edinburgh. In the meantime, however, the situation in Scotland had changed, and to his disadvantage. The Scottish king, James III, had been seized by a group of his nobles and Albany, Richard's ally, fearful of loss of support, changed sides. Richard, seeing the political horizon darkening, decided to pull back. By the middle of August he had returned to Berwick. On the surface at least, his campaign had been a success. The recovery of Berwick, the main objective, had been achieved. Parliament in the following January offered him its congratulations, praising 'his manifold and diligent labour and devoir in subduing a great part of the border' with Scotland; and his brother rewarded him by making him a hereditary grant of the wardenship of the West March.

Yet there seems little doubt that Richard's achievement was exaggerated. There was only prize to show – the recovery of Berwick itself – although admittedly that was the goal on which most attention had been focused. At Edinburgh Richard had achieved virtually nothing; he had not even exacted any reprisals on the city's populace. Once his ally Albany had defected, he had no alternative but to retreat. At the end of the expedition the border was no more secure than it had been before. For all the bombast and self-promotion, his achievement had been insubstantial. The well-informed Crowland chronicler had a keen sense of this. He commented sourly on Richard's letting 'the wealthy city of Edinburgh escape unharmed'. The capture of Berwick itself he considered 'a trifle'.[37]

The significance of Richard's Scottish expedition lies not so much in his actual achievements – which were slight – as in the way in which they were made to appear so much grander. Richard took the opportunity of deliberately boosting his image. He wanted to present himself as a great man – a commander in the mould of Henry V. He probably saw himself as his father's heir as much as, or more than, his brother's. His father, as we have seen, had been a distinguished commander in France and successful in the defence of Normandy.[38] His brother, by contrast, in his later years had been hesitant in arms; in 1475 he had actually abandoned a campaign in France. Richard probably aroused high chivalric expectation. On his accession William Worcester's son rededicated his father's

Boke of Noblesse to him. As king, he quickly sent an aggressive message to his neighbours: Henry Tudor's spy said that he wanted to inaugurate his reign with an invasion of France.[39] Richard's ambition was to revive that old-fashioned style of chivalric kingship which was associated with England's heyday. War, in his estimation, was not merely ennobling; it was the essential foundation for successful kingship.

Yet by the late fifteenth century this particular conception of chivalric rule was beginning to look dated. Ideas of royal and aristocratic behaviour were changing. Nobility in the abstract, to which chivalry was related, was no longer identified principally with martial prowess and the performance of brave deeds. Increasingly its essence was found as lying in peaceful behaviour and service to the state. The model for this new definition was found in classical Antiquity. In the eyes of the humanist writers, who were now influential in this field, the real nobles were the Romans of old – Scipio, Caesar and Pompey: those who possessed the quality of *virtus*. One of the key texts for the dissemination of this view was Christine de Pisan's *Livre du corps de policie*, a work in the 'mirror for princes' genre which drew extensively on Roman history. In the 1470s an English translation of this work was made by Anthony Woodville, Earl Rivers, Edward IV's brother-in-law. Woodville, through the medium of his translation, promoted a view of the nobility as servants of the state. In particular, he urged the development of a professional civil service whose members, following the Roman example, 'had their hearts on the common weal' and governed through order and reason. Just how serious a challenge these new ideas represented to traditional conceptions of chivalry was recognised in a text which another Yorkist courtier John Tiptoft, earl of Worcester, translated, the *Controversia de nobilitate* (or *Declamacion of Noblesse*). In this work, the conflict between the old and the new ideas was expressed in the terms of a debate. A pair of suitors were pitted against one another. One displayed the traditional pride in ancestry and wealth, while the other, Guyus Flaminneus, a nobleman cast in the image of Tiptoft himself, argued the opposite: that true nobility rested on *vertu* and service to the state. Through Guyus's speeches Tiptoft articulated his own views and those of the fashionable elite at the Yorkist court. True nobility was to be found not in lineage, wealth and deeds of arms; it was to be found in service to the state.[40]

Although these ideas were winning rapid acceptance among humanists and the Woodvilles and their circle at court, they apparently held little appeal to Richard. Richard's own tastes rested firmly with the older tradition of chivalry. He showed little, if any, understanding of the concept of a 'civil' nobility engaged in service to the state. In his dealings with his retainers he stressed loyalty to his person, and not loyalty to the state. *Loyaulte me lie* ('loyalty binds me') was his motto. But, as events at Bosworth were to show, these ideas were no longer sufficient to guarantee him support. In his hour of need he was deserted by magnates who should have aided him: by Northumberland and Stanley. Pragmatism, not personal loyalty, determined their allegiance. Richard's reliance on chivalry showed the enduring power of chivalry in the English political tradition. But his failure showed that its day was finally passing.

As a knightly exemplar the first Richard – Richard the Lionheart – had commanded the admiring attention of contemporaries for his bravery, his prowess and his acts of valour. But he also commanded their admiration because of the cause to which he devoted a great part of his life – the crusade. Where other kingly rulers had made hollow commitments to go on crusade, Richard matched his commitment with deeds. He spent nearly a year and a half of his reign in the East. In the middle ages the cause of fighting to liberate Christ's land from the infidel was the highest to which a Christian knight could devote himself. In championing the crusade so boldly Richard brought lustre to himself and his line. The strength of his reputation owed much to his commitment to the crusading ideal. Chroniclers heaped praise on him for his achievements on crusade. Langtoft saw in him the ideal king behaving in the way that the ideal king should. He sketched a picture of him as a man of deep piety as well as superb courage.[41] Richard was the first English king to involve himself in, and to take the lead in, crusading. There had been little English involvement in the first two crusades, of the 1090s and 1140s.[42] Henry II, though committing himself to the crusade, had never gone. Richard, by his brave deeds and subsequent repute, placed his heirs and successors under a heavy burden of emulation.

For the two centuries after the Lionheart's reign, crusading enthusiasm was to be a constant accompaniment to the rhythms of English political life. Some of Richard's successors responded to it more warmly than others. His brother and immediate successor, John, responded hardly at all. Ignoring the calls which led to the Fourth Crusade, John donned the cross only at the very end of his reign in order to enlist papal support against his opponents. The attitudes of John's successors, Henry III and Edward I, however, were different. Henry III was deeply aware of the challenge to his dynasty's prestige posed by the crusading achievements of the Capetian dynasty in France and, in particular, those of Louis IX. Conscious that among his own ancestors only Richard I could boast a record comparable to that of Louis, he donned the cross himself in 1216, after his accession, and in 1250 and 1271. Yet true to form, despite repeated attempts to do so, he never departed for the East. One political difficulty after another stood in his way – first, the recurring danger to Gascony from the French and then his ill-advised involvement in the 'Sicilian business', while after 1258 the long struggle with the opposition barons over their reform programme put paid to his plans altogether. Henry's promise was in the end redeemed by his son. In 1270 the Lord Edward – the future Edward I – embarked on an expedition which took him to Tunis, Cyprus and eventually (in Richard's footsteps) to Acre, where he was active in relieving Moslem pressure on the town. He was still away from England when he succeeded his father as king in 1272.

The fall of the Latin kingdom of Jerusalem, only a matter of years after Edward's return, had a transforming effect on Europe's response to the Turks. Instead of the large set-piece *passagia* which had characterised crusading activity in the past, there were henceforth many smaller expeditions, each of them more limited in objective and virtually all in peripheral locations. Crusading in this new, less ambitious, age transmuted into an essentially pluralist institution, owing little if anything to the direction of kings and everything to the initiative of individual knights and nobles motivated by a mixture of spiritual zeal and appetite for adventure. In the 1360s a steady flow of English and French knights went to fight in Prussia, Lithuania and other remote parts. Twenty years earlier, knights from England, Germany and France had fought against the Moors in Spain. Over this same period not one English or French king or heir of the throne took any direct part in crusading at all.

When, in the mid-fourteenth century, the Turks began to advance rapidly into the European heartland, this decentralised pattern of activity had, however, of necessity, to change. No longer could the efforts of individual knights be considered sufficient to stem the tide. A major royally-led expedition was needed. By the 1380s a group of crusading propagandists were actively engaged in mobilising Europe's princely rulers into action. The king of England at the time was Richard II. Richard, while hardly a soldier king in the mould of his predecessors, showed himself more than sympathetic to their ideas. He was deeply conscious of the obligation that lay on him as a Christian ruler to assist in defending Europe against the infidel. In the course of his peace negotiations with the French, he showed a keen interest in the idea that he and his French counterpart should undertake a joint crusade to the East. As a king by the name of Richard, he could hardly avoid the burden of crusading expectation placed on him. He himself was aware of that burden.[43] The closing years of his reign provide a fascinating case study of the close interaction between royal policy and crusading endeavour that existed in late medieval England.

The essential spur to crusading activity in Richard II's reign was provided by the rapid Turkish advances in south-eastern Europe. In 1385 Sofia had fallen to the Turks, in 1386 Nis and in 1387 Thessalonika. In 1389 at Kossovo the once mighty kingdom of Serbia was destroyed. The Christian response to this infidel threat was confused. While princely rulers all paid lip-service to the need to offer resistance, few took actual measures. Europe at the time was riven by bitter political and religious division. Not only were the kings of England and France locked in a seemingly interminable struggle over the claim of the English king to the crown of France; worse still, two rival popes, at Rome and Avignon, were struggling with each other for the undivided allegiance of Christendom. Against this background, the rapid mobilisation of an effective resistance to the Turk was virtually impossible. A key role in ensuring that there was resistance was assumed by a man with wide experience of the East – Philippe de Mézières, a former chancellor of Cyprus and tutor to the young Charles VI, who had retired to live in the house of the Celestines in Paris. From his well-informed vantage point, de Mézières wrote a series of tracts urging the kings of England and France to reach an accord, heal the schism in the Church and join forces in a crusade.[44] In the *Songe du vieil pèlerin* (1389) he argued his case in the rich language of chivalric allegory, while in the *Epistre au roi Richart II* of six years later he wrote more specifically of the need for Anglo-French peace and for action against the Turk. By 1385 de Mézières was employing four assistants, or 'evangelists' as he called them, to assist him in his endeavours – John de Blaisy, Robert the Hermit, Louis de Giac and Otto de Granson, a man closely connected with the English court. These four were deeply involved in the diplomatic exchanges between the English and French courts. In March 1393 Robert the Hermit secured an audience with John of Gaunt at Amiens to urge the case for a crusade on him, while two years later on a visit to England he pleaded with Richard for an Anglo-French marriage alliance as the first step to closer Anglo-French cooperation. Encouraged by the support he received, de Mézières founded an Order, the Order of the Passion, specifically to recruit would-be crusaders. Among the many whom he enrolled were a number of English courtiers. The dukes of Lancaster and Gloucester and the earl of Huntingdon were among the Order's patrons, while the duke of York and the earls of Rutland, Nottingham and Northumberland were among its members. The earl of Huntingdon was the king's half brother, and the dukes of Lancaster and York two of his uncles. The remarkable interest in the Order evinced by the Ricardian courtiers highlights clearly the commitment to the crusade of the English nobility. A number of English nobles actually embarked on crusade in these years. Henry of Derby (later Henry IV) and Sir John Beaufort both undertook expeditions to Prussia, while Henry, Lord Scrope, accompanied the French to Tunis.

A remarkable characteristic of the crusading history of the late fourteenth century is the strength of support given to the crusade by the English and French governments. Richard II and Charles VI both regarded Anglo-French peace as the essential preliminary to the launching of a fresh *passagium*. Richard's own commitment to the crusade is powerfully indicated by the iconography of the Wilton Diptych, that most luminous expression of Ricardian kingship, which he commissioned around this time. Crusading references are to be detected at a number of points in the Diptych's web of allusion. At the heart of the elaborate gesturing in the painting is the banner held by the angel in the right-hand panel. It is tempting to associate this banner with the banner of the Resurrection of de Mezieres' Order of the Passion, for the device of a red cross on a white field is common to both. Arguably, the Christ Child may be thought to be in the act of blessing the banner as the ensign under which Richard will go on crusade to the Holy Land. It is possible that a further allusion to de Mézières' Order of the Passion is implied by the many references to the Passion of Our Lord. Not only are the Crown of Thorns and the Nails of the Cross stippled on the nimbus of the Christ Child; the Lamb, another common symbol of the Passion, is shown tucked under the arm of John the Baptist in the panel opposite. These references to the Passion would immediately have been accorded a crusading context by contemporaries, for the Holy Land was Christ's bequest to the Christian world, won for it with His blood, and it was the duty of Christian monarchs to win it back. Lastly, and perhaps surprisingly, crusading significance may be found in the personal devices of the two kings worn by the angels – the white hart of Richard II and the broom pod of Charles VI. For an angelic company to appear in such badges would have been considered sacrilegious had not their owners been dedicated to the cause of recovering Christ's own land. As numerous scholars have pointed out, there are other interpretations which can be put on the Diptych: it is suggested, for example, that the tiny painting of an island on the orb of the banner may hint at the tradition of England as the Virgin's dowry. The Diptych certainly cannot be seen exclusively, as it once was, as a crusading icon; but a crusading context may well help to account for some of its iconography.

As it happened, the crusading initiatives so carefully nurtured by the two courts in the early to mid 1390s ended in disappointment. Only one major expedition was put into the field. This was a Franco-Burgundian force which set off for the Balkans in the summer of 1396. Striking deep into Bulgaria, it initially enjoyed a measure of success, forcing the sultan to lift his siege of Constantinople; but as it approached the Danubian fortress of Nicopolis its progress stalled. A Turkish force of some 15,000 came north to oppose the invasion. On 25 September outside Nicopolis the crusaders were heavily defeated and their leaders captured. The fate which overcame the expedition dealt a bitter blow to crusading initiatives. The mood of optimism which had accompanied the planning of the 1390s immediately evaporated. Whatever plans were being entertained for a possible royally-led *passagium* were quickly abandoned. To the military setbacks of the time were added diplomatic ones. The

Anglo-French peace negotiations, on which any further crusading initiative hinged, began to founder: disagreements arose between the two sides over how to end the schism, with one side favouring the 'voie de fait' and the other the 'voie de cession'. Finally, in 1399, the Lancastrian revolution put an end to the atmosphere of idealism and cooperation which had underpinned the planning of the early and mid 1390s. The political background to the pre-Nicopolis period was irrecoverable.

Yet the problem of the Turkish advance into Europe remained. Not only were the Danubian states such as Austria and Hungary under threat; so too was the Greek (or Byzantine) empire to their south. By the end of the 1390s Constantinople itself was virtually cut off. Had it not been for the threat to the Turks from the Mongols in their rear, it would have fallen within months. The problem of how to save Constantinople was the issue which now forced itself before Christian rulers' attention. In 1400 and 1401 the Emperor Manuel undertook an extensive tour of European courts to elicit aid. In the Christmas season of 1400 he came to England and was entertained by Henry IV. Henry had to formulate a response. As a former crusader he felt duty-bound to offer support, but as a newcomer to the throne and beset with problems on all sides he was limited in what he could do. He therefore fell back on an initiative of his predecessor's. In the summer of 1398 Richard II had authorised the collection of 'voluntary' contributions to aid the Greek cause. A number of bishops and nobles had contributed, and Richard himself had given £2000. Henry now breathed new life into the appeal. He encouraged further donations, and significant sums were raised in local churches. Henry himself paid all Manuel's expenses during his visit. Englishmen were persuaded to look with greater sympathy on the plight of the Byzantine Greeks. But with the renewal of Anglo-French hostilities in 1415 whatever hope there may have been of giving more substantial assistance to the Greeks quickly disappeared. Despite promises of aid from western leaders, Constantinople fell to the Turks in 1453.

The crusading cause continued to exert an appeal over princely rulers in the fifteenth century long after the fall of the Byzantine capital – and even longer after the final demise of the tradition of formal *passagia*. A reported conversation of Richard III's nicely illustrates its continuing allure. In May 1484 Richard was told by a German envoy, Nicholas von

Poppelau, of an Hungarian victory over the Turks. Overjoyed, Richard replied: 'I wish that my kingdom lay on the confines of Turkey; with my own people alone and without the help of other princes I should like to drive away not only the Turks but all my foes.'[45] Richard's response captures many of the nuances of the western response to the crusade at the end of the middle ages – the continuing concern at the Turkish advance; the linkage between the crusade and political priorities nearer to home; the readiness to express a commitment in principle to fight; and yet the sheer impotence felt by a ruler far from the front. By the fifteenth century the gulf between western aspirations and crusading practice had become almost too wide to bridge. Among the princely dynasties of Europe, only the dukes of Burgundy still made the crusading tradition central to their vision of chivalry. Mid-century, Duke Philip the Good repeatedly reaffirmed his commitment to go on crusade. In 1454, for example, at the Feast of Swans at Lille, he had a live pheasant brought into the hall and swore on it that he would go on crusade, provided that at least one other ruler joined him. In the event, old age prevented him from keeping his word. But his bastard son Anthony took the cross and, later, Burgundian naval power was deployed against the Turks in the Black Sea.

In England, by this time, preparations for crusade rarely got beyond the stage of fund-raising. No English king in the late middle ages ever actually committed men to the cause. English participation in crusading was a thing of the past. So, ironically perhaps, the long tradition of involvement in crusading, inaugurated by Richard I, found its final expression in a chance remark of Richard III. From time to time, the third Richard indulged his fancy in crusading speculation. On one occasion the king enquired of the monks of Westminster if they would return to him the oil which, according to legend, would anoint the English king who regained the Holy Land.[46] On the eve of Bosworth, when he rallied his troops, he swore that if triumphant he would take on the Ottoman Turks.[47] On the occasions – and doubtless they were many – when he used his prayer book, his thoughts would have strayed to crusading: for included in it was a prayer of the votive mass against the heathen.[48] That in more than his idle moments he identified with Richard the Lionheart is attested by his patronage of All Hallows by the Tower, London, where the Lionheart's heart was (wrongly) supposed to be buried.[49] But wishful romanticising was one thing, and cold reality another. So far as the English monarchy was concerned, the days of active crusading were over. Priorities now were different.

Surprisingly perhaps, the demise of crusading left the chivalric tradition, to which it was related, relatively unaffected. Chivalric assumptions were to shape the character, values and ceremonies of the English monarchy for at least another century. Few courts were more chivalric in character than that of the Virgin Queen. Yet the chivalry of late medieval and Tudor England was a very different phenomenon from that in which Richard the Lionheart had grown up. With the growth in power of the national monarchies in the fourteenth century, chivalry gradually lost its international character. By the late middle ages it was becoming less common for knights of different allegiances to experience the fellow-feeling which they had felt centuries before. It was also becoming less common for them to feel with any intensity the obligation they had once felt to uphold the values and authority of a Universal Church. In England, as elsewhere, chivalry had turned into a national chivalry, a buttress and instrument of national monarchy. Outwardly, the habits and institutions of earlier times lived on, but within them new patterns of thought were forming. The third Richard lived in a very different world from the first.

7

Every Inch a King

Whatever his deficiencies in rulership, Richard II certainly knew how to impress. In 1396 he attended a meeting with the French king, Charles VI, at Ardres, near Calais, to set the seal on the new Anglo-French entente. It was a prestigious event, and well attended. Both sides had carefully prepared for it. Yet it was Richard who stole the show. He easily outshone his French counterpart. The gifts he exchanged were no more splendid or valuable than those of the French. Where he excelled was in his attire. His wardrobe was magnificent. As an anonymous English observer records, he turned out in a brand new outfit every day.[1] On the first day, according to the writer, he sported a fine full-length gown of red velvet adorned with the white hart and a hat loaded with pearls, while on his shoulders he wore a collar incorporating the French king's device of the broom-pod. The French king attended in a disappointingly plain outfit of red velvet. On the second day Richard presented himself in a magnificent gown of white velvet and red sleeves, while the French king wore the same unimpressive red gown as he had the day before. On the third day Richard again outshone his counterpart. He attended in a superb new outfit, of blue velvet and gold 'molle', while the French king turned up for yet a third time in his familiar red gown. The hapless French king was simply overshadowed by his English rival. Richard won the sartorial stakes hands down. Richard was a showman, an actor. He understood the importance of power-dressing; and he knew that impressions counted. The meeting at Ardres cost him a huge amount of money – perhaps a quarter or a fifth of his annual income. But there was no doubt that it was money well spent. People sang the praises of the king of England. In an age which, in Platonic fashion, saw the outer as the mirror of the inner, the power of the English monarchy stood revealed in all its glory.

The junketings at Ardres afford a valuable insight into Ricardian kingship in action. The English king and his staff spared no effort to outshine the French. Richard's household entourage created a brilliant piece of theatre. All the stage props, accessories and scenery were there: the marquees and pavilions, galleries and tiltyards. There was an endless round of entertainments, banquets and dances for the guests. The very showiness and glamour of the court was its strength. It made for a spectacle in which a vivid image of royal power was reflected.

It was the prime function of the court, of course, to provide an appropriately splendid setting for the display of majesty. The court can be likened to a set of unfolding tableaux. It was not so much a place or an institution as an occasion or series of occasions. Its daily routine was defined by the ceaseless round of ritual and ceremony. The king presided over crown-wearings, liturgical festivals, Garter ceremonies, banquets, audiences. From the rituals and ceremonies of the court, the king's subjects and those who visited him formed an impression of his splendour and thus of his power. But the court was also a place where business was done. It was at sessions of the court that the king received envoys, dispensed favours to his magnates, arranged marriages for his kinsfolk, and performed the myriad other duties of an active ruler. The court was the most vital institution of medieval monarchy. It was at once the means and the expression of royal power.

The institutional structures of the court were provided by the household; or, to put it another way, the household organised the court. A picture of the household's layout can be formed from a description written in the reign of Edward IV known as the Black Book.[2] Broadly speaking, two main categories of offices can be discerned – the 'below stairs' offices, the *domus providencie*, and their above stairs counterparts constituting the *domus magnificencie*. The 'below stairs' offices were the responsibility of the steward and were divided into three groups: the buttery, bakehouse and pantry; the kitchen, including the larder and scullery; and the marshalsea, which had responsibility for the royal stables. Above stairs, under the control of the chamberlain, were the ranks of the esquires, sergeants-at-arms, marshals of the hall and valets of the chamber, as well as more specialist groups like the clerks of the chapel royal. The chamberlain and steward of the household were both significant figures at court. The chamberlain in the 1380s was Sir Simon Burley, a powerful influence on the young Richard II.

The structures of the household can be described in this way because they have left an imprint in the sources; in particular, they are documented in the Black Book. It is otherwise, however, with the structures of the court. The court, lacking an institutional aspect, left no archive of its own. Contemporaries could recognise the court, and very often they could describe it, but in the last resort it was a mental or perceptual construct – the rationalisation of those who beheld it. The sources for court history are, to say the least, elusive. They are not concentrated in one place. Rather they are scattered across the chroniclers' accounts, the reports of foreign visitors, the occasional comments of critics, and the expenditure sections of the wardrobe books. The material in total hardly amounts to a great deal. But there is sufficient of it to allow a sketch in broad outline.

Life at the medieval court was life spent constantly on the move. The spectacle of courtly theatre was staged wherever the king happened to be, whether it was Woodstock, Westminster, or somewhere further off. It was through the constant process of journeying that kings kept in touch with their subjects. Those with grievances could petition them for redress, while the lawless and disobedient could be made to feel the weight of royal justice. The itineraries of the twelfth-century Angevin kings were particularly extensive because of the kings' holdings on both sides of the Channel. In one year, 1194 – to take a not untypical example – Richard I's itinerary extended across Germany, through England, to the Loire valley.[3] At the beginning of that year Richard returned to England from imprisonment in the German Empire. He left Speyer on about 23 January, reached Antwerp a month later, and dropped anchor at Sandwich on 13 March. After paying a brief visit to London, he headed north to Bury St Edmunds and eventually Nottingham, where he stayed for a week. On 2 April he went hunting at Clipstone, and on the 5th turned southwards again for his second coronation, at Winchester, on the 17th. On 12 May he left England for Normandy, disembarking at Barfleur. By the middle of June he was moving south to Montmirail and Tours. On 17 June he was besieging the town of Mirebeau-en-Poitou. In early July he returned north to Vendôme, Belfou and Loches. On 10 July he captured the castle of Loches from rebel forces. Later in the same month he headed southwards again to Poitou to bring the count of Angoulême to heel. On 28 July he arrived at Poitiers itself. He spent the greater part of August at Ville l'Eveque, probably enjoying the chase. Then in mid autumn he returned to Normandy, to Argentan and Alençon. After a brief visit to Chinon, he spent Christmas at Rouen, the capital of Normandy. In the remaining five years of his reign he was to spend all of his time on the Continent.

A typical year of Richard II's reign a couple of centuries later would likewise have been characterised by restless journeying – though by now in a more circumscribed orbit. Richard's itinerary for 1393 can be taken as representative of those of his middle and later years.[4] In the first few weeks of January the king moved restlessly between Eltham, Sheen and Windsor. On 17 January, or thereabouts, he began the journey south to Winchester for a session of parliament. Three weeks later, when the session was over, he returned to Windsor via Farnham. He spent most of the eight weeks from then until mid April moving between Eltham, Easthampstead and Sheen, fitting in a visit to Windsor for the Garter feast day on 23 April. In May and early June he undertook a lengthy itinerary of Kent, taking in Rochester, Ospringe and Canterbury. In the early weeks of the summer he occupied himself with the chase in the parks around Windsor. Then in July he embarked on a progress to Downton and Cranborne Chase for more of the pleasures of the chase. In August and September he returned to the London area via Corfe, Salisbury, Beaulieu and Winchester. He spent October at Windsor and November at Sheen. Christmas was celebrated at Westminster.

The itinerant lifestyle of monarchy inevitably put limits on the opportunities given to the king to display his greatness. Jewellery, tapestries, furniture and altar vessels all had to be packed and unpacked every few weeks, while sessions of the court might have to be staged in cramped or inadequate surroundings. When itineraries of the more remote parts of the realm were made, it might be difficult for the household to find any accommodation at all. In 1390, for example, when Richard II travelled from Woodstock to Oakham, he had to make do with the shelter of lodging houses and small priories, and on some nights it is likely that his staff camped out. Even when the court was staying in a great abbey conditions could be difficult. At St Peter's,

Gloucester, in 1378, when Richard and his counsellors moved in, the monks had to move out.

Despite its many drawbacks, however, the itinerant lifestyle was not altogether incompatible with the display of majesty. The medieval English monarchy was relatively well endowed with places in which the king could stay. The palaces of Eltham, Sheen, Windsor and Westminster, in or around London, all offered ample accommodation. Windsor was without doubt the grandest of the group. A vast pile covering thirteen acres, overlooking the Thames, and with a lavish set of apartments rebuilt by Edward III, it was a particular favourite of the Yorkists.[5] Westminster too could provide the king with some dramatic settings. The painted chamber at the centre of the palace was redecorated by Henry III, and the great hall, the largest royal hall of its day, was rebuilt by Richard II. Eltham, Clarendon and Sheen could also provide some splendid interiors.[6] But, as the meeting at Ardres showed, grand or palatial surroundings were not *de rigueur* if a king was to lay on a show. The mere presence of the royal person could command attention. When Richard I stood silent and impassive at his father's grave at Fontevrault a few days after his death, those watching knew that they were in the presence of a great man.[7] A few years later, at Messina, Richard was again to steal the show, though in very different fashion. Richard was approaching Messina by sea from Marseille. He wanted to arrive in the grandest possible style. So, as Howden records, he ordered his men to raise a massive din: 'There was such a noise of trumpets and clarions from the busses and other ships and galleys that a tremor rang through all in the city; the king of France and his men, and all the people of Messina on the shore wondered at what they had seen and heard about the king of England and about his power'.[8] King Philip of France could hardly have been very pleased with all this. But no one was left in any doubt of the greatness of his counterpart, the king of England. Richard certainly knew how to impress.

Attracting attention, commanding obedience and eliciting respect: these were arts that came naturally to a man born to the purple. It was as well that they did, for they were integral to the projection of the kingly image. All three Richards knew this only too well, for all three were showmen. Richard I was a showman even in death: he asked to be buried in his coronation robes. Indeed, it was probably he who was responsible for his father, Henry II, being buried with his regalia.[9]

Throughout his reign Richard cut a far grander figure than his father. The latter, indifferent to pomp, had dressed simply and cared little about appearances. But Richard was very different. Richard was vainer. He cared about his dignity. He liked to put on a good show. According to Ambroise, when he feasted, he insisted on the most valuable dishes.[10] He dined off gold or silver. He was profligate in his generosity to servants. In his cult of splendour, as in other respects, he set an example which many later kings were to follow.

One such who did was his namesake Richard II. Richard was a showman to his fingertips. A story told by the Westminster chronicler nicely illustrates his style.[11] According to the chronicler, one evening in January 1386 Richard took the king of Armenia to see the crown jewels in Westminster Abbey. The party went as dusk fell, with Richard splendidly arrayed as usual. Creeping around by candlelight, the kingly pair gazed at the insignia which Richard had worn at his coronation and peered at the abbey's collection of relics. As the chronicler knew, this was the way to create an impression of the magic and mystique of monarchy. But Richard was hardly less adept at the grander, more public, side of kingship. The Eulogium Chronicler, in a famous passage, tells how he presided at formal crown-wearings. On solemn festivals, the chronicler tells us, the king would sit enthroned in his chamber from dinner till vespers, talking to no one but watching everyone; and, when his eye fell on anyone, that person, whatever his status, had to bend the knee.[12] The ceremony described here was almost certainly a revival of the early medieval tradition of 'crown-wearings' – formal ceremonies at which the king sat throned in state at each of the three principal festivals of the year. Richard's behaviour at these formal courts appears to have owed much to this earlier practice. But a knowledge of other courts may have exercised an influence too. In general, the formality and ceremoniousness of Richard's court was heavily indebted to the rituals of the Valois court in France.

It is unfortunate that we can say far less about Richard III's court than about those of his predecessors. Richard III's reign was, of course, much shorter. But there is a further problem: we lack the chroniclers' accounts which bring those earlier kings' courts to life. What evidence there is, however, suggests that Richard delighted in ceremoniousness as much as any of his predecessors. In the summer of 1483, for example, he made a highly ceremonious visit to York in the course of which he was entertained by a series of pageants and by a Creed play staged in his honour.[13] In January 1484, while at Westminster, he laid on a magnificent feast to which he invited all the leading Londoners and over which he presided wearing his crown.[14] For Richard III, more than for most kings perhaps, the show of pomp and pageantry was vital to the projection of kingliness. Richard was a usurper, and his title to the throne weak. He needed to compensate for his weakness of title. And the way in which he did this was by stressing his possession of royal office. He wanted to let everyone know that he was king.

It should not be supposed that there was anything new in the kingly appetite for splendour. Kings had been showing their majesty for centuries. None the less, in the period that separated the reign of the first Richard from that of the third there were certainly significant changes in the character of the court and court life. The first and most obvious of these relates to size. Courts grew bigger.

Between the twelfth century and the fourteenth there was a general trend for households of all kinds to become bigger. Aristocratic households grew very considerably bigger. A noble household which in the thirteenth century might have numbered a hundred people or fewer would probably have numbered at least two hundred two centuries later. The households of kings and princes grew even faster and more substantially than most: not surprisingly, for they were the pacesetters. In England in the early twelfth century Henry I's household had numbered some 150 or so. By the turn of the thirteenth and fourteenth centuries Edward I's numbered some 500–700, and by two centuries later Henry VI's perhaps as many as eight hundred.[15] The English royal household did not stand alone in this respect. Most other European royal households grew at a similar pace: the Valois household in France, for example, had grown to roughly eight hundred by the fifteenth century. It needs to be added that this growth did not follow a simple or straightforward linear pattern. Households were constantly expanding or contracting in size. In some periods numbers would fall as a result of the absence of staff on the king's business, while at others there would be an expansion caused by the arrival of visiting nobles or foreign envoys and their accompanying retinues. None the less, it is doubtful if there was ever much of a reduction in

numbers over any length of time. Over the *longue durée* the trend
growth was upwards.

There was another respect in which the character of court life
changed in this period. Courts became more formal and hierarchical.
Their etiquette became more mannered, and their ceremonies richer
and more elaborate. These should not be seen as entirely new developments. In a sense, courts had always been hierarchical; it was in their
nature to be so. But there is evidence that in the later middle ages the
tendency to emphasise deference and hierarchy became more pronounced. Not only was the king accorded a more exalted standing than
before; a hierarchy of honour developed among the knights and nobles
who lived in his shadow.

Much of the evidence for the growing formality of court life in England comes from the reign of King Richard II. It was in Richard's reign,
for example, that the language of 'highness' and 'majesty' was first used
regularly in forms of address to the king.[16] In earlier times, kings had
been addressed in the traditional language of lordship. Typically, a petition to a king began 'to our lord the king' or 'to our most excellent lord
the king'. But at the beginning of the 1390s there was a sudden change.
As Thomas Walsingham records, Richard began to encourage 'flattering
new forms of address' to his person. In the parliament of 1397,
Walsingham tells us, Speaker Bushy addressed the king 'supplicating
with his hands, as if praying to him, entreating his high, excellent and
most praiseworthy majesty to concede these or those things'.[17] Similarly
extravagant forms of address were encouraged in the 1390s in petitions.
In 1391 the Commons addressed the king as his 'most excellent and most
renowned prince, and most gracious lord ... your highness and royal
majesty'.[18] The use of these new forms of address is also found in correspondence. In 1394, for example, the treasurer, Bishop Waltham of
Salisbury, writing to the king, began 'Tresexcellent, tresredoubte et mon
soverein seignur, je me recommanc a vostre haut roiale majeste ...'[19]
The effect of these grander address forms was to distance the king
from his subjects and to invest him with greater mystique: he was made
God-like; he was lifted to a higher plane. This novel language was
accompanied by a greater emphasis on physical expressions of deference. References are found more frequently to bowing and averting the
gaze. Even the mighty John of Gaunt in 1386, when he met the king, bent

1. Drawing of Richard I by Matthew Paris. (*British Library*)

2. The Wilton Diptych. (*National Gallery*)

3. Portrait of Richard II in Westminster Abbey. (*The Dean and Chapter of Westminster Abbey*)

4. The earl of Northumberland received by Richard II at Conway. (*British Library*)

5. The earl of Northumberland swearing an oath that he means no treachery to Richard II. (*British Library*)

6. Portrait of Richard III in the Royal Collection. (*National Portrait Gallery*)

7. Portrait of Richard III in the possession of the Society of Antiquaries. (*Society of Antiquaries*)

8. Edward V and Richard, Duke of York, the Princes in the Tower, by Sir John Everett Millais. (*Royal Holloway, University of London*)

the knee.[20] Richard's court was a more formal, a more ceremonious
society than his predecessors' a century or more before.

The growing formality of the court manifested itself in another way
– in the lengthening of the hierarchy of degree. New ranks were introduced into the peerage; the peerage itself was elevated as a distinct estate
in the nobility; and the royal kin – that is, the princes of the blood –
were raised in dignity above their non-royal peers. These developments
all had their origins in the mid fourteenth century. The title of duke was
introduced in 1337 (in favour of Edward, the Black Prince), that of marquess in 1385, and the rank of baron by patent in 1387, while the last new
title, that of viscount, appeared in the following century; before these
titles appeared, there had effectively been only two ranks in the peerage,
those of baron and earl. At the same time, the peers themselves acquired
sharper definition as a group. Previously a body of shifting membership,
they now became an hereditary caste. These developments all had major
implications for ritual and etiquette. With perceptions of status becoming sharper, so disputes arose between peers over precedence. In 1405,
for example, there was a bitter row between the earl of Norfolk (as earl
marshal) and the earl of Warwick over priority in seating in the House
of Lords, and the argument between them flared up again in the 1420s.[21]
Increasingly, those conscious of their status felt the desirability of having a set of conventions to govern such matters. By the mid fifteenth
century, an advice literature of etiquette was coming to their aid. In one
such book hosts were offered advice on the appropriate seating of their
guests at dinner.[22]

In one final area it is possible to notice an elaboration of courtly
ritual – the staging of civic ceremonial. From the late fourteenth century
it generally became the practice for the leading civic elites to stage elaborate pageants for the king on the occasion of his entry into their walls,
or some special event such as the coronation. The first pageant of which
a description has come down to us was that staged by the Londoners for
Richard II's coronation in 1377. The Anonimalle writer tells how Richard
was fêted and garlanded as he rode through the streets of the city to
Westminster, passing conduits decked out as fountains, and being
showered with bezants cast down by angelic maidens.[23] Five years later,
according to the Brut writer, a similar extravaganza was staged by the
Londoners in honour of Queen Anne of Bohemia, on the eve of her

coronation.[24] Again, the conduits were all bedecked, and coins were cast down by maidens. Later, such ceremonies became quite common. They might be staged to mark such royal rites of passage as weddings and coronations; or, alternatively, they might be held in honour of a conqueror. In 1415 on his return to his capital from Agincourt Henry V was greeted with a procession on the scale of a Roman triumph.

In all these ways – the employment of a richer vocabulary of address, the lengthening of the hierarchy of degree, and the staging of grand civic pageants – the trend to greater formality and ceremoniousness in the life of the late medieval court may be traced in the historical record. Many of these developments had their origins in the Valois court in France. This is most obviously the case with the civic pageants. The model for these events was almost certainly the French *joyeuse entrée*, the formal ceremony by which the king was greeted on his entry into one of the *bonnes villes* of the kingdom. French influence may well account for the introduction of the new and more formal language of address to the king: the French kings had long been addressed in a richer vocabulary than their English counterparts. French influence can be detected in other areas – for example, in the enrichment of personal attire. The high collars and long houpelandes popular at the English court in the 1390s owed much to Parisian fashion. The influence of French models lent a touch of cosmopolitanism to English court culture in this period. There is a sense in which the style of the European courts took on an international air. In cultural terms, certainly, no court could be considered an island on its own.

Yet, for all the effect of these homogenising influences, courts still remained remarkably varied in character. No two European courts were alike. Each was marked by its own style and culture, each by its own etiquette. And the reason for this was quite simple. The culture and routines of a court were shaped by the king whom it was the courtiers' function to serve. And all kings were different. Some, like Richard II, were highly ceremonious, while others, like Richard's contemporary the Emperor Wenzel, were not. Some were relaxed and informal, others quite the reverse. The etiquette and ceremony of a court were shaped essentially in the presiding king's image. Those who observed the Tudor or Stuart courts, and were writing a century later, were fully aware of this. In a well known passage of his *History of the Reign of Henry VII*

Francis Bacon remarked on Henry VII's kingly style. The essence of that style, he maintained, was 'the keeping of distance, which he did towards all'.[25] In Bacon's view, the 'keeping of distance' was something distinctive to Henry. It marked him apart. It was certainly a way of ruling that contrasted with that of his son, Henry VIII. Henry's style was more boisterous and sociable. It was participatory and intimate. Henry VIII, unlike his father, wined and dined with his courtiers; he even on occasion wrestled with them. The contrasting styles of father and son provide a convenient model for categorising kingly style more generally.[26] On the one hand, we can recognise a 'kingship of distance', a kingship of the kind practised by Henry VII, and, on the other, a 'kingship of intimacy', of the kind practised by Henry VIII. Into which of these categories may the personal styles of the three Richards be placed?

The case of Richard the Lionheart presents a number of difficulties. Firstly, and most importantly, the king's character is not clearly conveyed by the sources. Although Richard lived at a time of rich historical writing, we lack a good first-hand picture of him at work. The great majority of the chronicle accounts were written after his death, and many of these are informed by legend-making. Even the best writer of the time, Gerald de Barri, gives only a conventional picture of the king. Added to this problem is the difficulty that much of what we know about the king makes him hard to categorise. He gives the impression of exhibiting two styles at once; or, to put it another way, we observe him switching quickly between two styles. At one moment he is cold, distant and reserved, while at another he is exchanging friendly banter with his courtiers. Which is the true Richard? There is certainly much about his style that conforms to the model of 'distance'. As contemporaries commented, he loved ceremony: all were agreed on his splendour. Ambroise, who knew him on crusade, spoke of the magnificence of his court.[27] He was attracted to the liturgy of kingship. When Bishop Hugh of Lincoln met him in 1198, he found him throned in state amidst his chapel choir and bishops.[28] It is noteworthy that, when he returned from captivity in 1194, he insisted on being given a second coronation. Richard yielded nothing to his fellow rulers in his love of the pageantry of kingship. His chivalry also reinforced his sense of style. Conscious of his knightly rank, he insisted on a show of honour to his person. According to Bertrand de Born, he 'desired honour (*pretz*) more than any man, Christian or infidel'.[29] Alongside the evidence of 'distance', however, there is likewise evidence of a warmer and more intimate side. Richard could come down from his pedestal. Being a soldier, he necessarily developed a camaraderie with his fellow knights. He enjoyed close relations with William Marshal and with his mercenary captain Mercadier. The story of how he was discovered in prison in Germany also suggests close relations with the minstrel Blondel. On campaign he was always to be found in the thick of the fighting. He was never one to hold back in the rear. He was notorious for taking risks. At the siege of Chalus in 1199 he was out on patrol when struck by the fatal arrow bolt. The truth of the matter appears to be that he combined kingliness with camaraderie. He was always conscious that royal leadership called for a show of respect and he never let slip the aura and mystique of the kingly office. Yet equally he could exchange jokes and banter with his men. Coggeshall tells how he indulged in games and jokes with the members of his household. But, while capable of relaxed banter, he never let intimacy degenerate into familiarity. Everyone who entered his presence was conscious that he was every inch a king.

Richard II's kingship, like Richard I's, presents problems of categorisation. While Richard II was in many ways a very different king from his earlier namesake – he was not a great soldier – he too could display more than one style. At one moment he could be grand and stately, lording it magnificently over his court, while at another be could be mixing with base intimates. There is a similar difficulty in establishing which is the 'real' Richard. The Richard who is familiar to history is the stately ceremonious king. This is the Richard of the chronicles. The monk of Evesham describes vividly how he presided at a magnificent banquet at the end of the Smithfield tournament in 1390, dressed in the very finest robes and wearing his crown.[30] The Monk of Westminster, in the same year, tells us that when he paid a visit to the abbey on St Edward's Day he was attended by the whole of his chapel and sat during mass wearing his crown, with the queen, also wearing her crown, beside him.[31] Richard's taste for ceremoniousness is also attested by entries in the record sources. In September 1397, according to the Lancastrian account book, he attended a feast given in his honour by Henry Bolingbroke at the White Friars Hall in Fleet Street sitting on a dais under a magnificent canopy.[32] On several well-attested occasions he indulged his taste for elaborate processions. In 1392, for example, as the Westminster writer again narrates, he and Anne processed in state through the streets of the capital, past a series of carefully orchestrated pageants honouring his kingship, censed as they went by boys dressed as angels.[33] Richard's natural inclination for ceremony was reinforced by the increased formality of the late medieval court. Courtly etiquette had become much more structured over the previous century or so. It was common, for example, for courtiers to bow or to avert their gaze from the king. Richard's institution or revival of formal crown-wearing ceremonies needs to be interpreted to this background.

But alongside the evidence of Richard's taste for formality needs to be set that of his apparent 'intimacy'. This aspect of Richard's kingship finds its most eloquent expression in Shakespeare. In Act III of *The First Part of King Henry IV*, Henry, hearing of Hal's misdemeanours, recalls his predecessor's style:

> The skipping King, he ambled up and down,
> With shallow jesters, and rash bavin wits,
> Soon kindled and soon burnt, carded his state,
> Mingled his royalty with cap'ring fools,
> Had his great name profaned with their scorns,
> And gave his countenance against his name
> To laugh at gibing boys.

The suggestion here that Richard 'mingled his kingship' with inferiors is not without foundation. The Evesham writer, in his account of the later years of the reign, says that the king spent long evenings carousing with a small group of intimates, while John Strecche of Kenilworth, admittedly writing later, says that his Cheshire archers, who guarded him day and night, would refer to him as 'Dycun': 'Dycun, sleep securely, and fear not while we live'.[34] These suggestions of familiarity were echoed in Henry IV's first parliament of 1399. According to Walsingham, John, Lord Cobham, a much respected peer, accused Richard's favourites of referring to themselves as 'we, foster children to King Richard ... etc'.[35] The men of whom Lord Cobham was thinking were probably the leaders of the new courtier nobility – Aumerle, Wiltshire and Gloucester – and chamber knights like the notorious Bushy, Bagot and Green. Richard's overfamiliarity with his intimates sat awkwardly with his careful cultivation of distance. The image of a remote, God-like king was fatally compromised. Onlookers were puzzled. At one moment they would find the king acting the remote monarch, and at another the 'skipping' playboy. The confusion unsettled them. It left them insecure. In 1399 it was the cool, reserved Bolingbroke who won the favour of the crowds, not the theatrical, but confusing, Richard.

By comparison with the sources for Richard II's kingly style, those for Richard III's are disappointingly few. Not only is there a lack of good chronicle narratives – the account of the Crowland Continuator being the only major one to have come down to us; a further problem is the dearth of wardrobe and administrative material for the reign. None the less, a rough outline of Richard's kingly style can be formed. Richard, it seems, was drawn to the more distant model of kingship. In the light of what we know about him, this is hardly surprising. By virtue of his weakness of title, he was necessarily driven to stress the office or estate rather than the man. The pressure of circumstance was reinforced by personal inclination. Richard was by nature an introverted and secretive man. There was not a trace in him of the easy affability of his brother. In consequence of these factors, it was only to be expected that his court would be a very ceremonious one; and so it was. On his itineraries of the realm he encouraged the staging of lavish civic receptions (*joueuses entrées*). On his arrival at York in the summer of 1483 he was greeted by all the leading citizenry and burgesses, and no fewer than three pageants and a performance of the city's Creed play were staged in his honour.[36] He also attached importance to dressing splendidly. On the day of his coronation he was attired colourfully even by fifteenth-century standards. In the morning he wore a long purple velvet gown over a doublet of blue cloth-of-gold, while in the afternoon he donned a long gown of purple cloth-of-gold marked with the insignia of the Order of the Garter and the white roses of York.[37] Richard also used the day-to-day pageantry of the court to telling effect. In January 1484 he presided over a magnificent Epiphany banquet in the White Hall at Westminster splendidly arrayed and wearing his crown. Among his guests was a delegation of Londoners, and he presented the city's mayor with a gold cup set with pearls and gems.[38] Richard, like his flamboyant elder brother, wanted to parade the splendour of his court before the widest possible audience. In this way, he believed, he could secure the respect and allegiance of his subjects.

If any one impression is conveyed by these sketches of the kings' styles, it is this: all three knew how to project an image of splendour. Each one of them was practised in the art of impressing, each one of them in the knack of cultivating grandeur. To put the point another way: all three kings, to a greater or lesser degree, conformed to the model of 'distance'. This is not to suggest that they were always, or altogether, consistent in their behaviour. Nothing could be further from the truth. Richard II, as we have seen, displayed an eclectic mixture of styles. In broad terms, however, in their manner of acting the king they inclined to the model of 'distance' rather than 'intimacy'.

In any medieval polity the personal style of the king was bound to have a major bearing on the life of his court. Nowhere and at no time was it the only or the most important influence. Broader cultural patterns, and contact with other courts, could also work their effect. But for the most part it was the king's personality and taste that settled the tone and ambience of his court; and because the personalities of kings differed so much, this made for immense variety in courtly style. Some kings were keen patrons of music and letters, while others were not. At some courts there would be vigorous artistic and architectural patronage, while at others very little. How was the taste of the three Richards manifested in the cultural patronage of their courts?

The king about whose courtly culture we are least well informed is Richard I. Unfortunately, the source material for Richard's court is disappointingly meagre. There is a scattering of useful information in the pipe rolls (the annual account rolls of the exchequer). In total, however, this does not amount to a great deal, and it is inferior in quality to the evidence later provided by the wardrobe books; moreover, it is evidence of a rather impersonal nature. More valuable insights into Richard's court are provided by the chroniclers and by the *obiter dicta* of Richard's own servants. At least, however, the message conveyed by all these various sources is clear. Richard's court was one of considerable culture and sophistication.

Culturally, the tone of the Angevin court had been set earlier, in the 1160s and 1170s, by Richard's father, Henry II. Henry, as contemporaries recognised, was a man of considerable learning and intelligence. According to Gerald of Wales, he was 'remarkably polished in letters', while in the words of Peter of Blois, 'with Henry it is school every day, constant conversation with the best scholars'.[39] Among Henry II's staff and associates were to be found some of the most distinguished literary figures of the day – Walter Map, for example, the author of *De Nugis Curialium*, and Walter of Châtillon, a poet of note. Richard, though often at odds with his father, inherited his interest in letters to the full. He was literate and well educated: all of Henry's family, indeed, were literate. He could engage in dialectics and logic-chopping. On one occasion he got the better of the papal legate in argument.[40] His speech was usually direct and economical; yet, at the same time, his words were well chosen. He was probably familiar with the literature of government. If these chance vignettes suggest a somewhat dry character, the picture should be modified. Richard on his mother's side was an Aquitanian, a southerner; in other words, he was a romantic. This southern influence showed in his love of the troubadour lyrics. He is credited with the authorship of two troubadour songs: the 'rotrouenge' which he is said to have composed in captivity and a sirventes composed for the benefit of the Dauphin of Auvergne.[41] The familiar legend of Blondel discovering his master by his song probably had its roots in the latter's command of the troubadours' courtly lyrics. Richard's court with its close links with the culture of southern and south-western France would surely have yielded to none in its musical and literary sophistication.

If Richard I's court is perhaps the least well documented of our three, Richard II's is assuredly the best. Not only do we have a good run of wardrobe (or household) accounts which shed light on the size and cost of the court; there is also the evidence of its remarkable literary and artistic output – most notably, of course, the finest painting of the period, the Wilton Diptych. Richard's court has long been regarded as one of the most elegant and sophisticated of the age. The extraordinary magnificence of its art has been commented on.[42] The court's reputation for refinement is largely justified. Its distinctive characteristics are well known. A new emphasis was placed on the civilian arts, in particular on the cult of letters. Table manners were improved through the greater use of cutlery at dinner. And, above all, the presence of women in greater number brought a touch of gaiety to courtly activity. The elegance of Richard's court owed a great deal to influences from abroad. Richard's interest in the culture and etiquette of the contemporary French court is well attested. We have seen how he drew on the model of the French *joyeuse entrée* for his processions through London. The influence of Italy, however, should probably be set alongside that of France. Relations between England and the Italian courts were particularly close in the late fourteenth century and a number of Richard's courtiers, Chaucer included, had knowledge of those societies. The cosmopolitanism of Richard's court provides the essential background to an understanding of its most celebrated artistic product, the Wilton Diptych. The Diptych is a work of such outstanding quality that it has sometimes been attributed to a French or Low Countries artist. Today, the consensus of scholarly opinion is that it was almost certainly produced in England.[43] Nonetheless, the fact that the case for a non-English painter has been considered is itself significant. Its stylistic sources are eclectic. Whoever the painter was, he had a knowledge of artistic sources from across a wide area of Europe.

Significant though the external influences on the culture of Richard's court were, the character and taste of the king himself were probably the most important influences of all. Richard's refined but mercurial personality and his fastidiousness of taste had a bearing on nearly every aspect of courtly life. The growth of ceremony, the introduction of the new vocabulary of address, and the new emphasis on the sacral dimension of kingship, all had their origins in Richard's initiatives and endeavour.

The area in which the king's influence can most clearly be seen today is in the development of royal portraiture. It is hardly coincidental that more likenesses survive of Richard than of any English king before Henry VIII. Richard, indeed, is the first English king of whose personal appearance we can be reasonably sure. There are likenesses of numerous earlier rulers on their tomb effigies at Westminster, Gloucester and elsewhere. With the exception of that of Edward III, however, these are all conventional likenesses.[44] Richard II's effigy on his tomb in Westminster Abbey is different. It is the first such effigy to display a genuine seeking after portraiture. In the long nose, the goatee beard and high cheekbones we sense a genuine attempt to portray the king's face as it actually was.[45] Richard took a close personal interest in the monument. The two contracts for it – one with the marblers and the other with the coppersmiths – were placed after the death of his wife Anne in 1394.

In the contract with the coppersmiths he said that the effigies were to be made according to a 'patron' – a pattern, that is – which had already been made.[46] In other words, he had personally inspected and approved the design. His aim was to commission a monument which would embody the most up to date ideas of portraiture. At the same time, however, he wanted a likeness of himself which accorded with his own self-image. Richard was one of the most image-conscious rulers of his day, and the narcissistic streak in his personality reinforced this preoccupation. Richard was no Oliver Cromwell. Not for him, a 'warts and all' portrait. Rather, a Van Dyck in the grand manner, which reflected the sublimity of monarchy.

Altogether more mask-like is the other likeness of Richard to be found in Westminster Abbey – the so-called 'coronation portrait', which hangs in the nave.[47] This is a portrait which focuses less on the individual than on the office. Richard is shown crowned and holding the attributes of sovereignty – the orb and the sceptre. He gazes out expressionless. The portrait is one of the most remarkable of its age. No direct parallel to it can be found in any extant portrait of a European late medieval monarch. There are possible analogies in the lost portraits on the staircase of Charles IV's castle at Karlstein (Czech Republic), although these figures were shown three-quarter face. The origins of the painting are obscure. It clearly cannot be a 'coronation' portrait in the conventional sense, for it shows a mature man and Richard was only a boy when he was crowned. For the whole of its recorded history it has been associated with Westminster Abbey, and it appears originally to have hung in the royal pew in the choir. The suggestion has been made that it attested the king's presence when he was not actually present in the abbey in person. Yet can we suppose such a dramatic portrait really to have had so limited a purpose? It was usual in medieval art for the subjects of portraits to be shown in profile. Only the Almighty was shown, as Richard was here, face on. For Richard to have been depicted in such a boldly hierarchic pose was almost deliberately to invite comparison with the Godhead. It may be presumed that this was Richard's intention. He wanted to be seen by those who looked at the painting as the divinely appointed sacral ruler. As we have seen, Richard exploited the religious dimension to his kingship in a variety of ways. Rarely, however, did he do so more audaciously than here. In this extraordinary

painting he affords us the boldest and most authoritarian statement of
his kingly ideals.

The other extant visual representations of the king are more conventional. Artistically, the most accomplished of them is the portrait in the
Wilton Diptych. In the Diptych's left-hand panel, Richard is shown as a
pious suppliant – kneeling, attired in a gorgeous robe, and with his
hands extended to receive the banner from one of the angelic company
opposite. In a row behind him stand his saintly sponsors – St John the
Baptist, St Edward the Confessor and St Edmund – while in the panel
opposite the Christ Child bestows a blessing. The quality of the Diptych's artwork is quite outstanding: never has royal apparel been more
gorgeously depicted. But in general terms the Diptych is a work of
familiar type – that of the portable altarpiece used for private devotions.
Kneeling figures like Richard's are to be found in a great many other late
medieval votive panels. Richard is shown as a suppliant in one other
contemporary portrait. In a panel of the east window of Winchester
College he is represented again in profile and this time kneeling to St
John the Baptist.[48] This is the only extant portrait of him in glass. Most
of the other representations of him are to be found in illuminated manuscripts. The presentation copy of Roger Dymock's treatise against the
Lollards is a good example. These representations for the most part all
conform to a type. Generally the king is shown in historiated capital
letters, enthroned, wearing a tall crown and carrying the orb and the
sceptre. In the best of these representations, in the Shrewsbury borough
charter of 1389, he is shown with his wife, Anne, who is interceding for
the charter and kneeling beside him.[49]

Not all of these portraits of the king had their origins in Richard's
own initiative. The great majority of those found in illuminated
manuscripts were commissioned by people seeking his favour. None
the less, Richard's interest in his self-image is amply enough attested.
Of no other medieval king do we have so many contemporary likenesses. So what was the reason for Richard's interest in commissioning
portraits of himself? Part of the answer is to be found in his solipsism.
His experience of the world essentially revolved around his own person – his own body, his own needs and his own feelings. There is
something self-referential about his interest in portraiture. It is possible,
however, that other factors were involved. In the first place, Richard

saw in the commissioning of portrait images a way of conveying a sense of the reality of royal power. In 1392, for example, when he made a settlement of his dispute with the Londoners, he insisted that statues of himself and his queen be placed above the gate of London bridge.[50] The statues would be a constant reminder to the Londoners of the presence of royal power in their city. Secondly, Richard's fascination with his regal image owed something to his interest in history. He had a powerful sense of his place in the royal line of succession. In the 1380s he commissioned a set of 'thirteen stone images in the likeness of kings' for Westminster Hall in which he was represented as last in the direct line from Edward the Confessor. Artistically, the model for the statues was the very similar series in the hall of the Palais de la Cité at Paris.[51] But the spirit that informed them was Richard's – Richard's sense of the past and his affinity with his royal ancestors. Richard's intense preoccupation with his self-image, therefore, while owing much to his narcissism, can be interpreted as furthering the policy aims of his kingship.

If Richard's personal tastes were a major influence on the artistic and architectural creativity of his court, it is less easy to establish his role in the promotion and patronage of letters. On the face of it, there is a powerful case for seeing him as chiefly responsible for bringing together the remarkable concentration of literary talent at his court. Chaucer, for example, was retained as an esquire in the royal household and was on several occasions employed as a royal envoy, once to Spain, and once – perhaps twice – to Italy. Sir John Clanvow, another distinguished poet, was a chamber knight from the late 1370s, and may have written his *Boke of Cupid* for the St Valentine's Day festivities of the court. John Gower, 'Moral Gower' as Chaucer called him, the author of the *Vox Clamantis* and *Confessio Amantis*, although less close to the court, was on good terms with the chamber knights and from 1393 was a fee'd retainer of Henry Bolingbroke. Other men with a keen interest in letters were in the king's inner circle. Edward, duke of Aumerle, the duke of York's son and translator of Gaston Febus's *Book of Hunting*, was a key ally of Richard's in the last years of the reign, and on one occasion, according to Bagot, Richard said that he would like Aumerle to succeed him. John Montagu, later earl of Salisbury, a poet who received tributes from none other than Christine de Pisan, was another close ally of the king. Among various others who stood high in the king's favour were some distinguished book collectors. Sir Simon Burley, Richard's childhood tutor, had an impressive collection that included nine French romances and Giles of Rome's treatise on government, while Sir Richard Stury was familiar with the works of Froissart and a French poet, Eustace Deschamps. There can be little doubt that Richard's courtly intimates were a well read and highly cultivated group of men.[52]

What actually did Richard do to bring these men together and to create the conditions in which they could work? What was his role in the promotion and dissemination of literature? It is when we ask questions like these that the evidence, in other respects so promising, begins to fail us. Richard's own role in the cultural flowering of his reign is strangely obscure. Abroad, he appears to have been regarded as something of a book collector: foreign envoys who wished to court his favour would present him with books.[53] But only one major work of poetry can be shown to have had its origins in a royal commission – Gower's *Confessio Amantis*, of *c.* 1386–90. In a prologue to the poem, which he later replaced, Gower tells us that he was travelling with the king one day in the royal barge when Richard asked him to write a poem about love, which, in obedience to the royal will, he did.[54] The passage could possibly be a literary conceit. Even if it is taken as referring to an actual event, however, it is a statement which stands curiously alone. In the rest of the 'Ricardian' poetic corpus there are no references to royal patronage and no dedications to the king in autograph manuscripts. Nor in the ample financial sources of the period – the exchequer issue rolls and the wardrobe books of the household – is there any record of payments to poets for their work.[55]

When the records are so conspicuously silent, it is difficult to envisage Richard as an active patron of letters. With the questionable exception of the *Confessio Amantis*, a book of geomancy of 1391 is the only extant work which can be directly associated with his patronage.[56] None the less, it would be wrong to go to the opposite extreme of supposing that Richard played no role in the promotion of literature at all. Even if he did not commission poems, he was active in shaping literary culture as a reader or listener.[57] This role is reflected in the addresses offered to him by poets in their works. In the Chaucerian canon there

are a number of addresses or less specific references to the king. In the
ballade *Lak of Stedfastnesse*, for example, Richard is the addressee of the
closing *envoy*:

> O prince, desyre to be honourable,
> Cherish thy folk and hate extorcioun.
> Suffre nothing that may be reprevable
> To thyn estat don in they regioun.
> Shew forth thy swerd of castigacioun,
> Dred God, do law, love, trouthe and worthinesse,
> And wed they folk agein to stedfastnesse.[58]

Chaucer probably wrote *Lak of Stedfastnesse* as a bid to regain office after
the purging of the court by the Appellants, in which case he could have
seen the poem as a petition.[59] In a very different work, the 'F Prologue'
to *The Legend of Good Women*, Chaucer's reference to Richard is more
allusive. Chaucer sketched the God of Love in terms which suggest that
he had Richard in mind. He describes the God's hair as golden, just as
we know that Richard's hair was golden:

> His gilte heer was corowned with a sonne
> Instede of gold . . .[60]

The point could be added that the sun which crowns his head was one
of Richard's symbols.[61] In another passage of the work, which suggests
that Chaucer imagined a royal audience, the mythical figure of Alceste
commands Chaucer to:

> Goo now thy wey . . .
> And when this book ys maad, give it the quene,
> On my byhalf, at Eltham or at Shene.[62]

A third poem for which Chaucer probably envisaged Richard as listener
or reader was the *Tale of Melibee*, a political advice poem which he was
later to include in *The Canterbury Tales*. When translating the poem
from French to English, Chaucer tellingly removed a passage referring
to the evils attendant on a child king – which suggests that he saw
England's child king – Richard – as part of his audience.[63]

The implication of these references is that in at least some of his
poems Chaucer saw himself in a kind of lord-retainer relationship with
the king. Even if the king did not actively commission poems from him,

Chaucer none the less saw a nexus of patronage as linking the two of them. Whatever form that nexus took, however, it could only have been loose and informal. As we have seen, there is no evidence that Richard ever actually commissioned a poem from Chaucer. Richard's role in the promotion of literature is most likely to have been passive rather than active.[64] Perhaps it is for this reason that no foreign *littérateurs* ever paid tribute to him. Writers like Eustace Deschamps, Philippe de Mézières and Christine de Pisan certainly knew something of the literary accomplishments of the English courtiers. Yet not one of them ever praised Richard himself for his role in contributing to their achievement. Richard's court was significant to *littérateurs* for providing them with a source of livelihood and support. And Richard himself was significant to them as a sympathetic listener. None the less, the mainspring of their creativity was found in the support and stimulus which they received from each other.[65]

Richard's contribution to the literary flowering of his court may thus have been more limited than has sometimes been supposed. Certainly, it could not compare with the contribution of Charles V of France to his. Never the less, as we have seen, there is ample evidence for seeing the king as a major influence on the life of the court more generally. He encouraged a vigorous artistic cult of his own person, commissioning a remarkable series of portrait images. He was responsible for a magnificent new set of buildings at Westminster. The great hall of the palace of Westminster was rebuilt on his initiative, and work on rebuilding the abbey nave taken up again. He was also responsible for bringing a new refinement to the social life of the court. He pioneered the use of the handkerchief and promoted better manners at table.[66] If he cannot be seen as a royal Maecenas, he certainly succeeded in making the English court one of the most elegant and sophisticated of its day.

Richard III's role in shaping the cultural life of his court is, by contrast, much harder to assess. Not only are the sources for this Richard's court considerably fewer than for his predecessors'; the opportunities given to the king to make an impact on his court were more limited. He was on the throne for barely two years. Yet, despite the shortage of source material, a picture of sorts does emerge. Richard made few if any changes to his predecessor's court. For the most part, he worked within the structures which he inherited. Beyond a general liking for magnificence, his own tastes as king were relatively little in evidence.

The character of the Yorkist court was, in all essentials, established by the first Yorkist king, Edward IV, in the second part of his reign, after his return from exile. Edward was an admirer and a devotee of all things Burgundian. He had spent his months of exile in 1470–71 during the Lancastrian restoration in the Burgundian Netherlands. He knew the Burgundian court and was on intimate terms with many of the leading Burgundian courtiers. Thus it is unsurprising that it was the style and etiquette of the Burgundian court that exercised the strongest influence on his own after his return. The Burgundian character of Edward's court in the later years of his reign showed in all sorts of ways. Most obviously it was manifested in the growing interest which the king developed in chivalric ritual. The Burgundian court had long made greater play of chivalric junketings than any other in Europe. Jousting, tourneying and feasting were all central to its sense of cultural identity. After Edward's restoration in 1471 the ceremonies of chivalry became ever more prominent in the life of the English court. In 1478, for example, a series of tournaments and pageants was laid on to celebrate the marriage of the king's son Richard of York and Anne Mowbray. In a parallel and related development, the Order of the Garter was elevated as a focus for the harmonisation of relations between crown and nobility, in imitation of the Burgundian Order of the Golden Fleece. The use of chivalry to enhance the image of the court in this way had hardly been anticipated in the years before Edward's exile.

The influence of Burgundy was also to be seen in the liking which Edward IV developed for sumptuously illuminated Flemish manuscripts. Edward's interest in manuscript art had been whetted in 1470 during his stay with Louis of Gruthuyse, at Bruges. Gruthuyse, a noted patron of letters, had amassed one of the finest collections of books and manuscripts of his day and Edward resolved to build up a similar collection himself. In the course of his second reign he did this. Among the many fine volumes he acquired were no fewer than twenty-five from the workshops of Bruges and Ghent, a number of them copies of Gruthuyse's own. Edward's collection formed the nucleus of what was later to be the Royal Library at Windsor.[67] Burgundian influence and, more specifically, the influence of Louis of Gruthuyse showed in a second way, in the building of the royal oratory in St George's Chapel, Windsor. This remarkable structure is strikingly similar to Gruthuyse's own oratory in the church of Our Lady at Bruges. In each case, the oratory was built at first-floor level in the choir, looking down on the high altar.[68] Since no direct model for the Windsor oratory is to be found in English architecture of the time, it is natural to find the inspiration for it in Gruthuyse's oratory at Bruges. It is true, as has been pointed out, that the Gruthuyse oratory was not completed until after Edward IV had returned to England.[69] None the less, the similarity of the two structures to each other makes it virtually certain that Edward IV must have learned about Gruthuyse's plans while at Bruges.

The influence of the Burgundian court also showed itself in the trend to greater formality at its English counterpart. The Burgundian court under Duke Charles was renowned throughout Europe for its formality and protocol. Regulations were published, for example, governing how many paces nobles of varying ranks should advance to welcome a guest, and the number of times that a superior, out of politeness, should offer precedence to an inferior before himself leading the way. In 1473 a major codification of the Burgundian court ordinances was produced by Olivier de la Marche, Duke Charles's master of ceremonies – the so-called *Etat de la Maison du Duc Charles de Bourgogne*. In 1474, through the good offices of Richard Whetehill, the victualler of Calais, a copy of this highly esteemed document was obtained by Edward IV. It seems very likely that it provided the inspiration for the king's major reordering of the English royal household which found expression in the Black Book and the Ordinance of 1478.[70] The customs and structures described in Edward IV's books are almost all of English origin. None the less, there is evidence of Burgundian influence in the concern to set them down in writing and to clarify the delineations of status. A desire to emulate the Burgundian court formed a major element in the thinking of Edward IV and his brothers.

At the end of the middle ages, then, as at the beginning, the English court was exposed to waves of influence from abroad. And this is only to be expected. Courtly society was by its nature cosmopolitan. The fashions of one court were quickly picked up and copied or imitated in another. But alongside the currents of international influence were those of more local origin – in particular, the preferences of the king or prince himself. Each of the three Richards, to a greater or lesser degree, shaped his court in his own image. Richard the Lionheart's court reflected simultaneously the martial, aggressive side of the king's character and the softer, more civilian, influences of the southern parts in which he had grown up. Richard II's more formal and hierarchical court bore the imprint of this ruler's ambition to develop a more exalted model of kingship – an ambition which explains the exceptional emphasis which he placed on deference and the showing of respect to his person. Richard III's court, while essentially a continuation of his brother's, reflected the usurper king's need to develop a kingly style which went some way to compensating for the weakness of his kingly title. Each of the three kings, therefore, through the medium of his court sought to articulate a statement of the values and aspirations of his kingship. If the court was a setting for the theatre of kingship, it was also at the same time a mirror image of the character and personality of the king himself.

Brass of Robert Incent, servant of Cecily, duchess of York, and of Richard III, Berkhamsted church (Hertfordshire). (*Reproduced by H. M. Stuchfield from a rubbing by the author*)

8

Marriage and Family

The marriage of a medieval king was always a great event: a cause of national celebration and, for the king himself, a moment of emotional satisfaction. Because of its importance, and provided the royal couple were old enough, the marriage was invariably celebrated in style. When Anne of Bohemia married Richard II in 1382 the junketings matched those of Richard's coronation five years earlier in scale. Forty years later, Henry V's marriage to Catherine of Valois was made the vehicle for celebrating the genesis of the new dual monarchy of England and France.

At every level of society in the middle ages marriage was treated as one of life's rites of passage. For no group, however, was it a matter of greater consequence than for a realm's governing elite – as Henry VIII's reign was later to show. Marriage was important to kings and princes for two reasons. First, it was biologically important. It was through marriage that a smooth dynastic succession was secured, through marriage that the royal line was kept going. Secondly, marriage served a political function. Marriage was integral to the functioning of international diplomacy. It provided the means by which alliances were sealed, social ties reinforced and warring nations brought together. In the pre-modern period, when the worlds of private and public were merged, it was through marriage that diplomacy was conducted.

Largely as a result of this second factor – the connection between marriage and diplomacy – the arranging of high-status matches in the middle ages was generally taken over by parents. Most medieval English kings were betrothed when still under age. Edward I, while still the Lord Edward, was married to Eleanor, daughter of the king of Castile, at the age of fifteen; Edward III was married to Philippa, daughter of the count of Hainault, at the age of fourteen, and the future Henry IV to Mary Bohun at about the same age. In each of these cases the principal aim of the sponsors was to advance national or dynastic interest. Strikingly, a high proportion of English royal brides in the middle ages were French-born. The two Eleanors – of Aquitaine and Provence – Isabella of Angoulême, Catherine of Valois, and Isabella, Edward II's wife, were all French by birth. This predominance in the English royal line of French wives was a natural reflection of the long-standing Angevin or Plantagenet interests in France. For over two centuries from the 1230s, it was through marital alliances between the English and French lines that differences between the two competing dynasties were accommodated.

To this general pattern of French marriages, however, the marriages of the three Richards constitute notable exceptions. Of the four wives of these kings, only one – Richard II's second wife, Isabella – was French. Richard the Lionheart's wife was Navarrese, Richard II's first wife was Bohemian, and Richard III's wife English. In a second, and equally notable, respect the marriages of the three Richards stand out. Unusually for the Plantagenets, they were all, by the biological test, failures. None of the four matches, as the Crowland Chronicler was to point out in the 1480s, was productive of surviving issue.[1] This deficiency was not without major implications. Its inevitable consequence was to give rise to doubts and questioning about the succession. In these two respects, then, the marriages of the three Richards raise questions affecting our understanding of the medieval English monarchy. The kings' marriages may be taken as a point of departure for an exploration of the role of the king's family in the governance of the realm.

It is best perhaps to begin with the story of the making of the first of these matches – that of Richard the Lionheart. In May 1191 at Limassol in Cyprus Richard married Berengaria, daughter of Sancho, king of Navarre. Berengaria was not actually the bride whom his father, Henry II, had intended for him. Henry had envisaged a young lady much grander. This was Alice, daughter of King Louis VII of France. Henry wanted his children to marry into the very best royal houses of Europe and the proposed match between Richard and Alice fitted into this pattern. Yet, surprisingly, the betrothal was never followed by a sealing of the knot. After an engagement of some twenty years, the relationship was broken off. Richard married Berengaria instead. Why was this? And why was a fiancée from one of the most distinguished royal lineages of

Europe so unceremoniously treated? To answer this question, we need to look at the history of Angevin-Capetian relations at the time that the match was contracted.

The alliance which Henry negotiated for his second son formed part of a much larger scheme to allow him to embark on crusade. Henry had been anxious to set out for the East for some time. Before he could depart, however, he needed to ensure that his borders were secure. His strategy for looking after the southern border of Normandy was a very traditional one: he negotiated a marriage alliance with his chief rival, the king of France. Richard would take Alice as his bride.[2] A year after the deal was negotiated, Alice was handed over – but to Henry, not Richard. Richard was probably aged twelve at the time, and Alice perhaps the same. There was a natural expectation that when, in a few years, they reached the canonical age, the bond between them would be solemnised. In fact, however, this never happened. The act of betrothal was confirmed on a number of occasions over the next two decades, most publicly in July 1189 shortly after Richard's accession, but the two remained unmarried. This bizarre – and for the unfortunate Alice highly embarrassing – state of affairs became the subject of critical comment. Rumours quickly circulated to compensate for the lack of hard fact. Roger of Howden and Gerald of Wales both maintained that Henry had seduced Alice and that Richard had said that he would never marry his father's mistress.[3] Whether, or to what extent, there was any truth in the rumours is hard to say. But the signs are that the main reason for Richard's failure to solemnise the bond was political. Alice's fate had become fatally entangled with that of a border territory occupied by the Angevins, and which Philip was striving to recover – the Norman Vexin. A quarter of a century before, when Henry the Young King had married Margaret, another of Louis's daughters, an agreement had been reached that the Vexin would be assigned to the latter as dowry; and shortly afterwards the Vexin was handed over. In June 1183, however, the Young King died, and Louis's successor, Philip, demanded that the Vexin be returned. Henry refused, maintaining that the Vexin belonged of right to the duchy of Normandy; and to this position he stuck rigidly. Six months later, in December, at a meeting at Gisors, Philip agreed to allow Henry to retain the Vexin provided that it was held by Alice's husband: the implication being that, should Richard solemnise his bond and the

Vexin be designated Alice's portion, then one day it might revert to France. Henry and Richard realised that, if they wanted to retain the Vexin, then it would be wiser not to confuse the issue. Alice, for this reason, was left unmarried.

When Richard became king, a resolution of the matter could no longer be postponed. Richard was keen to go on crusade at the earliest opportunity. It was essential, if the safety of his lands were to be safeguarded, that he reach an accord with Philip. Yet, so long as his sister remained unmarried, Philip would be unlikely to oblige. The matter appeared insoluble. As an expression of goodwill, Richard suggested that the two rulers embark on crusade together. Philip, who was himself under oath to go on crusade, agreed on one condition – that Richard renew his betrothal to his sister; which Richard did. The Angevin-Capetian accord, which was essential to the success of the crusade, was thus, after a fashion, preserved. However, it is doubtful if Philip placed much trust in Richard. By the time that the two kings set off together from Vézelay Philip must have had his suspicions, and rightly so. Richard was conceiving plans for a fresh marriage alliance.

The kingdom of France was not the only threat to Richard's far-flung dominions. Down in the south there lay the county of Toulouse. Raymond V, the ruler of Toulouse, was a long-standing rival of the Angevins. For six years before Richard's accession, he and Richard had been at war. The principal bone of contention between them had been the lordship of Quercy, a territory belonging to Aquitaine, to which Raymond laid claim. Richard knew only too well that, once he departed for the East, Raymond would invade again. To safeguard his southern frontier, he needed a reliable ally among the princely rulers of the area. The person with whom he entered into negotiations was Sancho VI, king of Navarre. In 1190 he suggested to Sancho the idea of a marriage alliance. The precise course of the discussions between the two men is hidden, because at Richard's wish they were kept secret. Their progress, however, can be charted from the parallel consultations which Richard conducted among his own nobles. In February 1190 Richard convened a meeting of the southern lords at La Réole on the Garonne. Here, it seems, he secured the support of a crucial group of power-brokers for the scheme that he had in mind. A month later, Richard convened a parallel meeting of the northern lords at Nonancourt in Normandy.

We know from the chroniclers that family affairs were discussed at the meeting, and it is reasonable to suppose that the king's marriage was included among them. In May or June Richard turned southwards again, probably for a meeting with Sancho in person. By midsummer it seems that a decision in principle had been taken: Richard would marry Sancho's daughter Berengaria. But before vows of betrothal could be exchanged, Richard had embarked on crusade. The timing was inconvenient. There were still important matters to be settled: Sancho had to be persuaded to allow his daughter to undertake the dangerous journey east to marry her husband and, perhaps more importantly, Philip had to be told of the decision to break off the betrothal to his sister. By the New Year, with Berengaria well on her way to Italy with her mother, these issues could be postponed no longer. Richard broke the news to Philip at Messina in March 1191. He told the French king that, while he had no wish to discard Alice, he could never make her his wife because she had been his father's mistress and had borne him a son – adding ominously that there were witnesses who could testify to this. Faced with a challenge to his sister's honour, Philip gave in. In return for 10,000 marks he released Richard from his betrothal. On 30 March the two kings went their separate ways. Philip sailed on directly to the Holy Land. Richard, heading in the same direction, was blown off course to Cyprus. It was in the Cypriot city of Limassol that he and Berengaria were married on 12 May 1191.

The story of Richard's engagement to Berengaria affords a valuable reminder of the importance of Iberian affairs to the Angevins. As rulers of Aquitaine, the Angevin king-dukes had to keep a watchful eye on the world beyond the Pyrenees. The friendship of the rulers of north and north-eastern Spain was essential to the long-term security of their southern borders. The Spaniards could be valuable allies in the seemingly unending struggle to contain the ambitions of the princes to the south east of Aquitaine. This was the reason for Richard's enthusiasm to enlist Sancho's assistance in the campaign against Count Raymond. Sancho, as events were to show, would more than prove his worth. In 1192 he came to the assistance of the embattled seneschal of Aquitaine, who was under attack from the French.[4] In later years, however, some of the warmth was to drain from the Angevin-Navarrese relationship. The unconventional nature of Richard's marriage to Berengaria may

have been partly responsible for this. Richard and his young bride were
to spend very little of their married lives together; and, oddly in view of
the importance to the former of continuing the line, the couple did not
have any children. The suggestion has been made that Richard was, in
fact, homosexual. In this connection reference is sometimes made to the
occasion in 1187 when Richard and Philip bedded down together in the
wake of Richard's breach with his father. The evidence, however, relating to Richard's sexuality is decidedly ambivalent. It was by no means
uncommon in the middle ages for men – particularly young knights –
to sleep together. Richard's sharing of a bed with Philip should be seen
as a political, not a sexual, statement. Against it, moreover, should be
set the fact that Richard sired an illegitimate son, Philip – the Philip who
appears as Faulconbridge in Shakespeare's *King John*. It is conceivable
that Richard was bisexual, as, much later, Edward II probably was. But
beyond that speculation it is difficult to go.

Richard's initiative in seeking an alliance with a Spanish prince was not
the first bid by an Anglo-Norman or Angevin ruler to find a peninsular
ally. A number of ties with Spanish rulers had been made over the previous century. According to the chronicler Orderic Vitalis, a daughter of
William the Conqueror had been betrothed to a Spanish king.[5] In 1170
Henry II had arranged for his second daughter Eleanor to be married to
Sancho's neighbour, Alfonso VIII of Castile.[6] In the 1250s, a match was
to be arranged between Henry III's son Edward, and Eleanor, daughter
of another Castilian king Alfonso X. From the English perspective, the
forging of marital ties with Iberian rulers proved a cheap and effective
means of ensuring the security of Aquitaine. In the middle of the fourteenth century, however, this long-standing strategy of the English was
put in jeopardy. To steal a march on their rivals, the French began cast-
ing around for allies in the peninsula themselves. In June 1366 they
gained a decisive advantage with the seizure of the Castilian throne by
their ally Henry of Trastamara. The English reaction to this reversal was
to develop a second strand to their policy. To marital diplomacy were
now added plans for military intervention. The chief advocate of this
course, the king's son John of Gaunt, duke of Lancaster, had a claim to
the Castilian throne by his marriage to Pedro I's daughter Constance. In
1386 Gaunt embarked on full-scale military intervention in northern

Spain.[7] For nine difficult months in the winter of 1386–87 the duke campaigned against the Castilian forces in alliance with the Portuguese. But, when dysentery began to ravage his army, he was obliged to give in. In July 1388, by a treaty negotiated at Bayonne, he surrendered his claim to the Castilian crown. But not everything that he fought for was lost. As part of the general settlement with Castile it was agreed that a marriage alliance should be contracted between the two dynasties. Accordingly, at Palencia two months after the making of peace, Gaunt's daughter Catalina was betrothed to Henry, the Castilian king's heir. Twenty years later this couple's son, Gaunt's grandson, succeeded to the throne of Castile. A more fitting conclusion to the long tradition of dynastic alliances with Iberia it would be difficult to find.

While Gaunt was nurturing his territorial ambitions in Spain, however, it was to a different part of Europe that English envoys went in search of a wife for his royal master. The young Richard II had come to the throne in 1377 unmarried and unbetrothed. As a result of his father's long illness, his parents had given little attention to the matter of his marriage. The new king, however, could be counted one of Europe's most eligible bachelors. With the prestige of the English monarchy at its height, there was going to be no shortage of offers of brides for him. Within months of his accession, two offers had been received – one from Charles V of France of the hand of his daughter Marie, and the other from Charles, king of Navarre, of that of one of his own daughters. In 1378 two further offers were received, the first from King Robert of Scotland, which was quickly dismissed, and the second, more favourably received, from Bernabo Visconti, duke of Milan, of his daughter Catherine.[8] In the end, however, all of these attractive offers were rejected. The match on which Richard's counsellors settled was one which, to begin with, had appeared the least appealing – that with the emperor's daughter, Anne of Bohemia. To most Englishmen at the time, no less than to their successors later, Bohemia was a faraway land of which they knew little. Only in quite exceptional circumstances could such a match have been conceived. What were those circumstances?

The background to Richard II's marriage is to be found in the outbreak of the Great Schism in the Church.[9] In the summer of 1378 two popes had been elected in quick succession in rival conclaves. In April, on the death of Gregory XI, Bartholomeo Prignano had been elevated as Urban VI. But five months later, after Urban had offended many of the cardinals, a second election elevated Robert of Geneva as Clement VII. The rulers of Europe ranged behind one or other of these two claimants, the line-up roughly corresponding to the main political division in Europe. The rulers of England, Portugal and the Empire supported the Urbanist cause, while the French and their allies backed Clement. Urban and his entourage were keen to tie loosely-knit supporters more closely together by promotion of an interlocking network of alliances. Accordingly, at the end of 1378 a scheme was hatched by a key Urbanist adviser, Pileo de Prata, archbishop of Ravenna, for a marriage alliance between Richard and a princess of the imperial house of Luxemburg. The idea of such an alliance had been aired once before, by the Emperor Charles IV (d. 1378), but had attracted little support in England. On this occasion, when it received the backing of the curia, it was pressed more vigorously. Urban and Pileo initiated the process of diplomatic manoeuvring in the early months of 1379. In the winter of 1378 a group of English envoys had arrived in Milan to negotiate for the hand of Catherine Visconti. These envoys were now summoned by the pope to Rome and the new marriage proposal put to them. Urban presented it in terms of humbling the French and helping to eradicate the Schism. While the envoys sent word of the proposal to London, Pileo himself embarked on a visit to Germany to win the support of the new king of the Romans, Wenzel.[10] At a series of meetings with Wenzel in April he achieved his objective. Wenzel, a weak-willed man, quickly succumbed to Pileo's blandishments, and at the envoy's behest wrote enthusiastically to Richard urging an alliance to bring Christendom back under the Urbanist obedience. On this second occasion the English council showed itself more responsive to the idea of an imperial marriage than it had before. By this time, most of the other candidates for Richard's hand had been rejected, and there was growing support for a pact with one of the most distinguished dynasties in Europe. In June the two envoys in Italy, John Burley and Michael de la Pole, were given instructions to go north to discuss the idea of a marital alliance at greater length with Wenzel. In late September and October they had a series of discussions with both Wenzel and Pileo and reported favourably on their outcome to London. At the beginning of June the formal decision to open negotiations for a marriage was taken by the council. A new embassy was sent to Prague under the leadership of men close to the king: his secretary Robert Braybrooke, his tutor Sir Simon Burley, and a Bohemian-born knight, Sir Bernard van Zetles. The negotiations in Prague proceeded smoothly, and it was agreed that formal talks on the terms of betrothal should be opened early in the New Year in Flanders. A high-powered embassy led by the bishop of Hereford made the journey to Bruges in January and a few weeks later final negotiations began. By March 1380 most of the outstanding isues had been settled, and the two sides decided to cross to London. On arrival they were lavishly received by John of Gaunt, who dined them at the Savoy palace. On 2 May, in the presence of the king, the final text of the treaty was sealed.

As always in such documents, the main clauses of the treaty dealt with the formal arrangements for the marriage. First and foremost, it was agreed that Richard would take Wenzel's half-sister Anne as his wife. Then the details of the arrangements for handover were spelled out: Anne's journey to Calais was to be paid for by Wenzel, but thereafter the cost was to be borne by Richard; Wenzel was to provide the bride with a dowry, the size of which would be decided later. The bride's marriage was to be followed by her coronation as queen. In addition to these detailed clauses, however, there were clauses of a broader character. In particular, a perpetual alliance was pledged between the two rulers and their peoples, and a solemn union proclaimed against all schismatics. To the pope's disappointment, however, no mention was made of military action against the schismatics. A week after the sealing of the treaty, Burley set out again for Bohemia to complete the arrangements for Anne's passage. A few days after Christmas 1381 Anne arrived in England, and on the following 20 January she and Richard were married in Westminster Abbey. A couple of days later Anne was crowned in the same church.

Richard II was the only English medieval king to marry a bride from a German imperial dynasty. This is surprising, given the close relations that existed for much of the time between England and Germany. For centuries, traders had been ploughing the sea route between England and the north German ports. The rulers of England and Germany, moreover, had often united in resisting French aggression. But to concentrate exclusively on the marital ties contracted by kings is slightly

misleading. A variety of marital ties were forged between the ruling
dynasties and elites of the two lands more generally. In 1114, for example, Henry I had negotiated the marriage of his daughter Matilda to the
German Emperor Henry V: hence the title by which she was later
known, 'the Empress'. Some fifty years later Henry II's eldest daughter
Matilda was betrothed to Henry the Lion, duke of Saxony and Bavaria,
and first cousin of the emperor, Frederick Barbarossa. A century later
still, Richard, earl of Cornwall, Henry III's brother, was to take as his
third wife a German lady, Beatrice of Falkenburg, Richard being titular
king of the Romans. Thus it would be wrong to suppose that the marriage of Richard II to Anne of Bohemia was entirely without precedent
or context.

In one significant respect, however, it still stands out. In the mid to
late fourteenth century the ties between England and the German imperial line were far looser than they once had been. The Luxemburgs,
who had held the imperial title since 1308, were strongly francophile in
sympathy. The Emperor Charles IV, Anne's father, had spent most of
his early years at the French court; his first wife, Blanche, was a sister
of Philip VI, while his sister Bonne was the wife of John II ('the Good')
of France. His father John, the blind king of Bohemia, had actually died
fighting for the French at Crécy. There was little or nothing in the family's past to suggest an inclination to enter into an English alliance. Yet,
paradoxically, it was the very francophilia of the Luxemburgs that made
an alliance with them attractive to the English. It held out the prospect
that the family might be weaned from their French attachments and, in
consequence, the former network of Anglo-German contacts be rebuilt.
If these were the expectations placed on the alliance, however, the meagre results which flowed from it must have come as a disappointment.
Wenzel proved a fickle and unreliable ally. Unwilling to do anything
which conflicted with his own interests, he simply refused to honour the
obligations which the treaty placed on him. In consequence, despite
repeated requests from the English, he brought no pressure on the
French to make peace; nor did he initiate any firm action against the
schismatics. Hardly surprisingly, there was considerable criticism of the
alliance in England. If the chroniclers are to be believed, Wenzel was
seen as a money-grubber, mainly interested in squeezing as much
money out of the English as possible. According to Walsingham, the

purpose of the papal envoy's visit to England in 1380 was simply to relieve the realm of money, while, in the opinion of the Westminster monk, Richard laid out 'no small sum' to acquire his wife.[11] There was a measure of truth in the chroniclers' criticisms. Over the four years from 1381 no less than £7500 was paid over to Wenzel in subsidies.

Inevitably, some of Wenzel's unpopularity rubbed off onto Anne herself. When she arrived in England, it was to a poor reception from the people of her adopted country. The Westminster writer rudely described her as 'this tiny scrap of humanity'.[12] Part of the problem was that Anne brought with her a large train of Bohemian attendants, and foreign hangers-on were never popular in England. From the moment of their arrival the Bohemians were the butt of popular criticism, with all the usual complaints being made about foreigners' greed. Later, the Bohemians were dogged by scandal when Agnes Lancecrona, one of Anne's ladies-in-waiting, eloped with the king's favourite Robert de Vere. Richard's own attitude to his wife, however, appears to have been unaffected by the criticism. He and Anne enjoyed a deeply companionate relationship. Unusually for a medieval royal couple, they often undertook itineraries together. In 1382, immediately after their wedding, they went on a lengthy circuit of the western counties, while in the following year they visited East Anglia. The grief which Richard felt on his wife's death in 1394 is well attested. He ordered the manor house at Sheen where she had died to be razed to the ground. It was not to be rebuilt for some thirty years.

Yet within three years of Anne's death Richard had remarried. He knew that he had to: he needed an heir, and a male heir. His new bride was the six year-old Isabella, daughter of King Charles VI of France. The background to the match was found in the Anglo-French rapprochement of the early 1390s. In the years after Richard's recovery of power from the Appellants in 1389 the elites of England and France redoubled their efforts to resolve the issues that had separated them for fifty years. In June 1393 envoys from the two governments reached an agreement on the terms of a draft treaty at Leulingham, near Calais. The terms which they sketched out were submitted to the two kings and their councils for approval; however, they fell foul of the English parliamentary Commons. The marriage between Richard and Isabella was in a sense a substitute for the treaty. It served the function of an entente.

While it joined the two monarchs in friendship and set the seal on a long truce, it circumvented the issues that had prevented the Commons from ratifying the treaty. It offered a personal solution to problems which diplomacy alone could not solve.

Richard's second marriage thus represented a reversion to the earlier pattern of Anglo-French marriages. It stood in lineal succession to Edward I's marriage to Margaret of France and Edward II's to Isabella. While it was the product of narrower horizons than the Bohemian marriage, it still attested the European role of the English monarchy. All the marriages of the English kings of this period, in their different ways, attested the geographical range of the 'Plantagenets'' interests. The Angevin or 'Plantagenet' line, by virtue of their tenure of wide possessions on the Continent, were remarkably cosmopolitan in outlook. They were major actors on the European stage. Their wives were invariably foreign-born. In the middle of the fifteenth century, however, this pattern of relationships began to break down. The wives of the Yorkist kings and of the first Tudor king were all English-born. The English monarchy was beginning to turn in on itself. Whereas in the past it had invariably been outward-looking, it was now becoming more introspective. English cultural and political horizons were shrinking. The cosmopolitanism of the English monarchy, once one of its defining characteristics, had all but disappeared.

This is the background against which Richard III's marriage to Anne Neville should be interpreted. When Richard became king in 1483, England was no longer the great European power that she once had been. Her dominions in northern and western France were virtually all lost. Aquitaine had been conquered by the French in 1453, while only Calais and its hinterland were left of the mighty conquests along the Channel coast. In proportion as English political horizons grew narrower, so England's kings no longer thought, as they once had, in terms of continental marital alliances. In the 1460s the earl of Warwick made a major effort to interest Edward IV in a marriage to the sister-in-law of King Louis of France. In this, however, he failed. His botched initiative was one of the causes of his rift with the king in 1469.

The marriages of England's kings in the late fifteenth century were born of a different set of priorities from those of their predecessors. Their main purpose was the cementing of alliances with members of the domestic nobility. For over a generation from the 1450s England was riven by intermittent civil war. Regimes came and went, as first Lancaster and York and then York and Tudor battled for the throne. Politics became factionalised. In these circumstances, it was vital for any regime which wanted to survive to consolidate its ties with key sections of the nobility and upper gentry. For the most part, this could be done by the judicious distribution of patronage and favour. But invariably the seal was set on such processes of wooing by a marriage tie. The policy imperatives of war inward – the Wars of the Roses – replaced those of war outward – the Hundred Years' War. Henry VII's commitment to marry Elizabeth of York was an expression of this outlook. By marrying Elizabeth, Henry sought to bring the same harmony to domestic affairs as foreign matches had earlier brought to international.[13]

Richard III had not actually become king at the time that he married Anne Neville: the wedding took place in July 1472. For this reason his choice of a wife had much in common with the pattern of alliances considered appropriate for royal or semi-royal younger sons. It gave him, as he had wanted, the hand of a very well-born lady of means. Anne was the younger of the two daughters and co-heiresses of Warwick 'the Kingmaker', Edward IV's former ally, who had been killed at the battle of Barnet in April 1471.[14] Isabel, the other daughter, was married to Richard's brother, George, duke of Clarence. The match was arranged by Edward IV himself, very much at the brothers' own prompting. The two men, ambitious and competitive, were both keen to acquire a large landed estate. As younger sons, they needed to provide themselves with a good income. Edward's desire to accommodate them followed the time-honoured policy of his predecessors. For centuries, kings had provided for their siblings by fixing up matches with heiresses. In the 1260s Henry III had arranged the marriage of his second son Edmund to Aveline, heiress of the de Forz earls of Aumale. A century later, Edward III had arranged the marriage of his third son, John of Gaunt, to Blanche, the wealthy heiress of Henry, duke of Lancaster.[15] Edward IV was merely following where a line of royal predecessors had led.

Despite the similarity between Richard's marriage and those of earlier royal siblings, however, Richard's match can still be seen as expressive of a more inward-looking trend. A couple of centuries earlier, many junior royal princes had been married to foreign brides. In the thirteenth century Richard of Cornwall, Henry III's brother, had been betrothed (as his first wife) to Sanchia of Provence, and Edmund of Lancaster, Henry's second son, to the widow of the king of Navarre. A century later, Edward III's second son, Lionel, was married to Violante Visconti, daughter of the duke of Milan, and John of Gaunt (for his second marriage) and Edmund of Langley to the daughters of the deposed king of Castile. In the early fifteenth century, when the Lancastrians had been conquering France, Henry V, too, had arranged foreign matches for his brothers. John, duke of Bedford, was awarded the greatest prize of all, the hand of Anne, daughter of the duke of Burgundy. Given the long tradition of foreign marriages for junior royal offspring – broadly defined – there might well have been a chance, at another time, that Richard of Gloucester would have been found a foreign bride. That, in the event, he wedded a daughter of the house of Neville reinforces the argument for the diminishing horizons of the English monarchy in the late fifteenth century.

In the degree to which they delivered the political and diplomatic results expected of them, the marriages of the three Richards may be judged variously successful. Richard the Lionheart's marriage to Berengaria was perhaps the most satisfactory diplomatically, for it assured the king of a secure southern border in his absence. Richard II's marriage to Anne of Bohemia may be judged the least satisfactory, for it brought the king little or no international gain. Richard's second marriage, to Isabella of France, served him better in this respect: it set the seal on the long truce with France. Richard III's marriage to Anne Neville at least brought him, as he wanted, a slice of the Neville family's great inheritance.

By the biological test, however – the production of issue – all four of the marriages were failures. Richard the Lionheart sired no issue by Berengaria, nor did Richard II have any by Anne. Richard III had one son by his own wife, but the boy died young. None of the three kings left an heir of his body. In the middle ages the lack of such an heir bred uncertainty. It encouraged jockeying for position between rivals for the crown. It is true that by the later twelfth century there were generally agreed conventions governing the succession: as was shown long ago, this was one of the outcomes of the civil war of King Stephen's reign.[16] In the Treaty of Winchester, which ended the war, the principle was affirmed that the king should be succeeded by his nearest heir; in other words, the hereditary principle was endorsed. Indeed, from the reign of John the crown was to descend by heredity. But in the later twelfth century there was still room for doubt. It was at least arguable that a younger brother of a deceased king should be accorded precedence over a nephew by an elder brother who was under age. The matter of the three kings' childlessness thus raises questions of a general nature. How far was the issue of the succession a matter of debate in their reigns? And what were the kings' own views on who should succeed them?

Richard I's childlessness had one big and very obvious effect – to encourage the ambitions of his brother John. John was a slippery and untrustworthy individual, unscrupulous and lazy, but at the same time highly ambitious. Richard, in arranging for the government of England while he was away, aimed to minimise his potential for trouble by a careful balancing act. While, on the one hand, he loaded John with favours, confirming his father's grant to him of the lordship of Ireland and awarding him lands elsewhere, on the other he took security from him: he made him swear an oath that he would stay away from England for three years. Later, however, he changed his mind. In 1190 he withdrew his insistence that John take the oath, according to Howden, on his mother's advice. Doubtless, he thought that the oath would be unenforceable. Not surprisingly, as soon as Richard was gone, trouble broke out.[17] John took strong exception to the man whom his brother had appointed chancellor, William Longchamp, bishop of Ely. When in the spring of 1191 Longchamp seized the castles of Gerard de Camville, the sheriff of Lincoln, accusing him of harbouring criminals, John retaliated by seizing some of the bishop's castles. To win wider support for his cause, John presented himself as the champion of baronial interests. It is possible that John aspired to recognition in some sort of regency: certainly he did nothing to discourage talk of himself as the next king. Away in the Mediterranean, however, Richard, hearing of events, reacted quickly. He despatched to England one of his most reliable lieutenants, Walter of Coutances, archbishop of Rouen, arming him with the authority of a justiciar. Shortly after the archbishop's arrival in London, John's disaffection collapsed. Longchamp decided to withdraw from the realm, while John himself surrendered the castles he held. For the moment, John had no alternative but to accept his brother's authority.

Eighteen months later, however, John found himself presented with
another opportunity. Richard, returning from the Holy Land, was taken
captive in Germany by Leopold of Austria. Clearly it was going to be a
while before Richard returned to England – if he returned at all. John
seized his moment. He threw in his lot with the one man who could
lever him into power, King Philip of France. In January 1193 at Paris he
performed a feudal oath of homage to Philip. In all probability, the two
men hatched a plan whereby Philip would seize Richard's continental
dominions and settle them on John. On returning to England, John
invited the Scottish and the Welsh princes to join him in rebellion. For
the second time, however, his plans came to nothing. In the summer of
1193 Richard and the emperor reached agreement, and early in the next
year the king was released. 'The devil is let loose again', Philip is
reported to have said to John. The latter, shocked to find his plans again
in disarray, fled to France.[18]

John indulged in the worst of his troublemaking in Richard's early
years. By the middle of the 1190s he posed less of a threat. This was partly
because he had just been humiliated, so that few would now follow him.
But there was a second reason. His brother was now married. With
Berengaria at his side, there was a possibility that Richard might sire an
heir; and, if that were to happen, John would no longer be next in succession. But fortune's wheel was to turn again. Later still in the 1190s,
John's hopes rose a second time. As Richard and Berengaria spent more
of their time apart, it became clear that they would not, after all, have a
child. Accordingly, the question of the succession was reopened. By this
time, however, the political background was very different. There was
now another candidate to be considered – Arthur, the son of John's
deceased elder brother Geoffrey of Brittany. Arthur had been a mere
child when Richard had become king. Ten years later, however, he was
growing to adolescence and his claims could no longer be ignored.
There were plausible grounds for supposing that he had a better claim
to succeed than John. In some parts of the Angevin empire inheritance
customs favoured his case. In England, for example, preference was
given to the nephew over the uncle. According to the law book associated with Ranulf Glanvill, Henry II's justiciar, the son of a deceased
elder brother should, on balance, take precedence over the younger
brother in succeeding to an inheritance. In Normandy the position was

different: custom awarded priority to the younger brother over the collaterals.[19] At the very least, with so much local variation, John could not
count on automatic succession. Much would depend on the attitude of
the great men of the Angevin lands. A glimpse of the debates that went
on is given in the biography of William Marshal, perhaps the greatest of
all the lords. The news of Richard's death was brought to William at
Vaudreuil just as he was retiring to bed. He dressed hurriedly and called
on Hubert Walter, the archbishop of Canterbury, who was staying
nearby. 'My lord', he said, 'we must lose no time in choosing someone
to be king.' 'I think Arthur should be king', the archbishop replied. 'To
my mind, that would be bad', said Marshal. 'Arthur is advised by traitors; he is haughty and proud; and, if we place him over us, he will only
do us harm because he does not love the people of this land. Consider
rather Count John: he seems to be the nearest heir to the land which
belonged to his father and brother.' 'Marshal', said the archbishop, 'is
this really your desire?' 'Yes, it is', he declared. 'Then so be it,' said the
archbishop, 'but mark my words, you will never regret anything so
much as this.'[20]

Subsequent events, it could be said, would prove Archbishop Walter
right. In the end, however, the matter was largely settled by Richard's
death-bed bequest. In his last days at the camp near Chalus, Richard
bequeathed his crown to John and his jewellery to his nephew Otto of
Saxony. Despite his record of disloyalty to his elder brother, John was
awarded the whole of the Angevin inheritance. Only in Anjou was there
any resistance to his succession, and this was soon overcome. On 25
April the new ruler was invested with the duchy of Normandy at Rouen,
and a month later he was crowned king of England at Westminster.

It might be supposed that John's manoeuvrings in his brother's reign
had cost him very little. Indeed, it might be thought that the challenge
to him from his nephew was of little significance in the long term. But
to make such assumptions is probably unwarranted. There was a sequel
to the story of John's succession. John may have been the winner in 1199,
but he was the definite loser only a few years later. Towards the end of
1203 the Angevin dominions began to break up. And the cause of that
fragmentation was John's treatment of Arthur.

When John took over from his brother, Arthur had attracted remarkably little support. Most of the Angevin nobility, like William Marshal,

believed that those who surrounded him were ambitious self-seekers whose interests conflicted with their own. One of the leading Angevins, the Poitevin Hugh le Brun, the head of the Lusignan clan, had even made an attempt to capture Arthur. Hugh's attempt had misfired, but his gesture was significant. Lusignan support was crucial to John if he was to control the lower Loire valley. But the backing given to him by the Lusignans came at a price. Hugh wanted a big favour in return. Hugh's ambition was to annex the county of La Marche, a territory over which he was in dispute with the count of Angoulême. In the summer of 1200, when he thought John's position was weakened by Arthur's threat, his troops moved into, and took over, the county. In the circumstances, John had little alternative but to acquiesce. A few months later, however, he got his revenge. He announced that he was marrying Isabella, the daughter and heiress of Count Adhémar of Angoulême.[21] Isabella, as he well knew, was already betrothed to Hugh. So Hugh, having secured the promise of Angoulême, faced the prospect of losing it again. He was understandably furious with John. In the following autumn he submitted an appeal to King Philip of France. Philip summoned John to appear before him and, when he failed to respond, confiscated John's fiefs and took Arthur's homage instead. The war of the Angevin succession had begun again.

The confiscation was the prelude to a desultory series of skirmishes on the border between France and the Angevin lands. John lost a series of major castles in and around the Seine valley. Yet paradoxically the fatal blow for him was not a defeat but a victory. On 30 July 1202, in a surprise attack on Mirebeau in Poitou, he took Arthur prisoner. John was exultant at his coup: 'God be praised for our success', he said. Yet he was presented with a dilemma: what was he to do with Arthur? If he were to let the boy go – he was fifteen – he would be taking a terrible risk for the future. Yet if he were to execute him, he would be implicated in what would amount to murder. According to Coggeshall, John wanted him blinded and castrated.[22] What happened to Arthur cannot now be established. The most that can be said is that he was never seen again. According to one tradition, John murdered him himself and threw the body into the Seine. Most contemporaries had little doubt that he was the victim of John's cruel vengeance. In England few tears were shed for him: he was seen as a traitor and deserving of his fate. On the other side of the Channel, however, reactions were very different. In the Angevins' continental dominions, and in particular in Arthur's Breton homeland, there was widespread anger at his disappearance. Support for John's rule crumbled, and in 1204 the French took possession of Normandy. John's erstwhile triumph at Mirebeau had miscarried. His terrible ill-treatment of his nephew had united his enemies against him. Arthur was no young innocent; he was not of the same blamelessness as the later 'princes in the Tower'. He was fifteen, two years older than the senior of the nephews whom Richard III was to murder; and he was definitely more worldly wise. But what John did to him was considered murder. In Normandy and Brittany in the early 1200s opinion was far less equivocal on these matters than it was to be in fifteenth-century England. Cruelly disposing of opponents whose presence was thought inconvenient was not morally acceptable. The summary executions that accompanied first one side's and then another's triumph in the Wars of the Roses found no parallel in this period. It was allowed that an offender might be imprisoned or made to abjure the realm, but he could definitely not be murdered. John's loss of his Angevin 'empire' in 1204 was to some degree at least the by-product of the unfortunate Arthur's death.

A couple of centuries later the succession was likewise to be an issue in Richard II's reign. Richard failed to produce an heir by either of his two marriages. His first marriage to Anne of Bohemia had at no time given indication of being productive of issue. The likelihood is that Anne was barren or Richard infertile. His second marriage, to Isabella of France, held out no prospect of issue in the short run, for Isabella was still only a child at the time of the marriage. Well into Richard's reign, the succession to the crown was still wide open. It seems that the descent of the crown was more openly talked about in this Richard's reign than in his predecessor's. At least, there are many references to the matter in the chronicles. The reason for this is clear. In Richard II's reign there was no obvious candidate for the crown – no equivalent of John waiting in the wings.

On the face of it, this state of affairs is surprising. Edward III headed a very large family. He sired more legitimate sons than any other king before George III. But at the end of his reign there was a sudden

narrowing in the direct line of descent. A year before his death, his son
and heir, the Black Prince, died after a long illness, while a few years
before this, in 1371, the prince's elder son (Richard's elder brother),
Edward of Angoulême, had also died. The direct line of succession now
hung on the slender thread of Richard's own person. In 1376 concern
about the descent of the crown had led the aged Edward III to make an
unprecedented declaration of the succession. In letters patent issued, it
appears, in the closing months of 1376, Edward settled the crown in tail
male – in other words, to the exclusion of the heirs general. The terms
of the settlement sat somewhat inconsistently with his long-standing
claim to the French crown, which was based on descent through the heir
general (that is to say, through his mother). Nonetheless the settlement
was fully in line with the growing practice of the nobility at this time to
settle their estates on their heirs male. The main beneficiary of the settlement was the duke of Lancaster – John of Gaunt, the king's third son.
If Richard were to die without male issue, it would be Gaunt or one of
his male issue who would succeed. In Richard's reign the settlement
appears to have been largely overlooked: not once was it referred to by
the chroniclers or in parliamentary debate, nor was it invoked in 1399
by the Lancastrian propagandists in support of Duke Henry's claim to
the crown. The reason for the oversight is likely to have been Gaunt's
deep-seated unpopularity. For much of Richard's reign Gaunt's standing in public opinion was so low that the prospect of him succeeding to
the throne was remote. Right to the moment of Richard's deposition,
therefore, the matter of the succession was wide open. For the first time
since the end of the civil war of Stephen's reign it was genuinely unclear
who was going to be the next king.

The person with much the best claim to succeed, in terms of custom,
was the heir general. This was the head of the Mortimer family, Roger
Mortimer, earl of March. Roger, who had succeeded to his title in 1382,
claimed descent through his mother from Lionel of Antwerp, duke of
Clarence, Edward III's second son. There are signs that by the 1380s
Richard had come to favour his claim to the succession. According to
the continuator of the *Eulogium* chronicle, in the parliament of 1385
Richard formally nominated Roger as his successor.[23] But there are
problems with this narrative, as commentators have pointed out: the
chronology is confused and many of the details inaccurate. In broad

outline, however, it may well be correct. In the mid 1380s Richard was on particularly bad terms with Gaunt and may have wanted to spite him by promoting the cause of his young cousin.[24] Moreover, there are signs of a new interest in the fortunes of the Mortimer family among the well-informed. The Monk of Westminster, in an otherwise inexplicable passage, maintained at this time that, if the king died without issue, the crown would pass by hereditary right to the Mortimers.[25] In other words, on Richard's death the next king would be the earl of March.

As the Monk of Westminster was to say in another context, however, human affairs can change quickly. The Mortimers' star was not to be dominant in the political sky for long. In the course of the next decade the rival Lancastrian star was to eclipse it. In the autumn of 1389 Gaunt returned from Spain to an enthusiastic welcome from the king. Richard, weakened politically by the Appellant triumph two years before, welcomed the return of someone committed to maintenance of the prerogative. From this time on, Gaunt was to become one of the king's most significant allies, a buttress of royal power. Gaunt took full advantage of his new influence to press his family's claims to the royal succession. According to John Hardyng, the historian of the Percies, sometime in the 1390s he petitioned to have himself recognised as the heir apparent, only to be rebuffed by his fellow lords.[26] Hardyng, was writing some forty years after events, and his recollection may have been confused. There are grounds for supposing that, rather than advance his own cause, Gaunt was actually advancing his son's. This is what a near-contemporary writer, the *Eulogium* continuator, maintains. According to this writer's witness, in 1394 Gaunt submitted a parliamentary petition to have his son recognised as heir to the throne, but ran into opposition from the earl of March. Both men were silenced by the king.[27] It is difficult to know quite how much importance to attach to these narratives. It would be wrong, however, to dismiss them *tout court*. In the 1390s the problem of the succession can never have been far from people's minds. Anne of Bohemia had died without issue in 1394 and the king's second wife was still a child. Even if Richard were to sire an heir by Isabella, he would not do so for a number of years. Aspirants to the succession naturally started jockeying for position. Gaunt, although doubtful of his own prospects, may well have been keen to promote those of his son. It is interesting to see how very carefully he cultivated his son's public image, for example by ensuring full reportage of his feats on his Baltic crusade.[28]

Richard's reaction to all this manoeuvring is hard to establish. At no time did he publicly nominate a successor. Indeed, he may well have regarded any discussion about the succession, hinting as it did at his own mortality, as distasteful. His chosen policy appears to have been to keep people guessing. He did everything in his power to prevent the emergence of a front-runner. When the earl of March won the favour of the crowds at Shrewsbury in 1398, Richard reacted by condemning him to effective exile in Ireland.[29] Yet oddly, according to his friend Sir William Bagot, at the same time he spoke teasingly of abdicating in favour of his cousin the duke of Aumerle – a most surprising course.[30] Richard was, in classic fashion, employing the tactics of divide and rule. He was deliberately sowing uncertainty in people's minds. In most other reigns, such a policy would have been eschewed as conducive of disorder; as we have seen, Edward III made his settlement of the crown in 1376 precisely to avoid this danger. Richard's attitude, however, was very different. Richard thought that, by creating insecurity in others, he would find the security that he craved for himself. It was a high-risk strategy. It would be wrong to say that it could never have worked. Two centuries later, Elizabeth was to pursue a not dissimilar course. But it was one that called for strong nerves, and the risk of failure was great.

In Richard III's reign the problem of concern to political society was not the total absence of an heir but the premature death of an heir. Richard III, unlike his two namesakes, did sire a son – an only child, Edward of Middleham, who was born in 1474. Edward was a sickly child, however, and died at the age of ten. Just nine months before his demise, his father had become king. For a newly-crowned monarch to lose his one begotten son was a crippling blow. Just as when King Stephen's son, Eustace, had died three centuries before, it cast a shadow over the reign. The Crowland Chronicler interpreted the event as an ill omen: God, he suggested, was deliberately punishing Richard for his usurpation.[31] When in the following year the queen also died, this view seemed confirmed. Richard was now alone in the world – without wife, and without issue or sibling: his direct line would die with him. To provide himself with an heir, Richard, according to one source, initially recognised Clarence's son, Edward, earl of Warwick.[32] Quickly repenting of this decision, however – probably because it implied the precedence of Clarence's line over his own – he decided to recognise his nephew John de la Pole, earl of Lincoln. In the last year of his reign, Richard cut a sad and lonely figure. In the thirteenth century King John had paid for the murder of his nephew by the attrition of noble support. Now in the 1480s Richard paid for it, in contemporary eyes, by the loss of his kin. A perjurer and infanticide, he had gained his just deserts.

Richard's isolation highlights the importance of the 'royal family' as agents and supporters of royal power. A king who was lacking in close kin was weaker and more vulnerable than a king rich in kin. Richard III was left painfully exposed by the deaths, in quick succession, of his son and his wife. A century earlier Richard II had stood coldly isolated after the death of his wife Anne in 1394. Two centuries before that, Richard I was embarrassingly short of allies to resist the machinations of his slippery brother John. How did the three kings compensate for their lack of kin? And how far, if at all, were they able to create substitute kin?

The three Richards differed sharply in their relationships with their families, and their wider kin. To some extent, this was a matter of personality. Richard II, for example, was quite simply a more uxorious man than Richard I. He enjoyed a deeply companionate relationship with his wife, Anne.[33] But there was another factor at work – the changing notion of the 'royal family'. In the twelfth century the notion of a royal kin group – a 'royal family' – was still ill-defined. Two centuries later, by Richard II's time, it had acquired sharper definition. For much of the middle ages understandings of the family centred on the concept of lineage. The lineage can be seen as overlapping in meaning with 'dynasty'. It was the family conceptualised in vertical terms: a unilateral descent group stretched out in a straight line. Richard I had a strongly developed sense of lineage. We have seen how he embarked on the Third Crusade at least partly out of a concern for his family, the house of Anjou.[34] When he presented his demands to Saladin, he did so, according to Ambroise, claiming right of inheritance: for it was from an Angevin that the kings of Jerusalem were descended.[35] Unlike later English monarchs, Richard did not see his lineage as confined in membership principally to one land. He not only regarded his collateral kinsmen in distant Jerusalem as members of his family; he also regarded his nephew, Otto of Saxony, from 1198 king of Germany, in the same light. For Richard, lineage was a loose construct, bringing together kinfolk stretched across a network of lands and dominions.

The process by which the king's kin came to be identified with his kin in his homeland had its origins in developments of the thirteenth and fourteenth centuries. The loss of Normandy and the consequent break-up of the Angevin 'empire' naturally represented a major turning-point. If nothing else, the separation paved the way for the emergence of a more clearly defined national political elite. While the 'Plantagenet' royal line still remained highly cosmopolitan and, in terms of political ambition, outward-looking, it none the less became more closely identified with one particular realm. In the fourteenth century a further significant development occurred when the notion of a royal family was given sharper definition by developments in England itself. In the course of this century a stratified parliamentary peerage gradually emerged. A previously undifferentiated nobility was sorted into a series of discrete ranks – those of duke, earl, marquess and baron. Once this new peerage had emerged, as it had by the third quarter of the century, it became possible to single out the princes of the blood for recognition. From his knowledge of French aristocratic society Edward III would have been aware of the French notion of the 'princes of the fleur-de-lys' as a discrete social elite. In the course of his reign a not dissimilar conceptualisation of the king's close kin developed in England. Edward himself took the first step to creating such an elite group when he made his eldest son, Edward (the 'Black Prince'), duke of Cornwall. Over the next twenty years he created three more dukes, two of them his sons, and by the end of the century the title of duke was recognised as that appropriate to a member of the blood royal. The special place of the king's close kinsmen was acknowledged in another way: they were given the right to bear the royal arms of England and France differenced only by a label or emblem. By the middle of the fifteenth century the notion of the 'royal family' – the 'blood royal' – was fully established. In 1450 Jack Cade's rebels begged Henry VI to 'take about him his trew blode of his ryall realme, that is to say, the hyghe and myghty prynce the Duke of Yorke ... the Duke of Exceter, the Duke of Bokyngham, the Duke of Norffolke ...' The princes of the blood were perceived as the necessary pillars of royal power.[36]

The recognition of the blood royal as peculiarly honourable gave

Richard II a means to develop a response to his kinlessness. He created what amounted to a substitute royal family out of the half-blood and collaterals. In the 1390s he elevated two groups – firstly, the Holands, the offspring of Richard's mother by her first marriage to Sir Thomas Holand, and secondly the Beauforts, John of Gaunt's illegitimate offspring by Katherine Swinford. Both groups were treated as if they were full members of the royal stock. Their superior status, for example, was given heraldic expression. In 1394 they were authorised to use the distinctive royal arms impaled with the arms of St Edward the Confessor. Their lofty status also found expression in other ways. Thomas Holand, earl of Kent, on his death in 1397, was given the honour usually reserved to members of the royal family of a funeral in Westminster Abbey.[37] The Beauforts, when accorded legitimation in 1397, were referred to in royal letters as 'our most dear kinsmen ... sprung from royal stock'. By virtue of their special rank, the royal kinfolk were conceived as enhancing the king's majesty and strengthening the royal line.

The value of the royal kin was also appreciated by Edward IV when he came to the throne in 1461. At the earliest opportunity Edward raised each of his brothers to a dukedom – George in June 1461 and Richard five months later. Edward conceived of his kin, as Edward III had his, as allies and associates in government. Just as Edward III had employed his son and heir as lieutenant in the duchy of Aquitaine, so his namesake employed his younger brother as vicegerent in the north of England. When Richard suddenly took it upon himself to seize the crown, he found himself conspicuously lacking in such allies: for in the course of the usurpation he had removed them all. Initially, his chief agent was a distant collateral, Henry, duke of Buckingham. But the duke's rebellion in the autumn removed him, too, from the scene. Richard, from that point on, stood alone. His lack of kin after the death of his son – lack even of collateral kin – once again drew attention to his political isolation.

At the centre of the 'royal family', however defined, stood the person of the queen. The queen was the king's consort, the partner chosen by him, or for him by his parents. The queen was also – assuming the biological success of the marriage – the bearer of his children. What importance attached to her position? And how did her role change in the course of this period?

Late medieval queens were given two biblical role models – first and foremost, that of the Virgin Mary, the queen of heaven, and, secondly and further back, that of Esther, the young Israelite woman who married the king of Persia. According to the behaviour patterns legitimated by these models, the queen should be obedient and merciful. The queen's task was to intercede with the king on behalf of his subjects. The queen should restrain the king; she should counsel him. Chaucer twice lavished praise on Esther in *The Canterbury Tales* for the counsel which she gave to her kingly husband.

As a counsellor and intercessor, the late medieval queen occupied an essentially subordinate role in political life. She occupied no formal governmental position. A few centuries earlier, however, her standing had been more exalted. In the eleventh and twelfth centuries queens had often been highly significant figures in political life. In some states – Portugal, Sicily and Jerusalem, for example – queens had actually ruled in their own right. Elsewhere, even as consorts they exercised considerable political influence. The queen's household was often merged with that of the king; queens had their own chanceries and seals, and their status was recognised in royal charters. In the Angevin world, Eleanor of Aquitaine, admittedly an heiress, Henry II's queen, ranked as a major figure in politics. In the late middle ages, however, queens declined in power and importance. Their households were generally separated from their husbands', and they were excluded from affairs of state. The compensation given to them was greater symbolic recognition. In public ceremony and ritual, in the size and magnificence of their households, they were accorded honour as contributors to royal dignity. But the reality was an increasing dependence on royal sponsorship. No longer did they have a role in government; their lot was to act as petitioners and intercessors. Like Esther, they were to plead with the king for his subjects.[38]

The role of the late medieval queen found clearest expression in the English career of Richard II's consort, Anne of Bohemia. Anne was brought to England in 1382 as the representative of the papally sponsored alliance between England and the Empire. Her arrival aroused little or no enthusiasm in the people of her adopted land. To the Monk of Westminster, not usually a sour commentator, she was 'this tiny scrap of humanity'.[39] Over the years, however, attitudes changed. Slowly but surely she won the affection of her husband's subjects. The main reason for this was undoubtedly her skill as an intercessor. As has been shown, she made intercession a regular part of her royal routine.[40] In 1381, even before her arrival, she was credited with obtaining mercy for one of the rebels in the Great Revolt. In 1384 she pleaded with her husband to spare the life of the turbulent London mayor, John Northampton. In 1388 she pleaded, unsuccessfully this time, with the Lords Appellant for the life of the condemned royal favourite, Sir Simon Burley. Most famously of all, in 1392 she begged her husband to show mercy to the London citizens, whose privileges he had confiscated in retaliation for their refusal of a loan.[41] Anne's work in the Londoners' cause was celebrated in August 1392 in a richly choreographed pageant at the end of which, in Westminster Hall, she prostrated herself before her husband to plead the city's case. In the light of her remarkable success in the mediatory role, it is not inappropriate that the only surviving representation of her should show her in this capacity – kneeling before her husband, receiving from him a charter for the borough of Shrewsbury.

Although Anne's career has often been interpreted as if it were typical of the time, it would be wrong to see the history of medieval queenly power simply as a narrative of decline. In reality, the story was more complex. In the twelfth and thirteenth centuries there were queens who showed little or no interest in politics, just as later there were queens who were highly dynamic. From the twelfth century an obvious example of a queen seemingly of little ambition is the Lionheart's consort, Berengaria of Navarre. Berengaria contributed virtually nothing to the governance of her husband's sprawling dominions. She and her husband lived their lives largely apart.[42] While Richard travelled far and wide in the Angevin lands, quelling rebellions and fending off the threat from France, Berengaria lived with her household at her castle of Beaufort en Vallée. Unable to give her husband a son and heir, or denied the opportunity to do so, she could not even aspire to succeeding Eleanor of Aquitaine in the office of the next king's mother. Nor, indeed, living as she did in the late twelfth century, could she aspire to the consolatory prize of symbolic elevation. Richard made no effort to accord her a position of honour at all. In the Angevin political system, she was without role and without recognition.

From the end of the middle ages an excellent example of a more assertive queen is provided by Margaret of Anjou, the wife of Henry VI.[43] Margaret was brought to England in 1445 as the symbol of her husband's policy of seeking peace and reconciliation with France. From the first she was identified with faction. She quickly became a confidante of William de la Pole, duke of Suffolk, Henry VI's minister who negotiated the marriage. In the 1450s, after Suffolk's fall, her influence at court greatly increased as criticism of her husband's government simultaneously grew louder. According to a letter of the late 1450s in the Paston correspondence, she was the prime mover in seeking the exclusion of the duke of York from the king's counsels.[44] In 1458, after her husband's mental collapse, she took full control of the court. Abandoning Westminster, where she viewed with distaste the strong Yorkist influence, she settled with her husband at Coventry in the Lancastrian heartland. For nearly three years until the final demise of the Lancastrian cause at Towton in 1461, she fought doggedly to save her husband's crown and to secure the succession of her son. Yet, in the end, she failed. After the Yorkist takeover she was condemned to the life of an exile. Even then, however, she did not give up. In 1469 she negotiated the pact with Warwick which brought her husband back to the throne for a few months in 1470. At Tewkesbury, in May 1471, she was at his side when his (and her son's) cause finally collapsed. Margaret's interventions in politics broke all the boundaries conventionally delimiting queenly behaviour. It is true that her case was exceptional to the extent that her husband was incapacitated. None the less, it should not be supposed that it was entirely unique. In the thirteenth century Eleanor of Provence, Henry III's queen, made skilful use of her household staff to intervene with effect at court and in national politics generally. It is clear that, if a queen was determined to create a role for herself in politics, in some circumstances she could do so.

A valuable insight into contemporary attitudes to female political involvement is found in Chaucer's 'Tale of Melibee' in *The Canterbury Tales*. Melibee and his wife Prudence are debating what punishment to visit on some miscreants who have assaulted their daughter. Melibee's strong preference is to hit back hard at the miscreants, but Prudence, urging caution, argues for composition and reconciliation. In the end Melibee, persuaded by his wife's arguments, is won over. Chaucer's poem, a close translation of a French original, almost certainly reflects

Chaucer's own views, since he chooses it for himself. What is significant about it is that Prudence is seen as politically the equal of her husband; indeed, she is shown to be a major influence on his conduct. It is true that she is only a noblewoman, and not a queen; and a queen's role may have been limited somewhat by the formalities of the court. None the less, in many ways a queen was simply a noblewoman writ large – a consort with a social and political space of her own, and enjoying the capacity to influence her husband. To judge from the approval with which Chaucer writes of Prudence, it is apparent that he did not expect a woman's influence to be confined to the bedchamber.

It is clear, then, that the potential existed for a late medieval queen to be politically active. In Margaret's case the spur to activity was her sense of dynasty – her urge to advance the fortunes of her only son. Margaret's instinct, however, was one which the queens of two of the Richards would have found it hard to understand, for those two were childless, while the son of the third died young. In biological terms, the marriages of the three Richards were failures. In each case, the fact that the king lacked a surviving son had major political consequences. Most obviously, it generated uncertainty. As we have seen, in each reign there was questioning over which royal kinsman would succeed to the throne. One of the three kings – Richard II – turned such doubt to advantage by deliberately sowing confusion among his rivals. His tactics, however, were unsuccessful. Invariably, when a king lacked a son, a question mark hung over his dynasty's future. It is easy to suppose, judging from the Hanoverians' experience, that sons caused nothing but trouble for their fathers. Generally in the middle ages, however, this was not the case. A healthy brood of sons could be a source of strength to a king. Edward III was well aware of this. And so too, a century later, from a different perspective was Richard III. The fact we have had eight Edwards but only three Richards is partly a result, quite simply, of their lack of kin.

9

Kingship and Piety

The theoretical basis of monarchy in England changed very little in the middle ages. Kingship, it was believed, was divinely ordained. Kings were God's deputies, and they exercised God's authority on earth. The king's rule was to be God-like in quality, rewarding the good and protecting the weak. The king was answerable to God alone: his subjects had no power to bind him. Yet his kingdom was not his alone to enjoy. His subjects had a stake in it, and accordingly he was under some obligation to them. He had to cherish and protect them; he had to further their interests and to work for the common good. His duties were a Christian responsibility. He had to make of his realm a Christian commonwealth and a preparation for the kingdom to come. One of his duties was the promotion of orthodoxy.

The Christian conception of the kingly office intersected at points with the king's own sense of piety. In the middle ages, religion for a king could never be an entirely private matter. The king had a public persona. The nature of his piety had a bearing on the way in which he conceived of his kingly duties. Since the king was the mediator of God's favour to his people, that people's wellbeing was dependent in part on his own acceptability to God. Provided he was obedient to God's will, his people would thrive and prosper. To many, the great victory which Henry V won at Agincourt was Henry's reward for his obedience to the divine will. Not uncommonly, monarchs appropriated particular saints' cults to further their political ends. Edward III, for example, associated himself with the cult of St George to legitimate his war of conquest in France, while his grandson Richard II patronised that of the unmartial Edward the Confessor to validate his attempts to end it. Piety, moreover, could play a role in boosting or enhancing the royal image. In this connection, church building occupied a position of considerable importance. When Henry III began remodelling Westminster Abbey on

French lines in the 1240s, it was at least partly to make the English
monarchy the equal in prestige of the French. In the 1470s, Edward IV's
massive rebuilding of St George's Chapel, Windsor, was designed in
large measure to strengthen the Yorkist monarchy's association with
chivalry – St George's being the chapel of the Order of the Garter. The
piety of a medieval king was rarely disinterested. It had implications for
public policy, even if these were not always intended.

The king's own expressions of piety were a matter largely separate
from that of his relations with the institutional Church. A king of quite
intense personal religion could find himself engaged in sometimes bitter disputes with the pope or the archbishop of Canterbury. In the
thirteenth century Henry III found himself at odds with the pope over
appointments to senior positions in the English episcopate; yet no one
could doubt the depth of Henry's inner devotion. In the reigns of the
three Richards quarrels between kings and popes or major churchmen
were very few. Richard I's most serious problem related to the nomi-
nation of his half brother Geoffrey to the archbishopric of York.
Geoffrey, an unsavoury character, was an unfortunate choice, for he
was not even tonsured when nominated; and, as the York canons
pointed out, he was warlike, conceived in adultery and born of a whore.
Yet Richard insisted on his appointment. Howden tells us that he did
so in deference to his father's wishes.[1] On the whole, the Lionheart's
other nominations to the episcopate were unexceptional.[2] Richard II
and Richard III encountered few, if any, difficulties in the business of
managing the Church.[3] By the later middle ages, papal power had weakened vis-à-vis the national monarchies from its peak in the thirteenth
century, and in the period of the Schism, which coincided with Richard
II's reign, it became weaker still. Increasingly, appointments to the episcopal bench fell under royal control. Most senior diocesans of the age
were retired ministers or civil servants. Richard III had no problem in
swinging the churchmen behind him on his usurpation. John Russell,
for example, the influential bishop of Lincoln, served under him as a
minister.

Personal piety, a private matter by definition, is not easily subjected
to historical enquiry. The documentary sources, which are the historian's staple, can illuminate only the outward manifestations of belief.
But those outward manifestations can sometimes allow us an insight

into inner spirituality – for in the medieval, broadly Platonic, view of the world, inner was held to be reflected in outer. Among the sources for outward piety are a number of some value and importance. For Richard the Lionheart's time, for example, we have the narratives of chroniclers who knew or observed the king and were able to comment at first hand on his piety. From the time of the two later Richards, in addition to the chronicles, we have the records of the royal administrative offices. By their nature, these are often rather impersonal, recording minor acts of alms-giving and charity, gifts to churches and shrines, and sometimes payments to favoured court preachers. Alongside them, however, may be set more personal sources – psalters, prayer books or devotional tracts commissioned or used by the king. Of particular importance for us is a book of Richard III's – his Book of Hours, now in Lambeth Palace Library. Finally, we should take note of the not inconsiderable body of physical and architectural evidence. In the chapels of the royal palace and in the rebuildings of monasteries and cathedrals we see images in stone of the kings' personal piety, mirrors of their devotional tastes and religious aspirations. The varying degrees of commitment to the royal mausoleum, Westminster Abbey, are of particular interest in this connection. By sensitive use of these bodies of material, we can succeed in forming a reasonable impression of the kings' piety. The picture will hardly be a complete one; but at least it will be a reasonably clear one.

The main impression to emerge from the evidence is that of the quite exceptional religiosity of the three kings. Their piety was deeply felt – even by the standards of the age. In the case of none can devotional commitment be said to have been merely token. The three kings were in a sense driven: the intensity of their piety had a deep influence on their practice of kingship.

The clearest indication of the Lionheart's devotion is found in his commitment to the crusade. Richard's vigorous prosecution of the war in the East constitutes his greatest single achievement. For Richard the *crucesignatus* the crusade was a just war – a campaign undertaken with papal authority to liberate Christ's patrimony. His enthusiasm for the *passagium* had been evident even before he became king. He had donned the cross almost as soon as he had heard the news of the fall of Jerusalem in 1187. North of the Alps he was the first major prince to do so. On succeeding his father in 1189 he subordinated everything to the task of equipping and provisioning an army to go east. Within less than a year he was ready to leave. Although his journey out was slow, and there were many distractions en route, he never lost sight of his overriding objective of liberating the Holy Land. Once he had arrived in the East, his prosecution of the campaign was consistent and single-minded. At Acre he concentrated on reducing the town and the citadel; and under his leadership a siege which had dragged on for years was wrapped up in a matter of weeks. After the capture of Acre, his aim was to eliminate the threat to the crusader kingdom from Egypt – hence the march on Ascalon. Although balked of the ultimate prize of capturing the Holy City, he left the crusader state secure – more secure, indeed, than it had been for decades. His dogged commitment to the crusade contrasted sharply with the half-heartedness of the other princely commanders. King Philip of France departed soon after the taking of Acre, while Leopold, duke of Austria, did the same months later. The strength of Richard's commitment also formed a contrast to the laggardly attitude of his father. The latter, although taking the cross, never set off at all.

Richard's piety was also reflected in another way characteristic of the age – in his patronage of monasticism. He founded no fewer than three monastic houses: a Cistercian abbey at Bonport in Normandy; a Premonstratensian abbey at Le-Lieu-Dieu-en-Jard further south; and a Benedictine priory at Gourfailles in the Vendée.[4] He was particularly notable as a patron of the Cistercians. At his coronation he gave an annuity of 20s. to the general chapter of the Cistercian Order, and he later made grants to the Cistercian houses of Le Pin and Pontigny.[5] Ralph of Coggeshall thought it worthwhile mentioning that he employed a Cistercian as his almoner.[6] Notwithstanding his favour for the Cistercians, his monastic patronage was widely spread. He was a keen patron of the Benedictines. At St Albans the monks were long to cherish the memory of the warmth with which he regarded their house.[7] But Richard's attitude to the monastic Orders was by no means uncritical. When Fulk de Neuilly taxed him with having three wicked daughters, pride, avarice and sensuality, he is reported to have quipped in response: 'I give my pride to the Templars, my avarice to the Cistercians and my sensuality to the Benedictines'.[8] It is not easy to know how to interpret this remark. Conceivably it was less a criticism of monasticism as such than of those whose conduct brought it into disrepute. There is evidence that Richard had considerable admiration for those who upheld ascetic ideals. In 1198 he yielded, admittedly under sufferance, to Hugh of Avalon, bishop of Lincoln, when the latter challenged him to restore his episcopal estates. Bishop Hugh was a saintly man, renowned for his humility. After he had protested to the king about the seizure of the manors, he demanded a kiss from him, but Richard refused. Hugh asked again, this time tugging at his cloak. Eventually Richard gave in. As he later said, 'If the other bishops were like him, no king would dare to raise his head against them'.[9]

For the most part – at least, if the chroniclers' stories are to be believed – Richard's outward piety was fairly conventional. There is little in what we know of it to suggest that he had a taste for the *avant garde* or for the spiritually adventurous. His preferences, while clearly formed and intense, were broadly consistent with those of the upper classes of the day: goodwill to the monks, enthusiasm for the crusade and a concern for intercessory prayer.

If there is one aspect of Richard's devotional life that stands out, however, it is his interest in saints of English origin. For someone of Angevin descent and whose early years were spent in Poitou and Aquitaine, this interest is remarkable. Yet it is well attested. Particularly noteworthy is Richard's devotion to the cult of the ninth-century East Anglian king, St Edmund. In 1191, after he had conquered Cyprus, Richard sent the Emperor Isaac's banner back to the saint's shrine at Bury Abbey as a trophy; and three years later, after safely returning to England from Germany, he offered thanks at the saint's shrine for his deliverance.[10] Richard's devotion to the cult of St Edmund was the subject of comment by the chroniclers. The Cistercian Ralph of Coggeshall praised him for it.[11] Richard may well have been the first post-Conquest ruler of England to show more than a passing interest in the cult. It is not inconceivable that he showed an interest in some other early English saints. On one occasion, shortly after his accession, he visited St Albans, where the English proto-martyr was buried.[12] Certainly he took care to associate himself with the spiritual traditions of the Old English monarchy. When he had himself crowned again in 1194, on his return from Germany, he did so not at the obvious place, Westminster, but at Winchester.[13] The choice was significant. Winchester was the old English capital, the ceremonial centre of the Wessex monarchy, and Richard wanted to associate himself with the city's – and, through it, with the kingdom's – traditions. Richard's interest in the saints of pre-Conquest England was paralleled by that of the higher nobility generally. The king and his fellow nobles were fascinated by the shadowy saints from England's remote past. Their interest can be interpreted as a measure of how English they had become: and it is worth remembering that Richard had himself been born in England. By the middle of the twelfth century the old racial distinctions of English and Normans were fading, and the descendants of the Norman settlers had to all intents and purposes become English by adoption. Yet in a sense Richard and his men still felt uncomfortable about their origins: they were not native, and they yearned for a legitimising link with the past. What drew them to the English saints was the cultural legitimacy that these figures conferred. By honouring the likes of St Edmund Richard and his nobles overcame the awkward discontinuities of conquest and settlement.

If it is possible to see Richard's devotion to Edmund as rooted in a search for legitimacy, then Edmund also had something else to offer Richard. Edmund stood as a representative of the traditions of Christian monarchy in England. In the ninth century, at the height of the Viking onslaught, Edmund had given his life fighting the heathen Dane; and now Richard was devoting his own energies to combating an infidel foe. The two kings were separated from each other by nearly three centuries. But in Richard's mind they were joined in a common enterprise – that of championing Christian kingship. Later still, Richard II was to identify with the cult of St Edmund for largely the same reason. He included him in the Wilton Diptych.

More remarkable still than Richard's interest in the English saints is his interest in the cult of St Thomas Becket. This interest too is well attested. In 1194, in the course of his brief visit to England, Richard fitted in a pilgrimage to Canterbury. The local chronicler, Gervase of Canterbury, describes the visit. He tells us that Richard paid his respects to the martyr's shrine. And, very pointedly, he adds that Richard visited Canterbury before going to Bury: he got his priorities right.[14] Richard's interest in the cult of Becket found expression not only at Canterbury but in the unlikely location of Portsmouth. Richard was the effective founder of modern Portsmouth: he made the town the headquarters of his fleet in the 1190s, and he established a base there. In the light of this, it is more than a coincidence that the great church in the town should be dedicated to St Thomas Becket. Becket had barely been in the grave more than a few years when work on the fabric was begun. Back in 1180 the Norman manorial lord John de Gisors had established a chantry on the site dedicated to Becket.[15] In 1194 this chantry was reconstituted as a church, and the dedication was transferred.[16] The church, completed probably by the early 1200s, is a mightily impressive one, almost certainly paid for by the king.[17] Richard's involvement in the project is an implicit acknowledgement of his interest in Becket. But what in that case could have inspired him? In the twelfth century, as later, Becket's cult served as a rallying-point for those who were critical of royal authority. In part, Richard's interest may have been tactical: by honouring Becket he was doing something to neutralise those aspects of the cult which threatened the crown. But probably, too, he was moved by a genuine respect for the saint. Richard had a liking for men of principle. He even liked awkward men of principle, like Hugh of Avalon. And it is worth remembering that his own relations with his father had been testy. Conceivably, he saw Becket as a fellow sufferer at the hands of a heavy-handed and often unsympathetic tyrant king.

It is sometimes suggested that Richard was instrumental in introducing the cult of St George to England. St George was admittedly the kind of saint who would have appealed to Richard: a fourth-century Syrian soldier martyred for his faith. The evidence for the king's sponsorship of the cult is, however, slight. Ambroise says that Richard invoked the saint on one occasion on crusade before he and his knights attacked a caravan. But that is the only indication in the sources of any interest on his part. Contrary to what has been said, Richard never placed his army under the saint's protection. Nor is there any hard evidence that he flew the saint's red and white banner. It is very likely that Richard saw the saint as one of his patrons in the saintly pantheon. But it is doubtful if he was at all active in propagating his cult in England or the other Angevin lands in Europe.[18]

A couple of centuries later, by Richard II's time, modes of religious expression in England were changing. Personal piety was finding expression in more private and individualistic ways.[19] The faithful looked for a more direct and immediate relationship with the Creator. In the north of England in particular there was a fascination with the writings of the mystics and contemplatives: the works of such writers as Richard Rolle and Walter Hilton enjoyed wide popularity with the nobility.[20] The spread of literacy among the laity generated a demand for a wider range of religious texts. Books of Hours (books of private prayer) joined psalters as widely read works of private devotion. Confession, made obligatory by the Fourth Lateran Council in 1215, played an increasingly prominent role in the shaping of individual consciences. Confessors, often chosen from the ranks of the Dominicans, were retained in every royal and upper-class household, and the penances which they set formed the basis for good works. After the Black Death, an anti-materialist strain is noticeable in upper-class piety. Funerary pomp was increasingly frowned upon (military accoutrements being prohibited), and the most popular of the monastic Orders was strikingly the most austere: the Carthusian Order.[21] At the same time, new liturgical feasts were admitted to the calendar. The cult of St Anne was introduced by Queen Anne of Bohemia in 1382, and the mass of the Holy Name was to attract a significant following in the next century.[22]

Yet it would be wrong to suggest that in the late middle ages patterns of religious devotion were entirely transformed, for they were not. For most of the faithful, religion was still a religion of the saints. By appealing to the saints people sought to draw down the Almighty's mercy, as they had done for centuries. The shrines of the major saints were still regular centres of pilgrimage. Canterbury and Rome were two of the most visited cities in Europe. The rise of personal relic collections, it is true, led to reduced pilgrim traffic at some of the lesser shrines, for people were now assembling relics in their homes. New cult centres were always appearing, however, to take the place of old: in Norfolk, for example, the shrine of Our Lady at Walsingham took the place of that of little St William at Norwich. At the same time, traditional monasticism continued to flourish, attracting a flow of bequests and privileges from benefactors, even as the range of intercessory foundations broadened. And the crusading ideal still figured prominently in the body of ideas which people held dear. In Richard II's reign, as we have seen, there was a considerable upsurge in popular enthusiasm for a new campaign against the infidel.

The themes of continuity and change in personal piety are reflected in Richard's own piety. On the one hand, it is possible to identify aspects of the king's devotional life which invite comparison with that of his predecessor and namesake. Yet, on the other, we can also detect characteristics distinctive to his own age and predilections. The balance between the old and new, and the traditional and the innovative, gives Richard's piety its particular interest and character.

Continuity with the piety of the Lionheart is most clearly evidenced by the king's interest in native-born saints. The second Richard, like his namesake, was deeply fascinated by the obscure galaxy of the Old English pantheon – St Edmund, St Etheldreda, St Winifred, St Erkenwald: all of these saints received the king's attention. His devotion to the Anglo-Saxon saints is one of the most noteworthy characteristics of his piety. In general, it is an interest with roots in the heightened sense of Englishness which can be observed in this period, itself largely a by-product of external war. None the less, its origins may also, to some extent, be found in the king's own piety and historical interests.

Richard's devotion to St Edmund, whom the Lionheart had admired, is particularly well documented. St Edmund is shown as one of Richard's three saintly sponsors in the left-hand panel of the Wilton Diptych. St Edmund stood for the Christian traditions of kingship in England; he also stood for Englishness. The king visited his shrine at Bury on a number of occasions. He paid a particularly ceremonious visit in 1383 as part of a wider itinerary of all the main East Anglian shrines. He also made grants of privileges to the abbey. In 1396 he provided the abbot with a writ of aid for the construction of a new cloister.[23] Each year he was assiduous in his observance of St Edmund's feast day (20 November). In 1390 he celebrated the feast at Westminster Abbey, arriving for vespers and midnight matins on the vigil and staying for high mass on the feast day itself.[24] Afterwards he gave the convent 10 marks for its pains. On the occasion of a later celebration he granted the abbey a set of liturgical banners of St Edmund.

Among other pre-Conquest saints, St Etheldreda appears to have had an especial claim on his favour. The reason for this was a remarkable miracle which she performed in his presence. In the early summer of 1383 Richard and his court were staying at Ely, where the saint was buried. One day, during a terrible storm, Sir James Berners, one of the king's chamber knights, was struck by lightning and left blind. Richard gave orders that the monks pray at the shrine for a cure. At the same time, Berners himself was taken to sit by the shrine overnight. By dawn on the following day his sight was restored. Richard showed his gratitude to St Etheldreda by granting her community at Ely confirmation of its claim to all forfeitures within the range of the cathedral's liberty.[25]

Richard was also devoted, albeit to a lesser degree, to a number of other pre-Conquest saints. Richard Maidstone mentions his interest in the cult of St Erkenwald, bishop of London and founder of Chertsey Abbey. Richard visited the saint's shrine at St Paul's in 1392, and it was probably at his behest that his anniversary was made a major service at the cathedral at this time.[26] In the final years of the reign Richard developed an interest in the cult of St Winifred, a Welsh virgin, who had spent the greater part of her life at Holywell (Flint) and was buried at Shrewsbury Abbey. Richard is recorded as visiting her shrine in 1398, and very likely Archbishop Walden's order for the celebration of her feast (along with those of David and Chad) owed something to royal patronage.[27] Another saint to whom Richard was devoted was the tenth-century king of Wessex, St Edward the Martyr. St Edward, like St Edmund, stood for the Christian traditions of the English royal line. A boy king, like Richard himself, he was assassinated at Corfe (Dorset) in 979 and quickly canonised. Richard stayed at Corfe for ten days in 1393 and in all probability visited the saint's burial place nearby at Wareham. It is reasonable to see Richard's sponsorship as the prime influence behind the promulgation of the saint's Martyrdom and Translation as principal feasts in Canterbury Cathedral in 1395.[28]

The cult, however, which elicited from Richard the deepest and most personal response was that of another royal predecessor – the saint, to whom the post-Conquest English monarchy looked for a legitimising link with the past: St Edward the Confessor.[29] St Edward had been canonised on Henry II's initiative in 1161. His reputation for saintliness was based partly on his chaste lifestyle (he was childless) and partly on his foundation of Westminster Abbey. But he had a very particular appeal to Richard. He stood for peace. Richard regarded peace as one of his main political aims: peace in both senses – peace with France, and also peace in the sense of internal unity. The Confessor's cult provided him with the necessary spiritual validation for both. But the Confessor also stood for dynasticism. Richard had a deeply felt sense of lineage. He saw his ancestors as a living presence in his midst. In this respect, he was not unlike the Richard the Lionheart. The Lionheart had embarked on his crusade at one level in the interests of the house of Anjou: for half a century between the 1130s and 1186 his Angevin kinsmen had been rulers of the Latin kingdom in the East.[30] The sense of ancestral obligation was a powerful influence on the actions of both kings.

Richard II's devotion to the Confessor is most clearly evidenced (like his devotion to St Edmund) by the saint's inclusion in the Wilton Diptych. The Confessor is shown in the left-hand panel as the second of the three saints commending the king to the Christ Child. In his left hand he carries the ring, the attribute by which he was generally identified. This emblem refers to a story which was widely circulated at the time. The Confessor is supposed to have given a ring one day to a beggar near Westminster. Some time later, a group of English pilgrims in the Holy Land were addressed by an old man who said he was St John the Apostle. He gave them the ring and told them to return it to Edward and to warn him of impending death. This widely known story was often alluded to in late medieval iconography of the Confessor.

Richard's devotion to the Confessor – and, with it, his interest in Confessor myths – found expression in a number of ways. Most obviously, there were the many expensive gifts which he lavished on the Confessor's shrine. On one occasion, he gave a magnificent portable altar enamelled with the story of the Confessor and the ring. At various times he also made gifts of jewellery. In November 1388, while visiting the shrine, he presented a gold ring (another reference to the story) with a valuable ruby set in it. He made the gift on unusual terms: he laid claim to the ring for his lifetime, but said that when he left the realm he would restore it and recover it on his return.[31] According to this arrangement, he should by rights have restored it when going to Ireland in 1399, but apparently he did not; it was left to Henry V to return it in 1413.

Equally suggestive of the king's piety as his gifts to the shrine were his gifts to the community at Westminster, which was its custodian. On various occasions – sometimes when visiting the abbey – Richard presented the monks with magnificent sets of vestments. In 1389, 'at the shrine of St Edward the Confessor', he donated a set consisting of a chasuble, three copes, three albs, three maniples and two stoles. In 1395, in somewhat bizarre circumstances, he gave the convent another set. As Abbot Colchester was later to recall, at the burial of his former treasurer Bishop Waltham in the Confessor's chapel, Richard, moved by the sight of the body, promised to give a vestment embroidered with the tree of Jesse in the bishop's memory.[32] Over the years Richard gave many other fine vestments, altarpieces and liturgical banners which, all told, must have been worth several thousand marks.

Richard showed himself the most generous royal patron of the convent at Westminster since Henry III. In the last decade of his reign the lavishness of his favour was especially striking. His many gifts to the shrine aroused wonder. But perhaps his most remarkable act of favour was something else again: his sponsorship of the rebuilding of the abbey church.[33] The long process of reconstruction had been begun by Henry III in the 1240s. Henry had been responsible for raising up a magnificent new choir and transept arm. These works were substantially complete by the time of his death in 1272. But in the reigns that followed little if anything was done to further the project. Royal patronage was mainly directed to the rival project of St Stephen's in the palace of Westminster, and work on the abbey languished. The initiative to resume activity was taken in 1375 by Cardinal Langham. In that year the cardinal, a former monk of the house, promised £200 a year to a building fund should work on the nave be set in hand. In the following year work began, but again proceeded slowly. Richard stepped in in 1386. In that year he granted the abbot and convent £100 a year to carry on the work. Three years after that – the Appellant tide having subsided – he put financial provision for the project on a firmer basis. He made over to the abbey two alien priories in his custody because of the French war – Folkestone, which was worth £20 a year, and Stoke-by-Clare (Essex), which was worth £100. The income from these was to support the rebuilding for the next ten years. Periodically, the endowment was supplemented by further gifts from the king. In 1394, for example, after Queen Anne's death, he paid a total of £106 13s. 4d. to the fund from his own pocket, and in the following year the sum of £100 exactly. Furthermore, he helped with the provision of materials for the work. In 1393, in response to a petition from the abbey, he provided for the impressment of labourers in Dorset to hew Purbeck marble for the columns and carry it to the sea. This was because in the years of falling population after the

Black Death finding labour was not easy. By the time that he was deposed the physical skeleton of the nave stood virtually complete. The walls of the side aisles were finished and the double row of columns had been raised up. Richard provided for continuation of the work in his will: he ordered his jewellery to be sold to pay for it. But not until a century after his death was work on the abbey church as a whole rounded off.

Over the years it is likely that Richard spent at least £10,000–£12,000 on Westminster Abbey. It is impossible to estimate precisely how much he spent, but the financial worth of his favour could hardly have been less. As we have seen, however, the bulk of that expenditure was concentrated in the later years of the reign. In the early years – the 1380s – his patronage had been more meagre. A number of reasons may be offered for the shifting pattern of his favour. In the first place, in the 1380s his relations with the abbey had been complicated by the monks' struggle with their rivals, the canons of St Stephen's, over jurisdictional rights, and Richard had given his support to the canons. Once the bitter dispute had been settled, as was the case by 1386, the king's instinctive affinity with the abbey reasserted itself. Equally significant, however, may have been a second factor – Richard's need in the years from 1389 to reaffirm the sacral character of his rule. In the later 1380s, the period of Appellant upheaval and rebellion, the aura of mystique surrounding his kingly estate had been badly tarnished. The Appellants' triumph had exposed the hollowness of his authoritarian ambitions. If Richard were to restore and enhance the prestige of the kingly office, it was essential that he recapture something of the mystical quality that had been lost. One of the most striking ways in which he chose to do this was by strengthening his relationship with Westminster Abbey: in other words, developing the liturgical aspect of his office. Accordingly, from 1386 he made the abbey the focus of many of his most significant actions as king. He processed there on his return to the capital from his 'gyration', or tour, of the realm in 1387. A decade later, at the end of the 'Revenge Parliament', he presided over an oath-taking ceremony at the Confessor's shrine in which he made the magnates swear to uphold the assembly's enactments. But the most elaborate ritual involving the abbey was staged between these two events – in 1392, when he made his peace with the Londoners. On this occasion, he walked barefoot with the monks from the abbey to St James, north to Charing Cross, and then back to the abbey – a distance of some two to three miles. At the end, footsore and tired, he spent time praying in the abbey before returning across the precincts to his palace.[34]

Richard's development of the liturgical dimension to his kingship is evident in almost every aspect of his governance in his later years. It can be seen, for example, in his encouragement of a new and more elaborate language of address. In the 1390s it became common – indeed, almost *de rigueur* – for the Commons to employ the language of highness and majesty in their parliamentary petitions: the point being that majesty implied a theocratic dimension to the king's rule. The liturgical dimension is also illustrated in the Westminster Abbey portrait of the king. Richard looks out frontally like an iconic close-up of the face of Christ. In this dramatic image courtly and celestial are merged in a liminal symbolism. Richard's new preoccupation with the sacrality of his office formed an element in a larger change in the character of his kingship in his middle years. He began to take a new interest in the religious responsibilities of his office. He placed a greater emphasis than before on the promotion of conformity; he made himself the defender of religious orthodoxy; and he placed the secular arm at the disposal of the Church. This sudden preoccupation with orthodoxy almost certainly had its origins in the outbreak of heresy. By the 1380s Wycliffite beliefs were spreading quickly in England. The outbreak of heresy was an entirely new experience for the ecclesiastical authorities. Not since the outbreak of the Pelagian controversy in the fifth century had dissident religious beliefs circulated north of the Channel. Richard's involvement in the enforcement of orthodoxy arose as a natural response to the challenge of heresy.

The man after whom the heretical creed was named was an Oxford academic, John Wyclif.[35] Wyclif was born in the north of England in the 1330s. He is first recorded in Oxford as a fellow of Merton College in 1356, and by 1360 he had become master of Balliol. By 1372, when he supplicated for his doctorate, he had established himself as one of the leading theological masters in the university. The background to his thought lay in the great debate between the rival realist and nominalist schools of thought – in other words, between those who believed in abstract concepts or 'universals' (the realists) and those who did not.

Wyclif was a leading realist. In his view, by peering through to the underlying reality of things one could gain an understanding of God, whose universal knowledge made a knowledge of things accessible to those made in his image. As a by-product of his realist beliefs, Wyclif was a committed predestinarian. He believed that an omniscient God knew from the beginning of time who was going to be saved and who would be damned. This led him to a radical conclusion. There was no justification for the visible Church and its hierarchy. Only those with a standing in grace could be counted members of the Church. The Church, in the sense of the Church on earth, had no authority. Authority, for Wyclif, lay solely in the scriptures, which accordingly ought to be made available in the vernacular. By a separate line of reasoning – a biblical literalism – he also came to reject transubstantiation. He argued that when Christ said, 'This is my body', he did not mean that there was a change of substance, only that faith receives the body as bread. Wyclif never denied the centrality or importance of the mass. It was rather that he saw its significance as representing the spiritual union of all the faithful in Christ's sacramental presence.

Wyclif quickly attracted a following among those seeking a more personal and immediate relationship with the Creator: one that was based on biblicism, not sacerdotalism. At court, he won the support of a body of knights associated with Richard's parents, the prince and princess of Wales. The leading members of the group were Sir John Clanvow, Sir Lewis Clifford and Sir Richard Stury. These were men who made no secret of their beliefs: they were known to the chroniclers as the 'milites capuciati' (the hooded knights) because they kept their hoods on during mass. Their presence in the prince's and the princess's entourage, and later at Richard's court, suggests that the king grew up in a distinctly radical religious atmosphere. The Black Prince's sympathies seem to have been strongly anticlerical, like those of his brother, John of Gaunt. He was critical, for example, of those churchmen, including Archbishop Whittlesey, whom he thought reluctant to help pay for the war, and he presided over an assembly in which Wyclif's anti-papal arguments were either anticipated or echoed. The evidence of Richard's mother's sympathies is still more explicit. In 1378 she sent a directive to the bishops, delivered by Clifford, ordering them to halt their proceedings against Wyclif. Seven years later, when she drew up her will, she conspicuously named as her executors three Wycliffite knights: Clifford, Clanvow and Stury.[36]

It would be surprising if some of this sensibility had not rubbed off onto the young Richard. The king's inner religious beliefs before the late 1380s, however, are remarkably difficult to fathom. The record or administrative sources are uninformative, and no devotional books of his survive. None the less, there is circumstantial evidence to suggest that, however orthodox his outward observances, inwardly he had absorbed some of his parents' views. In the first place, there is the strik-ing fact of his retention of the services of the Wycliffite – the Lollard – knights, Clifford, Stury, Clanvow and the others; these men all served in the king's inner sanctum, his chamber. There is no indication before the 1390s that any disciplinary action was taken against them. Secondly, and hardly less notably, there is the evidence of the king's failure to offer any significant support to the Church in its fight against the heretics. Before 1388 only one legislative initiative was taken. In May 1382, as a response to the Great Revolt, power was given to the chancellor to order the sheriffs to arrest unorthodox preachers and detain them pending their appearance in a Church court.[37] This measure offered a speedy and effective mechanism for dealing with elusive itinerant preachers. In the legislation of the early years of the reign, however, it stands alone. Not till the takeover by the Appellants were any further measures taken. To say the least, Richard had been lacking in energy in his support for the ecclesiastical authorities.

Towards the end of the 1380s, however, his attitude underwent a change. From being mildly detached, he became the vigorous and artic-ulate defender of orthodoxy that he was to remain till his death. The reasons for his change of attitude are hard to fathom, but it is likely that, in common with many of his contemporaries, he suspected a connection between Lollardy and popular unrest. In the aftermath of the Great Revolt there was considerable alarm about the unsettling effects of Lollard preaching. In the preamble to the 1382 statute it was asserted that the preachers 'made discord and dissension between the various estates of the realm, spiritual and temporal, to the commotion of the people and the peril of the whole realm'; and Adam of Usk a generation later said that Wyclif's disciples, 'by preaching the with-holding of tithes and offerings', had sown the seed of 'many disasters, plots, disputes and sedition, which last to this day'.[38] The Wycliffite creed fell victim to the timing and circumstances of its birth. Appearing when it did, it became associated with the phenomenon of popular unrest; and once that association was established, upper-class support for it ebbed away. Gaunt appears to have abandoned his interest from 1382, and Richard probably did so a few years later. Richard's progress to orthodoxy may have owed a little to the influence of Archbishop Arundel, the Appellants' chancellor. Arundel was socially and politically a thoroughgoing conservative. In the 1390s, when he served a second term as chancellor, he went the whole way in endorsing his master's views on the need for obedience. In Arundel's view, heretics were guilty of conspiracy and were thus enemies of the social order. As the king's letters on the close rolls show, this was essentially Richard's view too.

Evidence of the king's new interest in enforcing orthodoxy can be found in his enrolled correspondence. In 1393, when he thanked the archbishop of Canterbury for news of a miracle at Becket's shrine, he dwelled on its value in combating Christ's enemies. Miracles, he wrote, were essential for converting men 'from their errors back to the way of salvation'.[39] Four years later, in another letter to the archbishop, he stressed his role as protector of the Church. 'As to the maintenance of the Catholic faith and destruction of damnable opinions', he wrote, 'if there be such working contrary to our creed, we desire for the future, just as we have always done, by the grace of God, to do our duty; and the more Almighty God strengthens us with His power, the more we intend to strive and labour to show honour to the Holy Mother Church and to cherish and strengthen the faith.'[40] In a letter to the bishop of Chichester a few months earlier he stressed his responsibility for the spiritual welfare of his people. Urging the bishop to arrest all Lollards in his diocese, he said that he longed for the diocese to be purged 'of such heresies, lest the wickedness of the lurking enemy thereby infect the people of the whole realm, the ruling whereof is committed to the king from on high'.[41] Towards the end of his reign, probably in 1398, Richard expressed fears for the safety of the Church under any other defender than himself. Speaking to Sir William Bagot, he said that he was afraid that if Derby became king he would be 'as great a tyrant to the Holy Church as there ever was'. He and his ancestors, by contrast, had been 'good confessors', who had never persecuted the Church.[42] They had utterly 'cut off and abolished errors and heresies by the secular arm'.[43]

The king's zeal for the faith in his later years manifested itself in the more vigorous deployment of the secular arm against heresy. While no new legislative initiatives were proposed, the existing legislation was enforced more thoroughly. The council, using the powers given to it in 1388, had little hesitation in arresting and interrogating traffickers in heretical writings. It was particular watchful of activities in Wyclif's old university of Oxford. In 1392 a writ was sent to the university stating that the council had learned that the Cistercian doctor Henry Crumpe had been teaching heretical doctrines; the university was required to suspend him from teaching and order him to appear before the council. Three years later, in 1395, a further writ was sent to the university authorities: they were instructed to expel all who, after enquiry, were found to be of Lollard sympathy; and anyone opposing the proceedings was to be brought before the council for punishment.[44]

In February 1395 there was something of a Lollard scare at court. During a parliament held while Richard was in Ireland, Lollard sympathisers nailed manifestoes to the doors of Westminster Hall and St Paul's. The council wrote to Richard urging his return, and by the beginning of May he was back, taking measures to restore confidence. Walsingham tells how he made one of the 'Lollard knights' in his service, Sir Richard Stury, swear an oath to abjure heresy, warning him that if he went back on his word he would have him executed.[45] The king also took measures against some lesser officials in his service. A household esquire by the name of John Croft was arrested and interrogated, and made to submit before Richard at Windsor.[46] Even after the scare was over, Richard was vigilant in his stand against Lollardy. In March 1397, for example, he ordered Sir William Scrope to bring before him for his own examination all the Lollards whom he had in his custody.[47] By the later 1390s, however, the authorities were looking for new measures to stem the spread of the heretic weed. In one of the parliaments of 1397 a petition was submitted by the clergy asking for heresy to be made a capital offence. No statute to this effect appears to have been published, and the suggestion has been made that Richard was too busy with other matters to take action. But whatever the reason may have been for his caution, there can be no doubt of his general zeal for orthodoxy. Over the previous decade he had been unswerving in his support for the Church, and the popular perception of him was as an orthodox ruler. It was for this reason that Roger Dymock presented to him a copy of his anti-Lollard *Treatise against the Twelve Errors*.[48] While Richard may not have 'laid low the heretic, and scattered their friends', as he boasted on his tomb epitaph in Westminster Abbey, he had done all that could reasonably be expected of him to give the ecclesiastical arm secular backing.

In the century after the king's death there were fewer changes in lay religious expression than there had been in the longer period between the reigns of the first and second Richards. For the most part, devotional patterns remained the same. Everyday religion was still a religion of the saints. Brightly coloured images of the most popular saints, such as St Christopher and St John the Baptist, were found in every church or cathedral – on altars and rood screens, in stained-glass windows, and even on tombs and brasses.[49] The saints were generally seen as comforting figures: they were sources of protection, favour and mediation – intercessors for mankind with the Almighty. At the same time, the age-old conception of the afterlife held sway. In the late middle ages there was hardly anyone who did not view the sufferings of the soul in purgatory as a fate to be guarded against at all costs. Those who could afford it made provision in their wills for intercessory prayer. By the fourteenth century a whole apparatus of intercession had grown up in churches. Obits, trentals, anniversaries, perpetual chantries: whatever the financial means available to the deceased, there was a way in which his or her intercessory aspirations could be satisfied. As the enormous popular appetite for intercession shows, the majority of the faithful still readily accepted the mediatory role of the priesthood. Yet, at the same time, they were looking for a more direct and immediate relationship with the Creator. There were a number of ways in which this could be met. One was by following the prescriptions of the contemplatives, such as Richard Rolle, and seeking a more emotional and mystical understanding of God. The contemplatives attracted a considerable following in the fourteenth century and influenced patterns of devotion for much longer. A second, and more conventional way of approaching the Almighty was by reading works of personal devotion, in particular psalters and books of hours. Devotional works intended for private use were produced in enormous number in the fifteenth century. The late middle ages were a period of increasing lay literacy. By the second Richard's time, all of the upper and middle classes and many of the peasantry could read. As a result, probably for the first time a class came into being who were able to find their own way to an understanding of God. It might be supposed that these developments would have assisted the growth of Lollardy – Lollardy being a religion of the written word. In fact, however, they did not; or they did so only slightly. While there was a growing biblicism, traditional religion in England remained a genuinely popular religion. The threat from the Lollard sectaries was almost certainly exaggerated by the authorities – and exaggerated, it has been suggested, in order to strengthen their own hand.[50] At the time that Richard III became king, the Church in England could scarcely be considered under serious threat. Its hold on the affections of the faithful was still strong. Huge sums of money were spent by many of the faithful on the building and rebuilding of parish churches. Popular piety may well have been conventional, even undemanding, but that is not to say that it was necessarily superficial.

Richard III's private religious life is by no means as richly documented as that of his predecessor and namesake. We do not have for this king any objects of comparable importance to the Wilton Diptych for Richard II; nor, disappointingly, do we have many administrative instruments shedding light on his patronage of saints and shrines. On the other hand, we are fortunate in having a range of other sources. The most valuable of these is the king's book of hours, which includes a prayer added at his request, apparently conveying 'a sense of oppression and danger'.[51] Alongside this volume we can set the statutes drawn up for the king's proposed, but uncompleted, collegiate foundation at Middleham, and the slighter evidence of his plans for similar institutions at Barnard Castle and York – all of which reveal his concern for the afterlife. Further insights into the king's piety are provided by aspects of his policies – notably his support for the Cambridge colleges, his protection of the Church in England, and his interest in cults in the North. It would be wrong to suppose that these sources, even when taken together, will unlock for us the secrets of the king's soul. None the less, they provide us with some clues as to how he saw his relationship with his Creator.

The impression which has been formed by many historians who have studied Richard's career is that he was a man of sincere, if perhaps slightly austere, piety. To Professor Ross, he was 'a genuinely pious and religious man'.[52] In Ross's view, a key influence on him was his mother, Cecily, duchess of York, a lady famed for the purity of her life. In common with Cecily, he was attracted to the movement of pietism and mysticism which spread across Europe in the later middle ages. He owned a number of key texts associated with the movement – a vernacular (but non-Lollard) version of the New Testament, parts of the Old Testament in English, and a volume of *The Visions of St Matilda*, a saint who with St Bridget had been one of the leading figures in the movement. To Professor Ross, the much discussed prayer which Richard had inserted into his book of hours, while attesting a sense of danger, is of a piece with the evidence of his genuine piety.

A very different view of Richard's piety has recently been offered by Jonathan Hughes.[53] Hughes rejects the view of Richard's religious thinking as essentially conventional. In his estimation, it was much more personal; it was idiosyncratic and highly anguished. Hughes's Richard has something of the character of a religious fanatic. Hughes pictures him as introspective, puritanical and self-righteous. Like Ross, he sees Richard as in many ways his mother's son. He points to the fact that he read many of the same books as his mother. However, he believes that the conclusions which he drew from these were quite different. Whereas his mother, reading for example *The Visions of St Matilda*, would have understood this text as an invitation to accept providence, Richard understood it very differently, as a spur to action. In like fashion, Richard reacted in a highly personal way to the prayer which he inserted into his book of hours. Where others would have found solace in this Old Testament reflection, Richard found the strength to strike out in his own arbitrary direction. Richard, in Hughes's eyes, was thus someone with a sense of destiny – a man whose willingness to follow an unconventional course was reinforced by his personal religion. How does he justify this novel interpretation of the king?

To a greater extent than other historians, Hughes connects Richard's religion with the contemplative movement of the fourteenth century. In its English form, as he points out, this movement had roots in the north of England, Richard's own part of the world. Its leading figures were Richard Rolle of Hampole, John Thweng (St John of Bridlington) and Nicholas Love, the prior of Mount Grace. The twin characteristics of the contemplatives' writings were an emphasis on individual experience and an appeal to the senses. By resort to rich and emotive language, these men encouraged the growth of a highly developed sense of self-worth. Richard Rolle, for example, in a commentary on the canticles, described the experiences of *calor*, *canor* and *dulcedo* (warmth, song and sweetness), which he felt on invoking the Holy Name – taking these to be evidence of God's power. In another work, the *Incendium Amoris*, he described how, after hearing some melodies and enjoying the pleasant warmth, he saw the door of heaven swing open to reveal the face of Our Lord.[54] Such experiences, Rolle emphasised, set him apart from other mortals. Moreover, to experience them, he needed to be in a desert place, by himself, often facing suspicion and hostility. Any person reading the contemplatives would find himself nurturing a highly emotional and mysterious relationship with the Creator. A state of mind would be developed entirely different from that developed by the communal rituals of mainstream religion. The communal rituals (principally, the mass) by their very nature brought people together and bonded them. Contemplative religion, however, had the opposite effect: it drove men into isolation. Rolle's expectation was that his readers, having found a quiet place, would pray and, in this way, seek an accord with the Almighty. Among men of the world, however, reactions could be very different. When Richard reacted by embarking on a lonely course of political takeover, it was a response that could hardly be expected. But the strength that he needed for that course came from his reading.

Much of Hughes's book consists of an analysis of the circles in which Richard moved. He demonstrates that many of the king's northern supporters were descended from patrons of Rolle and his fellow mystics. The Nevilles, for example, had connections with the group going back nearly a century. One of the Kingmaker's ancestors, William Neville, archdeacon of Durham, was Rolle's original patron at Oxford. Margery Neville was a patron both of Rolle and his younger contemporary, St John of Bridlington. The Scropes of Masham, who were also to be numbered among Richard's friends, were likewise close to the eremitics. Various Scropes lent patronage to a disciple of Rolle's, Margaret Kirkby,

and were among the earliest lay owners of his writings. The leading clerical member of the family, Richard Scrope, archbishop of York, had
been involved in popularising Rolle's teachings and accommodating
them to the mixed life – the mode of life of which Richard's mother
Cecily Neville was one of the most celebrated exponents. Hughes maintains that a sharp contrast is to be observed between the piety of this
group and the more secular outlook of the Yorkist elite generally. The
circle around Edward IV and the Woodvilles, he argues, was imbued
with a taste for fashionable classicism. Cicero and Seneca were more to
their liking than eccentrics like Rolle and Thweng. Emphatically not for
them the ideas of mystical contemplation and detachment from the
world; the hearts of these men were set on honour, reason and human
achievement.[55]

In this view, a key role was played in the shaping of personal piety by
regular reading of books of hours. Books of hours were much the most
popular medium of personal devotion in the later middle ages. Their
contents were fairly standard by this time. Generally, they consisted of
collections of psalms, antiphons, lessons and prayers. Their attraction to
the reader was that they allowed the opportunity to enter into a fully
religious life. With the psalms arranged according to the monastic
hours, readers could pray in ways appropriate to changes in the day or
stages in the life cycle. The first psalms were usually those for matins and
lauds praising God's creation and the birth of Christ the redeemer.
Those for nones emphasised the range of achievements culminating in
the birth of the saviour, while at compline the emphasis was on the
longing of the soul: 'Hail Mary, we sigh groaning in this valley of tears,
turn to us your merciful eye ...' Prayer in the fifteenth century was an
emotional, individualistic and amateur activity that allowed worshippers
to relate their religious experience to their own secular worlds of family
and career. Through the psalms, in particular, it was possible for men
and women to reconcile themselves to the crises and sufferings of life.

Richard III's own book of hours survives.[56] The king acquired it second hand, probably after taking the throne. On stylistic grounds it can
be dated to *c.* 1420 and its contents suggest that it was made for a priest.
Its value to us is limited by the fact that the king did not commission it
himself, so it does not open a direct window onto his soul. As we have
seen, however, he did make additions to it. Hughes suggests that by

analysing the volume, and reconstructing the responses it would have evoked, we may be able to discover the mainsprings of the king's piety; more than that, indeed, we may be able to establish a link between the king's thoughts and his political actions.

The most distinctive feature of the volume is the prayer which Richard added at the end (fos 181–83). It is a version of a prayer found in a number of volumes of this kind and is usually attributed to St Augustine. In it, the supplicant appeals to Christ for deliverance from sin, captivity, grief, temptation, illness and immediate danger. A close identification is assumed between the supplicant and the heroes of the Old Testament. Just as the Old Testament figures were delivered from peril by prayer, so likewise will the supplicant be; his enemies will be scattered:

> Keep concord between me and my enemies ... Deign to assuage, turn aside, destroy and bring to nothing the hatred they bear towards me, even as you extinguished the hatred and anger that Esau had for his brother Jacob. And stretch out your arms over me and spread your grace over me and deign to deliver me from all the perplexities and sorrow in which I find myself, even as you delivered Abraham from the hand of the Chaldeans, Isaac from sacrifice by means of the ram, Jacob from the hands of his brother Esau, Joseph from the hands of his brothers, Noah from the waters of the flood by means of the ark, Lot from the city of the Sodomites, your servants Moses and Aaron and the people of Israel from the hand of Pharoah and the bondage of Egypt, and Saul from Mount Gilboa, and King David from the hand of Saul and of Goliath the giant. And even as you delivered Susanna from false accusation and testimony and Judith from the hand of Holofernes, Daniel from the den of lions, and the three young men from the burning furnace, Jonah from the belly of the whale, the daughter of the woman of Cana from the torment of devils, and Adam from the depths of hell, with your own precious blood, and Peter from the sea and Paul from chains; [therefore] Lord Jesus Christ, son of the living God, deign to free me, your servant Richard, from every tribulation, sorrow and trouble in which I am placed and from the plots of my enemies, and deign to send Michael the Archangel to my aid against them, and deign, Lord Jesus Christ, to bring to nothing their evil plans ... even as you brought to nothing the counsel of Achitofel, who incited Absolom against King David.[57]

This is a striking prayer. Hardly less distinctive, however, is one

addressed to Joseph, son of Jacob, which was added for the original
owner. This begins:

> 'O God who gave wisdom to the blessed Joseph in the house of his Lord
> and in the presence of Pharoah and freed him from hatred and from the
> envy of his brothers but also raised him in honour I pray to you Lord God
> omnipotent that similarly you deliver your servant from the plots of his
> enemies so that he finds grace and favour in the eyes of his adversaries ...'

As Hughes argues, we sense from this prayer, as from the one
which Richard himself added, that the supplicant saw himself embattled
on all sides, struggling against the odds in a hostile world. In Hughes's
view, Richard's identification with the heroes of the Old Testament
would have helped him to conceive of his religion in aggressive terms.
Many of the prayers included in the book are militaristic and call for
God's help in defeating enemies. One of them, for example – a prayer
to Christ by Berengar of Tours (d. 1088) – calls for Christ's assistance
against spiritual enemies or opponents, and opens: 'By thy right hand
that shattered Acheron's infernal gate, Break mine enemies into
pieces ...' But, Hughes argues, the most significant of the Old Testament figures with whom Richard identified was King David, who
appears prominently in Richard's own prayer. In a prayer to the cross
in Richard's book, the cross is pictured as a standard belonging to the
line of David: 'Behold the cross of our Lord: flee ye adversaries, overcome by the lion of the tribe of Judah, root of David, the wand of Jesse,
saviour of the world, save me ... Christ of cross, defend me.' King
David, according to this view, was a man with whom Richard could
readily identify. Not only was he a ruthless guerrilla leader, capable of
cold duplicity in sending Uriah to his death; he was also a genuine man
of God betrayed by those closest to him, including his predecessor Saul.
Richard's identification with this familiar Old Testament hero, it is
added, would have been reinforced by a reading of the psalms. Many of
the psalms associated with David are marked by a sense of struggle – of
struggle against enemies on all sides and the need to overcome them
with prayer. The David of the penitential psalms, Hughes reminds us, is
a David who feels persecuted: 'But many are my enemies, all without
cause, and many are those who hate me wrongfully, those who repay
good with evil oppose me because my purpose is good' (psalm 37). It is

not unreasonable, he concludes, to suppose that Richard would have identified with David the persecuted man of sorrows.[58] He would have seen David, like himself, as something of an outcast, and this would have lent support to his fighting spirit. When, as king, he found himself becoming ever more unpopular, he would have drawn from the psalms a sense that he alone was right and understood by God. His sense of isolation would have been reinforced. Where, for some laymen, a reading of psalms bred passivity, for Richard it led to a preoccupation with what he considered betrayal. Richard's devotional life led him to develop an embattled mentality: an aggressive sense that he alone was right.

Hughes accordingly gives us a picture of Richard as a man whose piety was essentially introspective and self-referential. In his view, Richard found in his personal religion a way of making sense of the hostility shown to him, and of overcoming it. But how convincing is Hughes's reconstruction? And how accurately has he read the mood of the age? Is he entitled, moreover, to make the use which he does of Richard's book of hours? His account of Richard's piety has aroused fierce controversy among those interested in the king's career. A number of scholars would take strong exception to the highly coloured interpretation which he offers.

Central to Hughes's reconstruction is his assumption that the mystical movement was unique to the north of England. Hughes believes that the religious world of the northern lords was very different from that of their peers in the midlands and south. Northern religion, Hughes argues, was marked by a strain of personal asceticism which encouraged individual isolation and reinforced introspection; Richard absorbed this during his long period of residence in the north in the 1470s. It is doubtful if Hughes's view can be sustained in its entirety in the way he presents it. In recent years a great deal of research has been done on popular piety in the later middle ages, and we now know that the mystical movement was far more widespread in England than Hughes allows. Yorkshire was certainly the seed-bed of its early growth in the fourteenth century. But scarcely inferior in importance was East Anglia, an area which produced two of the most celebrated early mystics, Julian of Norwich and Margery Kempe. Julian, author of the *Revelations of Divine Love*, like Richard Rolle, lived the life of a hermit, while Margery Kempe, a burgess's wife from King's Lynn, wrote an account of her life and journeyings which ranks as one of the great mystical treatises of the period. Away from East Anglia, we find evidence of mystical activity in the east midlands. Walter Hilton, for example, the author of the fine treatise the *Ladder of Perfection*, was a diocesan administrator at Ely and a canon of the Augustinian house of Thurgarton (Nottinghamshire.).[59] The late medieval movement of mystical piety was in fact a far more widely disseminated phenomenon than Hughes allows. Once we take this into account, we can appreciate that the influence of mysticism is likely to have been felt far beyond the north of England. We can take for example a major southern family, the Cobhams of Kent. From their wills we know that some of the Cobham family manifested a personal piety scarcely distinguishable in its essentials from that of their northern counterparts. In mood the Cobhams' piety was austere, penitential and bookish; in some cases too it was marked by a deep sense of personal unworthiness. Joan, the wife of Reginald, Lord Cobham, of Lingfield (d. 1369) was an early exponent of the mixed life. In her widowhood she established a 'holy household', a classic form of the mixed life, nearly a century before Cecily Neville did.[60] In the light of the current reassessment of the mystics, it is doubtful if the distinction between a northern and a southern piety can be sustained in quite the form that Hughes presents it.

Hughes may also be guilty of overstating his case at a later stage of the argument. Central to his interpretation is his view that the mental world of Richard and his circle was very different from that of most of Edward IV's courtiers. Richard and the northerners, he believes, were wedded to an austere piety of detachment, while Edward and the Woodvilles were drawn to the fashionable classical nostrums of fame and worldly honour. Again, it is doubtful if Hughes's argument can be sustained in precisely the form in which he argues it. It is highly unlikely that the distinction between the two groups was actually so sharp. Hughes, in discussing the court, chooses to focus principally on the Woodvilles and their faction. But the Woodvilles, although influential, by no means comprised the whole court. There were many in Edward's entourage who did not share their particular tastes. Moreover, Hughes overlooks the firmly traditional tastes of Edward himself. Edward shared with his younger brother a liking for grand intercessory establishments – colleges, in other words. Where Richard lavished his favour on Middleham and York, Edward did the same on St George's Chapel, Windsor. He refounded and reconstituted Edward III's college and embarked on a lavish rebuilding of the chapel as a Yorkist mausoleum. Nothing could be more traditional or less *avant garde* than that.

But the most serious objection to Hughes's interpretation relates to the use which he makes of Richard's book of hours. It is natural when a volume owned by the king has come down to us to want to make the fullest possible use of it. But interpreting the volume raises problems. As we have seen, it was not actually commissioned by Richard; it was acquired by him second-hand. He had no influence on the formation of its contents (although he did make additions). Any value which the book has for a study of Richard's piety must turn, therefore, on his response to it. And here we enter the realm of conjecture. We simply do not know how the king responded. We cannot even be certain that he read the book. He only acquired it towards the end of his life – perhaps in 1484 or 1485. There are no annotations or marginalia in his hand. It is hardly surprising that Hughes's pages are littered with words such as 'probably' or 'perhaps' or phrases like 'might have' and 'would have'.

But there remains Richard III's own prayer – the prayer with its heavy Old Testament incantations, which Richard added at the end of the book. Other historians besides Hughes have rested weighty interpretative schemes on this. But the prayer, no less than the volume as a whole, raises problems. In the first place, the prayer is not unique to the book. It is found in a number of other books of hours and devotional works of the period. The earliest versions of the text are found in a series of volumes which may be dated to the late fourteenth century. Nearer to Richard's time, it is found in volumes belonging to Ferdinand of Aragon, Prince Alexander of Poland, the Emperor Maximilian I and, in England, the duchess of Exeter.[61] In the light of the evidence for its dissemination, it is difficult to claim for the text any exclusive value as a source for Richard's piety. Moreover, it is difficult to come to any definite conclusions about the effect of the prayer on his actions. To understand how Richard would have reacted to the prayer, we need the rubric – and unfortunately this vital heading is lost: the leaf on which it was written is torn out. It was the rubric which guided the supplicant in his reading and determined how he would respond. Without it, we are effectively lost. We are justified in assuming that the prayer would have

appealed to Richard. And quite possibly he found its references to biblical stories attractive. But beyond that we cannot go.

   The evidence of the prayer book, then, must largely be set aside.
So what other sources are we left with? It is possible that there are lessons to be learned from Richard's intentions for his proposed college at
Middleham (Yorkshire). Richard secured a licence to establish an intercessory college on his chief Yorkshire manor in 1478. His plans were
ambitious.[62] He made provision for a dean, six chaplains, five clerks and
six choristers. In the preamble to the statutes he disclosed something of
the thinking behind his design. He spoke of the mutability of human
fortune, the unworthiness of the individual, and the trials and tribulations which a man faces in this world. The phrases are more than
conventional. Arguably, we hear Richard himself speaking in them:

> Richard, duke of Gloucester ... to whom these presents shall come, greet-
> ing ... Know that it hath pleased Almighty God, Creator and Redeemer of
> all mankind, of His most bounteous and manifold graces, to enable,
> enhance and exalt me His most sinful creature, nakedly born into this
> wretched world, destitute of possessions, goods and inheritaments, to the
> great estate, honour and dignity that He hath now called me unto, to be
> named, knowed, reputed and called Richard, duke of Gloucester, and of
> his infinite goodness not only to endow me with great possessions and of
> gifts of His divine grace, but also to preserve, keep and deliver me of many
> great jeopardies, perils and hurts, for the which and other manifold
> benefits of His bounteous grace and goodness to me, without any desert
> or cause [I] am finally determined, unto the loving and thanking of His
> Deity, and in the honour of His Blessed mother Our Lady St Mary ... and
> of the holy virgin St Alkild [patroness of Middleham] to establish, make
> and found a college within my town of Middleham ...

In this passage Richard articulates his sense that God had especially
favoured him. Although (he says) a younger son, he had been raised to
great heights and honoured with great riches; and thanks to God's
favour he had been delivered from all evil and hurt. Richard's emphasis
on 'great possessions' hints at his sense of destiny and his appreciation
of himself as an elect: an aspect of his piety which Hughes has found in
his prayer. But the contrast which Richard also draws between his present state and his 'nakedness' at birth points to a different aspect: that
fashionable contempt for the flesh which is found in so many wills of

the time. Repeatedly in the fifteenth century testators expressed a loathing and contempt for the flesh. Joan Beauchamp, Lady Bergavenny, for example, in 1435 spoke of 'her simple and wretched body' and Sir William Stourton in 1407 of his 'putrid body, naked as it came into the world except for a linen cloth'.[63] Testators who articulated such sentiments not uncommonly commissioned cadaver tombs – tombs which showed the commemorated as a decaying skeleton. The very wealthy countess of Warwick in 1439, for example, asked to be shown 'completely naked, with nothing on my head and the hair pulled back' on her tomb in Tewkesbury Abbey. To highlight this contrast between the present and future state of the body, testators sometimes arranged to be shown twice on their tombs – on one effigy, usually on the tomb chest, clothed in finery and on a second, beneath, represented as a decaying skeleton. The signs are that Edward IV had wanted to be commemorated in this way. In his will of 1475 he asked for burial 'low in the ground (under a stone) wrought with the figure of Death', with above, in a chantry at first-floor level, a tomb 'with an image of our figure, being of silver and gilt'.[64] If executed, this two-part monument would have been similar in conception to that of the duchess of Suffolk (d. 1475) at Ewelme (Oxfordshire) – which is likewise a double-decker affair. In the light of his statement in the Middleham charter, it is not inconceivable that Richard could have intended such a memorial for himself. It would certainly have given striking visual expression to his sense of the contrast between past and present and future states. But, if such had indeed been his intention, we can hardly conclude that his tastes were any different from those of the Yorkist courtiers. On the contrary, it would simply align him with the tastes of the king himself. In personal religion, there was less separating Richard from his contemporaries than might be supposed.

Even the apparently singular aspects of Richard's piety, then, are not without parallels in the religious mainstream of the age. Indeed, this is a point that can be made more generally. Richard's patronage of religious foundations shows little that distinguishes his taste from that of his contemporaries. Richard chose to bestow his favour on secular colleges. He set in motion the establishment of two grandiose colleges at Middleham and Barnard Castle. Colleges were the most popular form of intercessory foundation in the late middle ages. From the fourteenth century they took the place of the monasteries as the type of institution most favoured by the nobility and greater gentry. Richard's ancestor Edward, duke of York, had founded such a college at Fotheringhay (Northamptonshire.), close to the castle where Richard had been born. Richard's brother Edward IV had refounded the college of St George in Windsor Castle as a great Yorkist mausoleum. Richard was only espousing the conventional tastes of the nobility in establishing his own foundations to ensure the safety of his soul.

In a similar way Richard's attitude to the saints was mostly conventional. Just as most medieval kings looked to the saints to legitimise their ambitions, so too did Richard. An idea of the saints to whom he was most deeply devoted is provided by the Middleham statutes. On Richard's instructions, the two principal feasts to be celebrated at Middleham were those of St George and St Ninian. The provision for St George should occasion no surprise. St George had been adopted as a patron of the English monarchy in the fourteenth century because he stood as a representative of the martial values it espoused. The provision for St Ninian is initially more puzzling. St Ninian, a fifth-century bishop of Whithorn, had been an apostle to the Picts and was the focus of a considerable cult in the north west and on the Borders. Ninian's significance was that he legitimated Richard's ambitions in the north. In the 1470s, when he ruled as a virtual viceroy from Middleham, Richard aspired to a mighty palatinate in Cumberland and Westmorland, and identification with St Ninian would assist in gaining him acceptance. Richard also arranged for Ninian to be honoured at his other projected foundations at York and Barnard Castle, and at Queens' College, Cambridge, to which he lent support. In addition to St Ninian, three other saints with connections with the north were honoured at Middleham. These were St Cuthbert, the patron of Durham and the pre-eminent saint in the north, St Wilfrid, the evangelist to the Northumbrians and focus of a major cult at Hexham and Ripon, and St William, a former archbishop of York whose cult was based at the Minster. The honouring of these saints reflected Richard's emphatically northern interests. Significantly, in his years as king his visits to Canterbury never coincided with any of Becket's feast days.[65] But it should not be supposed that the objects of his devotion were always or exclusively northern. He looked to other saints as well. At Middleham College he made provision for the observance of the feast of St Anthony of Egypt. Although his preference for saints of northern extraction set his piety apart from his brother's, his attitude to the saints' mediatory role was scarcely distinguishable from that of most aristocrats of his day.

If anything at all identifies his religious patronage as distinctive, it is not so much idiosyncrasy of taste as a different quality: a taste for doing things in style. Richard liked grandiosity. He went for gigantism. He never did anything by halves. This is illustrated by the sheer scale of his intercessory foundations. Where most aristocrats were content with calling one institution into being, Richard went for two. Perhaps he feared more for his soul. The communities he established were close to one another, at Barnard Castle and Middleham. Barnard Castle was the larger of the two. Lavishly endowed with lands worth £400 a year, it was fleetingly the grandest foundation of its kind in the palatinate, its establishment consisting of a dean, twelve chaplains, ten clerks, six choristers and a sacristan. Middleham, although less grandly conceived, was still ambitious, with a dean, six chaplains, four clerks and six choristers. But the two colleges did not represent the totality of Richard's patronage. He also proposed a college of no fewer than a hundred priests at York.[66] His intention, it seems, was to revive and re-endow the community of vicars choral at the Minster. His death in 1485, however, brought the scheme to a premature end. Had it been carried to completion, it would have created a clerical establishment without parallel at an English cathedral.

Richard's taste for grandiosity is one very striking characteristic of his piety: he certainly liked doing things on the big scale. But there is another characteristic which stands out – the almost complete absence from his religious patronage of any sense of dynasticism. Most medieval kings or aristocrats felt themselves bound by a rich complex of ties to their ancestors. They saw themselves under obligation to their forebears. They believed those forebears to be dependent on the power of their intercessory prayer. Richard III, however, seems to have been different from his contemporaries. For the most part, he lacked this body of sentiment. Where most of his fellow magnates would arrange intercessory prayer for their ancestors in the family mausoleum, Richard conspicuously did not: he arranged prayer specifically only for his immediate family and his parents; and where most magnates sought burial alongside, or in the midst of, their ancestors, he sought burial, it appears, by himself.[67] For well over half a century the Yorkists had had an established mausoleum at Fotheringhay (Northamptonshire), where he had been born. To this, Edward IV had added a new mausoleum at St George's Chapel, Windsor. But Richard had little or nothing to do with either of these churches.[68] He directed his favour to his northern foundations. In this respect, he showed himself very different from Richard I and Richard II. Both of these kings had evinced a strong dynastic piety. Richard III, by contrast, cut a highly individualist stance. The familial ties to which most of the nobility attached such importance seemingly meant little to him.

So how can we sum up Richard III's piety? And what relationship, if any, was there between the king's religious beliefs and his actions? These are very difficult questions to answer. On the one hand, the evidence of the 'king's prayer' in the book of hours points, however uncertainly, to a troubled mind. But much else that we know about his piety suggests no more than the usual concern for the afterlife. Richard's piety, like that of his contemporaries, was a religion of the saints: he looked to such patrons as Ninian, Cuthbert and Wilfrid to legitimise his ambitions in the north. The religious institutions which he founded were utterly conventional. Like most aristocrats of his day, he concentrated his munificence on chantries and colleges. The most distinctive characteristic of his patronage was its scale: he did nothing by halves.

Yet are we in danger of making Richard's personal religion look too ordinary? Are we in danger of underestimating the distinctiveness of his religious character? Here, after all, was a man who, in the space of a few months in 1483, flouted all the behavioural norms of his age. He overthrew a legitimate minority government, ordered the execution of the king's chamberlain and various other of his counsellors, and was responsible for the murder of two of his own nephews. How could he have justified such terrible deeds to himself? And how could he have overcome the constraining bounds of morality? Was there something strange or unusual about his personal religion after all?

It is hard to resist drawing parallels with the similarly extreme actions of Richard II. This Richard, like his namesake, flouted all the behavioural norms of his age. Richard II, like Richard III, thought nothing of resorting to murder, or semi-judicial murder, when necessary. Richard II,

like Richard III, struck down all who dared to stand in his way without warning. In each case, the key to understanding apparently erratic
political actions may be found in the interplay between politics and
piety. For both kings, piety powerfully reinforced personal political conviction. Both the second and the third Richards believed that they had
the Almighty on their side. Richard II, for example, in his letter to the
count of Holland in 1397 spoke in biblical terms of those rebelling
against him as rebels 'against King Christ the Lord'. Richard III in the
preamble to his Middleham charter articulated a sense of destiny as
God's elect: 'know that it has pleased Almighty God of his most boun-
teous grace to enable, enhance and exalt me ... to the great estate,
honour and dignity to which he has now called me ...' Both men's sense
of identification with the Almighty went further still. Both saw themselves as engaged on a divinely ordained mission of reform. Richard II
felt charged to strengthen and reaffirm royal authority. A century later,
Richard III felt obliged to restore morality to a corrupted political life.
Richard III's moral puritanism, in all likelihood, led him to regard his
brother's alleged pre-contract as an impediment to his nephew's claim
to the throne.

The parallel between the piety of the two kings should not be pressed
too far. There were important differences which should be taken into
account. If it is true, for example, that the piety of both kings was vehe-
ment and embattled, in Richard III's case there was a touch of
vulnerability which his namesake apparently lacked. When Richard III
added to his prayer book the prayer which bears his name, he was hinting at a need for protection which the earlier king did not feel. None the
less, it is the similarities which are bound to impress the observer. In
both kings' piety there was a touch of self-righteousness, even a seeking
after martyrdom. Both kings went to their deaths utterly convinced of
their rectitude. In the case of both kings too, a highly individualist piety
reinforced a sense of isolation. For both kings, it was the world they
inhabited which was at fault, and not they themselves. A piety at once
defiant and embattled translated into a self-conscious and aggressive
style of kingship.

10

Sad Stories of the Death of Kings

On his return from Ireland in the summer of 1399, Shakespeare's Richard II mused on the unhappy fate of so many of England's kings:

> For God's sake let us sit upon the ground
> And tell sad stories of the death of kings:
> How some have been deposed, some slain in war,
> Some haunted by the ghosts they have deposed,
> Some poisoned by their wives, some sleeping killed,
> All murdered.

Shakespeare, *Richard II*, III, 2, 155–60

Each of the three kings named Richard came to a violent, bloody end. Richard I was killed by a stray arrow shot at Chalus in the Limousin, Richard II was murdered in a dungeon at Pontefract, and Richard III was slain on the field of battle at Bosworth. The fact that all three kings died violently was the subject of comment after 1485. The chronicler known as the Crowland Continuator, as we have seen, reflected on this strange historical coincidence.[1] Generally, by the later middle ages Europe's rulers could reckon to die peacefully in their beds. The three Richards constitute notable exceptions. So how are we to explain their deaths? And can we identify a link between them beyond the coincidence of the victims' names?

The first and the third Richards both died in the course of military action – the first Richard while besieging a castle in France and the third while fighting for his crown. Their two deaths occurred nearly three centuries apart. Yet, interestingly, in both periods there was a general sense that the king should be seen at the head of his troops in battle. Kings and princes had always been seen pre-eminently as war leaders. The Conqueror had placed himself in the vanguard at Hastings, and Stephen in like position at Lincoln. In the thirteenth century St Louis was to be at the head of his troops on his Egyptian crusade. For as long as kingship was defined by martial valour, it was expected that the king should lead his men from the front. At Bosworth Richard III would have conceived no other position for himself. In this sense, there was broad continuity in what was expected of a king in the middle ages. It is true, of course, that the circumstances of the two Richard's deaths were in some respects different. Richard I was undertaking an evening patrol at a siege: he was not actually fighting; while Richard III was in the very thick of the fray struggling to vindicate his kingly title. What is important, however, is that both kings insisted on placing themselves at the head of their troops. There was a general belief that to be a king was to be an active commander. While undoubtedly important changes took place in kingship in the middle ages – among them the rise of what is called 'administrative kingship' and the gradual distancing of the king from his subjects – these had remarkably little effect on the martial aspect of kingship. In the fifteenth century, as in the twelfth, the essence of successful kingship was found in the successful practice of arms.

Yet a distinction needs to be drawn between the death of the first Richard and the deaths of his two namesakes. Richard I died as the result of an unfortunate mishap at a siege: he was so bold as to tempt fate by going on patrol without armour. The second and third Richards, however, were violently removed from their thrones. These two kings were the victims of homicide – Richard II murdered on his successor's orders, and Richard III slain by a challenger. It is the deaths of the last two Richards which actually raise the most interesting historical issues. To be a king in late medieval England was evidently to live dangerously. In the century from the 1390s no fewer than four English kings lost their thrones, one of them twice. So why, in this period, was the business of kingship such a risky occupation? Why did the second and third Richards meet such unhappy fates?[2]

At one level it is tempting to say that they were quite simply unsatisfactory rulers: their governance became intolerable to their subjects. By any standard, the two were guilty of appalling cruelty and political misjudgement. Richard II was responsible for the murder of his uncle and the judicial murder of one of his earls, while Richard III, a usurper, had murdered his nephews and executed those who stood by them. The two kings' arbitrary actions went well beyond the bounds what was politically acceptable. Yet it is doubtful if an explanation couched in terms of their insufficiency is by itself adequate. Many other kings in the middle ages ruled badly and yet survived. From the thirteenth century there is the obvious case of King John. John was, by any standard, a cruel and capricious tyrant, more than the equal of Richard II in his vindictiveness, and towards the end of his reign the realm was torn apart by civil war. Yet John died a natural death. Two centuries earlier, there had been the case of Æthelred the Unready. Æthelred's incompetent and factional rule sapped the strength of his kingdom, and left it open to harrying and conquest by the Danes. Yet Æthelred too survived.[3] Across the Channel, we might consider the cases of two French kings who notoriously failed in war against the English – John II and Charles VI. John II, oddly known to history as 'the Good', was defeated and captured by the Black Prince at Poitiers in 1356, while his grandson Charles VI collapsed before the rapid English advance in the years after Agincourt. Each king was utterly incompetent, and Charles, indeed, in his later years was insane. And yet both again survived. No French king between 987 and 1789 suffered the fate of deposition and death. In general, the French kings may be judged to have been no better and no worse in the art of rulership than the English. By itself, then, the fates of the second and third Richards cannot be explained solely in terms of their personal unfitness.

Yet the problem of unfitness cannot altogether be ignored. Somehow a place has to be found for it in any explanation of the kings' fates. Had the two Richards been well regarded by their subjects, or judged effective in the discharge of their duties, they would have survived on their thrones. In reality, they were neither well regarded nor effective; and so they were deposed. The question that has to be addressed, then, is this: why was resort to deposition a peculiarly English characteristic? What made English conditions so very different from French? A secondary level of explanation has to be introduced here. And that, it seems, must relate to the impact of the king's unfitness on his subjects. If the king's actions, however malevolent or ill-conceived, had little or no impact on his subjects, then the king could be left on the throne. If, on the other hand, by his actions he materially damaged his subjects, then he was likely to be removed. To put it another way: the key variable was the structure and organisation of the state. In a highly centralised polity a malevolent or ineffective king was more likely to be removed. In a polity of looser structure there was a greater likelihood that he would survive.

It is this point about relative degrees of centralisation which explains the contrasting fates of England's and France's kings. In the nature of the linkage between their respective centres and localities, England and France could hardly have been more different. England was the most centralised state of medieval Europe. Across wide areas of southern and central England the king's actions were felt by his subjects with a directness and intensity felt nowhere else in Europe. France, by contrast, was relatively decentralised. In large areas of the country a regionally organised layer of princely or noble power separated the king from the local communities. Outside the royal domain, the French king could only initiate action by forging alliances with ducal and comital rulers. In England, certainly, the greater nobility had their zones of influence – or 'countries' as they were called. With a few exceptions, however, these were both scattered and loosely organised. Intermarriage between families and the exercise of royal policy brought about their dispersal. They never formed compact territorial blocks in the way that they did in contemporary France.

The tight administrative mesh which characterised the government of medieval England was largely a creation of the Wessex kings in the late ninth and tenth centuries. A notable characteristic of that government was that it combined the principle of local self-direction with the exercise of supervisory control from the centre. The unit on which the entire system hinged was the shire. The shiring of England, which was effectively complete by the eleventh century, represented an attempt to create a series of units which were both large enough to serve the needs of government and yet small enough to be lacking a regional identity. At the next level down from the shire were units called generally in southern England hundreds and in the north wapentakes, which drew on a long tradition of local corporate action. It was at the level of hundred or wapentake principally that responsibility for peacekeeping lay. In the course of the tenth to the thirteenth centuries, a network of officials came into being to link the localities to the centre. In the shires the pivotal figure was for long the sheriff, an officer who was appointed by the king and was answerable to his ministers for his actions. It was the sheriff's duty to execute writs, levy taxes, collect the county farms, inspect the tithing groups and perform a variety of other duties. By the thirteenth century, as the sheriff's responsibilities increased, he was joined by other officers. The coroner was appointed in 1194, the escheator in 1232, and the keepers (later justices) of the peace in the 1260s. Through the increase of local officialdom, the shires were drawn ever more tightly into the fabric of national government. In the thirteenth century a further important step was taken when the shire was chosen as the unit of representation for parliament. Each time a parliament was called MPs were elected by the shire, and each time one ended statutes were read out to a shire audience. By that slow but seemingly inexorable process by which royal government became stronger, centre and locality were drawn closer together. At the same time, and largely in consequence, the control which the barons exercised over their tenants became weaker. After Henry II's reign, once the royal courts were opened to all free men, the baronial courts went into decline. Judicial power became power exercised by the king's officers. Increasingly, the localities danced to a tune composed at the centre.

In England, then, by the standards of medieval Europe the king's hand rested unusually heavily on his subjects. As early as the tenth or eleventh century, England was a much governed country. It follows that there was considerable potential for a malevolent or incompetent king to damage the interests of his subjects. Yet, if we lay aside the exceptional case of Harold, there is no instance of a king being successfully deposed until the fourteenth century. As we have seen, it can hardly be argued that no unsatisfactory king ruled in those years. The cases of Æthelred II and Stephen spring to mind.[4] So how is the time lag to be explained? If royal government was really as powerful as we have argued, why was no 'bad' king deposed?

Part of the answer is that the pressure of government was neither uninterrupted nor of even incidence. There were safety-valves. In the immediate post-Conquest period the most significant of these was the king's periodic absences in Normandy. On average, the Norman and Angevin kings were in their cross-Channel dominions for between a third and a half of their reigns. These absences did not mean that the pressure of government in England was entirely lifted – the English government, under the direction of the king's chief minister, the justiciar, could operate largely by autopilot. But it did mean that some of the more oppressive burdens were eased. For example, the demands for money and prises made by the itinerant household were removed, while the king's arbitrary interventions in the doing of justice would be much reduced.

A second safety-valve was the admittedly crude one of rebellion. Rebellions by groups of the aristocracy were a regular feature of the political life of medieval England. At the end of Edward the Confessor's reign, the northerners rose in rebellion to secure the removal of Tostig as their earl. In the years after the Conquest, rebellions erupted under the leadership of whoever had a claim to the throne – Duke Robert in the reigns of William Rufus and Henry I, and Matilda in the reign of Stephen. In the reigns of Henry II and Richard I rebellions took the form of violent feuds within the ruling Angevin family. In 1173–74 a mighty rebellion was provoked by Henry II's treatment of his sons: virtually all of the Angevin lands were drawn in. In the next reign a lesser fracas was provoked by the ambitions of Richard's younger brother John. Generally, in the Norman and Angevin periods noble rebellions were never serious enough totally to unsettle the realm, for the forces of crown and opposition were too evenly balanced. Moreover, once a rebellion was overcome, the rebel leaders, after temporary eclipse, were generally restored to favour and a process of reconciliation would take place. Every king found it in his interests to restore harmony. So rebellion, while briefly disruptive, could serve to defuse tension. It provided a means by which resentment and anger found an outlet. A king with a sense of the politically possible would adjust his policies in consequence.

But in the century after the Conquest, as political society became more sophisticated, a less crude means had to be found of seeking release from the pressures of government. By the end of Henry I's reign, one of the most popular of these was the purchase of pardons. In the 1170s and 1180s Henry II's subjects were regularly buying pardons from his officers for a variety of transgressions such as trespass. A not dissimilar tactic was the purchase of exemptions. The wealthier landowners in the twelfth century paid fines to the king to be freed from the geld or to have their assessments reduced. Yet another tactic, in the reign of Richard I, was to purchase a royal office from the king. By the device of purchasing an office – the shrievalty, perhaps – a country gentleman could turn himself from poacher into gamekeeper.

By John's reign, however, there was one source of protection above all which was sought – the purchase of a liberty. When a king granted a liberty, invariably in return for money, the beneficiary gained respite from a particular set of burdens or exactions. Take, for example, suit of court – the obligation on certain landowners to attend sessions of their local court, a burden widely resented. By Richard's reign, the crown was selling exemptions to hundreds of suitors every year. It was much the same with jury service. This too was an obligation widely disliked, and hundreds of exemptions were sought out, and routinely granted, each year. In similar fashion, it was becoming common for individuals to seek release from the operation of the feudal prerogatives of the crown. In the pipe rolls we commonly come across widows paying fines for permission to marry whomever they wished. Shortly after John became king, Nicola Hermingford paid £100 for this right.[5] Where individuals led, communities, in particular urban communities, were not slow to follow. Most of the leading English towns by the mid twelfth century were paying for the right to govern themselves and to elect their own officials. In the countryside local communities came together to defend their own interests. In 1190 the men of Surrey paid Richard I 200 marks for the partial disafforestation of their county, while the men of the Ainsty in Yorkshire paid £100 for the total disafforestation of their wapentake.[6] The securing of local concessions or charters of liberties was an initiative commonly undertaken by towns and countrymen in the twelfth century. It was but a short step from this to securing a national charter of liberties – which is what the barons did, on behalf of the national community, when they sought Magna Carta in 1215.[7]

The growth of demands for immunities points to the growing need of the king's subjects for protection against the increasing intensity of government. The expansion of royal government was a double-edged affair. On the one hand, it brought order to the realm and offered benefits to the subject; on the other, it provoked opposition from communities accustomed to self-regulation. The problem in the twelfth century was that the powers of the crown were effectively unlimited. In the Angevin period, the king was restrained in his actions only by the practicalities of what he could achieve. There was no formal machinery of restraint, no means by which the powers of the crown were balanced against the rights of the subject. The king was accountable to no one.

The only judge of his actions was the Almighty on the Day of Judgement. In the later Saxon and Norman periods rebellion had provided an outlet for the frustrations of the subject, while under Henry II and Richard the purchase of privileges served a similar purpose. But each of these actions sprang from feelings of desperation; each was an admission by the subject that there was no better way of restraining the king. In reality, administrative growth had far outstripped the growth of a culture of political accountability. Not even among the governing elite was there any agreement on the parameters within which the king should operate or on the norms that should govern his behaviour.

Gradually, however, and particularly at the end of the twelfth century, political thinking began to catch up. Paradoxically, the rapid bureaucratisation of Henry II's government was the main contributor to this. The effect of the king's measures – principally, the provision of regular judicial procedures, the standardisation of weights and measures, the growth of a more settled pattern of government – was to encourage the view that the standards of political behaviour which the crown expected of its subjects should be accepted by the crown itself. The confidence of the English political elite in challenging royal demands was much enhanced by the experience of Richard's reign. During the Lionheart's long absences the magnates and ministerial class had governed the realm largely by themselves, indeed discharging their duties with considerable distinction. This experience was to strengthen their resolve in the crisis of John's reign. After John's accession, one by one the traditional safety valves were closed off. The king was now resident in England, Normandy having been lost to the French. At the same time, the price of rebellion had been pushed up: John's fury promised terrible retribution for failed rebels. The baronial class responded in the only way they knew how. They demanded a charter of liberties. Just as they had once demanded charters to secure their own interests, so now they demanded one to protect the interests of the national community as a whole.

Magna Carta, the outcome of this crisis, represented the triumph of one particular response to the growth of royal government in the eleventh and twelfth centuries – the belief that the monarchy could be restrained by constitutional means: by law. Before this time, England had lacked anything resembling a constitution. The king had been free to act in accordance with his will. While it fell to him to enforce the law, he could also override or ignore the law. He could, and did, flout regular or customary procedures through interventions of *vis* and *voluntas* (force and will).[8] There was much debate in this period about the relationship between the king and the law. While it was generally agreed that the king, like everyone else, was subject to God's law, it was unclear how he stood in relation to man-made law. Was he bound by it or not? Before the making of Magna Carta in 1215 the answer was unclear. After it, however, there was no longer any room for doubt. The king operated under the law. The body of rules which applied to the king's subjects applied to the king himself. As the legist 'Bracton' said a generation or two later, 'while the king is below no man, he is below God and the law'.[9] A good deal of English late medieval debate can be seen as revolving around this issue. What kings and their critics were arguing about was the precise relationship between royal authority and the law. Edward II and his critics were certainly at odds on this issue. So too, at the end of the century, were Richard II and those who were ranged against him.

In the circumstances of 1215, however, King John found Magna Carta deeply objectionable. No sooner had he given his assent to it at Runnymede than he was plotting its overthrow. In August 1215 he secured papal release from his oath to uphold the Charter, and in so doing plunged his country into war. The bitter struggle between the king and his opponents was still going on when he died in October 1216. The process by which Magna Carta became a statute had its origins in the minority government of John's son, Henry III. To halt the bitter war with the opposition lords, the minority government needed to make a dramatic gesture. Accordingly, they took over the Charter and reissued it in a form with a broader appeal. The tactic worked. The rebel lords made peace and the war was brought to an end. The Charter was launched on its distinguished career as the foundation stone of the constitution.

A charter which solved the problems of one moment in history, however, might not solve the problems of another. Conditions will always change. Governments face new challenges; and, at the same time, those on whom they bear down seek new safeguards. So it was in the thirteenth century. Magna Carta served the needs of the barons of 1215. Half a century later, however, when the impact of government was very different, its protective value was more limited. Henry III's governments from the 1230s, prevented by Magna Carta from exploiting traditional feudal perquisites, increasingly turned for money to the localities. Ministers found that impressively large sums could be raised by tightening the crown's grip on the shires. So the sheriffs' tourns, hitherto held twice yearly, were held more often; the forest law was tightened up, and eyres (judicial visitations) initiated more frequently.

Against these multiple assaults, the Charter afforded no protection. A new and more radical initiative was needed to bring royal government under control. In the spring of 1258 a set of Provisions was drawn up at Oxford, in response to a crisis provoked by the uneven distribution of royal patronage, which went very much further than the Charter. The entire apparatus of royal government was brought under public supervision. A council was appointed to oversee the king, and the king could initiate no significant act without its approval. As has famously been observed, the king was humiliatingly reduced to a mere figurehead.[10] No measures so radical had been attempted in the Charter. Indeed, it was the fact that the Provisions went so far which was to be their undoing. The king and his friends would never willingly accept them. In 1264, when Henry and his son Edward rallied the royalist lords, they overturned the constraints, and in the following year, after Simon de Montfort's death, the Provisions were abrogated. But the tradition of subjecting the king to accountability by means of statutory or conciliar checks lived on.

When next a crisis broke, half a century later, and a king had to be coerced, it was through much the same machinery. In 1310, just three years after he had become king, Edward II was forced to give assent to the first of the Ordinances. By this major set of proposals he was restrained in a variety of ways: he was limited in his ability to declare war; he had to accept limits on his exercise of patronage, and he was prohibited from levying prises. But Edward always insisted that his assent was given under duress. So predictably, once he had recovered power, as he had by 1321, he threw off the yoke. At Boroughbridge in March 1322 he defeated his hard-line opponents, Lancaster and Hereford, and abrogated the Ordinances. Yet paradoxically Edward's very success was the cause of his ultimate failure. The collapse of the Ordinances showed that constitutional restraint would never succeed. If a king showed himself incorrigibly malign, the only solution was to remove him: which was what Mortimer and the opposition did to Edward five years later. It is hardly coincidence that the last king on whom a statutory check was imposed was the first to suffer deposition.

Deposition, though effective as a remedy, was an admission of constitutional failure, a recognition of the sheer scale of the problems raised by trying to legalise coercion. For a medieval king was, in reality, beyond control. As God's appointee he had full, free and absolute authority to carry out his duties as he saw fit. His exercise of his office was a matter for him and the Almighty alone; he was answerable to no earthly tribunal. His subjects might well expect him to be guided by virtue and to accept their counsel in his exercise of his duties. In practice, however, no means was given to them of obliging him to do this. In an age of personal monarchy, the king was near absolute. He drew on all the authority of his office. He alone could initiate political action. All decisions flowed from him, and all orders were given in his name. No one, not even the most irreconcilable critic, could challenge the rights belonging to him as God's anointed. Moreover, the king was the source of all patronage and the fountainhead of favour. His ability to enrich and reward men gave him immense power. At a practical level, it gave him a decisive edge in any struggle with those opposed to him. For, as any recalcitrant critic like Lancaster must have realised, to cut oneself off from the king was an expensive act of self-denial; the critic could only impoverish himself as a result. The sheer resilience of medieval kingship meant that no opposition lords could make their will prevail for long. In most reigns, most of the time, the monarchy was undoubtedly a force for good. Monarchy was the most dynamic and experimental force in English political society. Yet, in the hands of an incompetent or a malevolent ruler, its influence could be malign, even destructive. The matter of deposition was emphatically not one that jurists and thinkers were keen to talk about. It raised all sorts of difficulties. But there were times when, at least for those who suffered at the king's hands, deposition could not be avoided. In England such a time came at the beginning of 1327, when Edward II was deposed. Edward's rejection of the Ordinances, and the failure of repeated conciliar and statutory attempts to restrain him, made his forcible removal the only available response to the problem of his kingship. Another such moment of decision came three quarters of a century later, when

Richard II was deposed. In Richard's case, as in Edward's, conciliar supervision had been attempted but had not succeeded. Deposition, as on the earlier occasion, was the only course open to those seeking an end to the king's tyranny.

Oddly, although it was the first deposition of a king, that of Edward II was the easier to accomplish. A number of factors assisted Edward's opponents in their efforts to bring about his downfall. In the first place, there was a popular rising on the streets of London, which gave the king's enemies control of the capital and thus of the machinery of government. It was as a result of this that they were able to summon a parliament without the king's consent and even though he was still imprisoned in the midlands. Secondly, Edward himself gave up the struggle to keep his crown early on. Unlike his great grandson three-quarters of a century later, he did not hold out until the very last moment. When he was captured in South Wales, he simply burst into tears. Thirdly, and most importantly, the direct line of succession to the throne was not broken. When Edward was deposed, his son simply took his place. The dynastic principle was not challenged. It is true that Isabella and Mortimer were embarrassed by what they had done. They and their advisers, like their Lancastrian heirs later, dressed up what was a deposition as effectively an abdication; the pretence was made that Edward's resignation had come before his deposition by the estates.[11] But there was virtually no opposition to what the two did: they were carried along by a tidal wave of popular approval. Nor was there a great deal of theoretical debate about the deposition. The attitude of most contemporaries was akin to Macbeth's: 'If it were done when 'tis done, 'twere well it were done quickly'.

The situation three quarters of a century later, on Richard's downfall, was very different. Not only was Richard altogether more resistant to the humiliating fate which his enemies wished on him. There was also the problem that this time the royal line of succession was being diverted. Henry was not Richard's heir apparent. He was not even the closest male to him by the common law rules of inheritance: Edmund Mortimer, earl of March, a descendant of Edward III's second son, Lionel of Clarence, took precedence over the scions of Lancaster. Though of the blood royal, Henry was really just the leader of a successful coup. Richard's removal raised far trickier issues for the victorious party than his great grandfather's had in 1327. The questions avoided in 1327 could be ignored no longer. How could the act of deposition be justified? How could something wholly illegitimate be dressed up to look legitimate? These were the issues with which the Lancastrian propagandists grappled in the summer of 1399.

Fortunately, one member of the Lancastrian group has left us an insider's account of the debates and deliberations that took place.[12] Adam of Usk, our informant, was a doctor of laws and a clerk in the service of Archbishop Arundel. Joining the Lancastrians in Cheshire, he was appointed to the committee that advised on the procedure for deposition. He tells us that consideration was given to the Crouchback legend, the fiction that Edmund Crouchback, first earl of Lancaster, had been the elder and not the younger brother of Edward I, but had been passed over for the crown because of an alleged deformity. The advisory committee, however, Adam says, decided not to make use of the legend because it would have challenged the legitimacy of England's kings over the previous century. Instead, a different way of proceeding was found. It was decided to follow the precedent of Pope Innocent II's deposition of the Emperor Frederick II in 1245. Frederick had incurred the pope's enmity for a range of reasons – his political independence, his dominance of southern Italy, and his opposition to papal policy in the peninsula. It would have been possible for Innocent to deprive him of the government of the empire (while allowing him retention of his title) by claiming that he was 'useless' and 'insufficient'. He settled, however, on removing him from the throne altogether; and, to do that, he needed to demonstrate his cruelty and tyranny. A list of charges was accordingly drawn up accusing him, among other crimes, of tyranny, perjury, sacrilege, and suspicion of heresy. The sentence against Frederick was published by the papal chancery in the bull 'Ad apostolicae dignitatis', under the title 'De re judicata'. Adam tells us that the bull was known to members of his committee. There can be little doubt, as Caspary has shown, that it provided the model for Richard's deposition.[13] There were echoes, conscious or unconscious, of the articles of 1327 in the emphasis laid in the opening declaration on the king's insufficiency. However, the case against Richard was essentially one that had its basis in canon law.

That case was summarised in thirty-three somewhat randomly

assorted articles.[14] If they are rearranged in thematic order, it can be seen that they fall into three groups. A number refer to the Appellant crisis of thirteen years before, when the king had connived at the destruction of the opposition lords: that he forced the judges to give compliant answers to the questions put to them about the legal basis of royal power (clause 2); that he assisted Robert de Vere, duke of Ireland, in plotting the destruction of the lords (clause 3); and that he was involved in the deaths of the duke of Gloucester and the earl of Arundel (clause 4). Many other of the clauses related to his conduct of government in the last years of the reign: that he had appointed personal retainers of his as sheriffs (clause 13); that he had kept those sheriffs in office for longer than the statutory one year (clause 18); that he had raised loans which he had not repaid (clause 14); that he had imposed taxes in time of peace which he had spent on his own pleasure (clause 15); that he had acted in accordance with his own arbitrary will, even proclaiming that the laws were in his mouth and, at other times, that they were in his breast (clause 16); that he had extracted 'blank charters' from his subjects (clause 18); that he had manipulated parliamentary elections (clause 19); that he had suppressed open expressions of counsel from his magnates (clause 23); that he had taken the crown jewels with him on his expedition to Ireland (clause 24); and that he had contravened the clauses of Magna Carta in his use of the court of Chivalry (clauses 26 and 27). A final group of clauses related to his treatment of Duke Henry, his cousin and supplanter. These were clause 11, that he had halted the duel with Mowbray at Coventry; and clause 12, that he had revoked the letters allowing Henry to claim his inheritance on the death of father, John of Gaunt.

What legal purpose the charges were seen as serving is hard to say. As in the charges against the Emperor Frederick a century before, the general aim was to prove that the king was a tyrant. Yet, strangely in the circumstances, the word tyranny never once appears. The omission may have been deliberate. The charge of tyranny would probably have been difficult to sustain; and in the eyes of 'men of action', it was an issue probably best passed over in silence.[15] It is interesting that charges of tyranny were never brought against any kings of France either. Nonetheless, there was a widespread perception among his subjects that Richard was a tyrant. Walsingham articulated the general view when, in his account of 1397, he said that in that year Richard began to 'tyrannise' his people.[16] So what did contemporaries understand by the notion of tyranny? And how may the deposition articles be understood as an indictment of tyranny?

The contemporary view of tyranny was clear: tyranny was a perversion of legitimate rulership. Rulers, it was held, were instituted for the sake of peoples, and not peoples for rulers. Rulership was based, if no more than implicitly, on the general consent of the governed. Rulership was subordinate to the laws, to which legitimate rulers were themselves subject; and its sole purpose was the protection and advancement of the common good. When a ruler abandoned advancement of the common good for personal aggrandisement, employing arbitrary rule in the process, he became a tyrant. The legitimate ruler – the true ruler – was a servant of right and justice, neither harsh nor familiar. The tyrant, on the other hand, was a second Herod, the slave of his arbitrary will.[17]

This body of ideas lay at the heart of virtually all late medieval discussions of tyranny. Some of the most elaborate treatments of the subject were written in Italy. The reason for this was very simple. It was in Italy that writers could treat the subject by direct observation. In northern and central Italy tyranny and legitimate government existed side by side. Milan under the Visconti was perhaps the most striking example of tyranny, while Florence to its south saw itself as the exemplar of constitutional legitimacy – in this case, republican legitimacy. But most late medieval discussions of tyranny drew not only on direct observation; they also drew on the writers of Classical Antiquity. The works of Aristotle and Plutarch were particularly influential. The description of tyranny offered by Bartolus of Sassoferrato, a fourteenth-century jurist, was essentially second-hand Plutarch. Bartolus listed ten characteristics of tyrannical rule: the destruction of rivals, banishment of wise men, ruin of study and education, prohibition of private associations and lawful public meetings, maintenance of informers, impoverishment of citizens to keep them supine, the use of foreigners as a personal bodyguard, and the provocation of wars abroad to weaken internal resistance at home. This list of characteristics had direct antecedents in Plutarch. None the less, it is undeniable that many of those characteristics could be recognised in fourteenth-century Italy. At the end of his treatise, Bartolus added his own summing-up. The test of a tyrant, he said, is that his actions 'are not directed towards the common good but to his own advantage, and that means to rule unjustly – as is the case *de facto* in Italy'.[18] Forty years later the chancellor of Florence, Coluccio Salutati, argued much the same, laying stress on the distinction between legitimate and illegitimate rule:

> A tyrant is either one who usurps a government, having no legal title for his rule, or one who governs proudly and unjustly, or does not observe law or equity; just as, on the other hand, he is a lawful prince upon whom the right to govern is conferred, who administers justice and maintains the law.[19]

Contemporary writing on tyranny by the Italian jurists and others found ample reflection in the articles drawn up against Richard. It appears to have been the general aim of the articles to prove that Richard was a tyrannical ruler. Accordingly, nearly every aspect of the contemporary lexicon of tyranny was alluded to. The notion that Richard was a tyrant who ruled not for the common profit but in accordance with his own interests was embodied in the articles relating to his misuse of taxation (clauses 1, 15). The connected notion that he sought the destruction of his domestic enemies was reflected in clauses 2 to 4 (that he encompassed the destruction of the duke of Gloucester and the earls of Arundel and Warwick). The further aspect of tyranny that the tyrant appropriated his subjects' property was reflected in clauses 7, 14, 15, 21 and 22 (that Richard charged twice for pardons, exacted forced loans, levied taxes in time of peace, extracted 'blank charters', and seized transport equipment for his expedition to Ireland). A final characteristic of tyranny – that he placed himself above the law, ruling in accordance with his own will – was the subject of the last set of clauses, 16–20, 26, 27 (he declared that the laws were in his mouth, kept sheriffs in office for longer than the statutory twelve months, interfered with parliamentary elections, made sheriffs swear an unaccustomed oath, overrode the terms of Magna Carta, and declared that lands and tenements were held by his will).

Taken together, the deposition articles provide a comprehensive indictment of Richard's unjust kingship. Surprisingly perhaps, there appears to have been little or no factual distortion in them. They simply recorded what the king had done. In his last years Richard had behaved as a tyrant; so he stood condemned as a tyrant. None the less it would be wrong solely to interpret the articles to the background of contemporary debates about tyranny. As has been shown, the articles also show an awareness of larger principles.[20] They assumed, for example, that the king should abide by the Great Charter, accept counsel from the magnates, and rule for the common good. They also affirmed parliament's unique status in England as the setting for lawmaking and the offering of redress; and, while they recognised the freedom of the king's estate, they never the less maintained that there were limits to the exercise of the king's prerogative. The principles underlying the articles were principles of universal validity. Yet in the end it is the indictment of tyranny that makes the deepest impression on the mind. English writers and politicians had hitherto contributed relatively little to the contemporary debate about tyranny. This is not to suggest that they were necessarily unaware of it. Quite the contrary: Chaucer, one of the sharpest commentators of the age, had considered the character of tyranny in the Prologue to the *Legend of Good Women*, while more significantly in the present context Archbishop Arundel, a key actor in 1399, had actually met Chancellor Salutati of Florence in Italy that year and may have discussed tyranny with him.[21] If Chaucer's work may be said to attest a general familiarity with ideas of tyranny in England, Arundel's meeting points to the possibility of direct influence from abroad; for, through Arundel, Italian ideas may have found their way to England. At the very least, it should occasion no surprise that it was in England that the act of deposition was carried out. For in the highly centralised English polity the potential for tyranny was greater than in almost any other polity of the age.

Richard II's deposition in 1399 ushered in almost a century of unparalleled political instability in England. For the act of deposition once carried out – or, rather, carried out twice – was easier the third, fourth or fifth time. In the ninety or so years following Richard's removal, no fewer than three kings were forcibly removed – Henry VI (twice), Edward V and Richard III. England acquired an unenviable reputation among her neighbours for instability. In 1444 Jean Juvenal des Ursins, archbishop of Rheims, spoke of 'the habit of the English of evilly killing their kings', while forty years later Guillaume de Rochefort, the chancellor, claimed that the English had had twenty-six changes of dynasty since the foundation of their monarchy.'[22] Both men thought the English habit of deposition 'odd'. Frenchmen were, by contrast, more loyal to their kings. Yet the realm of England was both rich and well ordered. For the peasantry and skilled artisan class, indeed, the period was one of unparalleled prosperity. So what, in the state of England, had gone wrong?

The new dynasty – the Lancastrian – had got off to a promising enough start. Henry IV was swept to power on the crest of a great wave of popular goodwill. Although in his early years he was plagued by repeated challenges to his title from the Percies, who were over-ambitious in the north, he successfully withstood their assaults. When he died in 1413, he passed a secure crown to his son Henry V. The latter in the course of his brief reign raised the dynasty to unparalleled heights of renown. His remarkable triumphs in France seemed to indicate the blessing of the Almighty on his cause. Yet in the next reign the curse of factional discord reappeared. Henry VI's incompetence and increasingly partisan rule led to the dynastic question being reopened. After a popular uprising in 1450 and an attempted Yorkist putsch two years later, the legitimacy of the Lancastrian line was finally challenged. In 1460 Richard, duke of York claimed the throne. His claim was rejected by the Lords, and later in the same year he was killed in battle. But in the following year his son became King Edward IV. The long period of intermittent civil strife known as the Wars of the Roses had begun.

The Wars of the Roses were to be far less productive of constitutional novelty than earlier civil struggles. No radical new constitutional thinking emerged; nor were any innovative ways of dealing with the problem of an inadequate king proposed. In the crises of the thirteenth and fourteenth centuries fresh ideas had been broached on how the king could be held to account by the political community. As we have seen, in 1399 Richard II's deposition had led to the elaboration of a doctrine of tyranny. But no such advances in thinking were made in the fifteenth century. When a king was removed, it was for quite different reasons from those invoked a century before.

The principal justification offered for deposing a king in this era was dynastic right. Kings were removed not for being tyrants but for being of the wrong lineage. The key issue was their blood line. It may have been the case that a king had ruled tyrannically or incompetently; and his tyranny, or incompetence, moreover, may very well have been the real reason for his deposition. But his failings as a ruler were never given as the public reason for deposing him. The public justification was different: it was that another claimant had a better title. Once that rival claimant was put on the throne, all would be well.

The dynastic issue, which dominated the politics of the fifteenth century, had its origins in the events of 1399. Henry Bolingbroke's seizure of the crown had broken the direct line of succession. Henry's claim to the crown came through his father John of Gaunt, 'time honoured Lancaster', the third surviving son of Edward III.[23] But there was another nobleman (very young at the time) with a better claim – Richard II's heir male, Edmund Mortimer, earl of March. Mortimer was descended from Lionel of Antwerp, duke of Clarence, Edward III's second son; his grandmother was Clarence's daughter. In the middle of the fifteenth century the representative of the March line was Richard, duke of York, Earl Edmund's nephew. It was of no consequence that York's claim came through the female line: in England, unlike France at this time, transmission through females was allowed. Technically, the Yorkist line enjoyed precedence over the Lancastrian. Accordingly, when the duke finally challenged Henry VI's kingship in 1459, he did so in terms of blood: he claimed to be king by direct descent from Edward III. When his son repeated his claim – successfully – in the following year, he did so on the same grounds. The attraction of couching a claim in these terms was that it left the position of the crown intact; the only matter in dispute related to the question of its holder.

The tactic of challenging the king's title made it possible for Edward IV to snatch the crown from the Lancastrians in 1461. A generation later, it provided the means for another claimant, this time a less obvious one, Henry Tudor, to snatch the crown from Richard III. In each case, what was involved was a transfer of power from one dynasty to another. But how could the deposition of a king by another member of the same family be justified? This was the problem which Richard, duke of Gloucester (as he then was) faced in 1483. How could his removal of his own nephew be justified? Would not a challenge to his nephew implicitly be a challenge to his own position?

Richard's appreciation of his difficulty is indicated by his shifting response to it. Initially, it appears, his tactic was to challenge his nephews' claim through their father. According to Mancini, Richard maintained that Edward IV had been a bastard and, as a result, his sons could not inherit the crown; Richard himself was his father's only legitimate son: the physical resemblance between them bore witness to this. Accordingly, the argument concluded, he should be the next king 'as his legitimate successor'.[24] The difficulty with a claim couched in these terms was that it constituted a shameless assault on the virtue of Richard's own mother, the Duchess Cecily – a lady who was renowned for her piety. Doubtless for this reason, in the later propaganda the grounds for the claim shifted. In the later version, it was actually Edward's *sons* who were bastards. According to the Crowland writer, Richard had the story circulated that Edward IV's marriage was invalid because he was already pre-contracted to Lady Eleanor Butler, a lady at court.[25]

The fully developed version of Richard's claim, however, rested on more than just a challenge to the legitimacy of his brother or nephews. Richard launched a frontal assault on the very morality and integrity of his brother's regime. He presented his case with almost puritanical fervour. Edward, he claimed, was under the immoderate influence of the Woodvilles. In former times, kings had been surrounded by God-fearing ministers and councillors, men committed to impartial justice and the common good; and as a result there had been order at home and victories abroad. But more recently those 'who had the governance of the land, delighting in adulation and flattery, followed the counsel of persons insolent, vicious and of inordinate avarice, despising the counsel of good, virtuous and prudent persons'. Because of this, the prosperity of the realm had been decreased, felicity turned to misery, and 'the Law of God and Man confounded'. The laws of the Church had been broken and justice set at nought, with a consequent growth of murders, extortions and oppressions, so that no man was sure of his life, land and livelihood, nor of his wife, daughter or servant, 'every good maiden and woman standing in dread to be ravished and defouled'. Still worse, there had been inward discords and battles, and the destruction of the nobility of the land. In the wake of all this, the matter of Edward IV's pre-contract was invoked almost as an afterthought. Edward and Elizabeth, it was alleged, were never validly married; their life together was conceived 'sinfully and damnably in adultery'. In consequence, their children were illegitimate. And since Clarence's children were disqualified by their father's attainder, Richard was the rightful king of England.[26]

In the composition of this remarkable piece of special pleading Richard drew on every weapon in his armoury. While denouncing his brother in terms of moral righteousness, he pitched a plea for his own qualities: his 'great wit, prudence, justice, princely courage and memorable and laudable acts in divers battles'. But the case as a whole was unconvincing. Although it was possible to accept Edward's lust and perhaps, too, the Woodvilles' greed, the general picture of Edward's regime, which his brother presented, was a travesty. Moreover, there were no certain grounds for supposing Edward's sons to be bastards. Richard himself never produced any evidence to substantiate his charge. The French writer Philippe de Commynes named Bishop Stillington of Wells as the king's source, but whether or not this was the case is unclear.[27] At any rate, no other contemporary is recorded as making the allegation, and there was no shortage of those hostile to Edward who could have done so. There can be little doubt that the charge was a fiction.

In choosing to traduce his brother's regime in this way, Richard consciously claimed the moral high ground. Very likely, he was driven by the strong moral puritanism which was a characteristic of his piety. But he was sensible enough to appreciate that he was likely to be judged on the same high ground himself. Accordingly, he deliberately cultivated an image of the virtuous prince. It was a task that he accomplished with some skill. From the outset, he stressed his concern for proper justice. He set a reforming agenda. In June 1483 he summoned the judges, 'commanding them in right strait manner that they justly and duly minister his law without delay or favour'.[28] A couple of weeks later later, 'he sent the lords into their countries', instructing them to see that 'the countries where they dwelled [were] well guided and that no extortions were done to his subjects'. In the aftermath of Buckingham's rebellion in October he again stressed his concern 'to see due administration of justice' and to ensure that everyone 'finding himself grieved, oppressed or unlawfully wronged' should 'make a bill of his complaint'. The king's commitment to good justice found expression in the legislation of his only parliament. Measures were taken to prohibit benevolences (arbitrary taxes), to give suspects the right of bail, and to protect the rights of purchasers of lands by outlawing secret fines. More than a few of the king's contemporaries were impressed by his efforts. John Rous, chaplain of the earls of Warwick, said that Richard earned 'the thanks of God and the love of all his subjects, rich and poor', while Bishop Langton of St David's remarked that he had never approved 'the condition of any prince as well as his; God has sent him to us for the weal of us'.[29]

Yet, for all his efforts, Richard failed in his attempts to present a positive image. For one insuperable obstacle stood in his way – his association with the murder of the princes. The princes had last been seen in the grounds of the Tower during the summer. According to the *Great Chronicle* of London, they 'were seen shooting and playing in the garden sundry times' in the mayoralty of Edmund Shaw (before 28 October). After that time, by implication, they were seen much less – or not at all. Mancini, an Italian visitor to England, was concerned for their fate as early as mid July. Well before he left England in that month, the princes, he later wrote, 'were withdrawn into the inner apartments of the Tower and were seen more and more rarely behind the bars and windows, till at length they ceased to appear at all'.[30] Rumours of the princes' deaths were already circulating by the year's end. George Cely reported that he had heard that Edward V might be dead not long after 13 June, and certainly before his uncle claimed the throne.[31] The Crowland chronicler, writing in about 1486, recalled how the rumour arose in September 1483 that 'the princes, by some unknown manner of destruction, had met their fate'.[32] Some early reports went further, stating quite categorically that the princes were no longer alive. Robert Ricart, recorder of Bristol, entered in his *Kalendar* under the year ending 15 September 1483 that 'in this year the two sons of King Edward were put to silence in the Tower of London'.[33] Shortly after 1485 the anonymous compiler of a genealogy of English kings concluded his work by accusing Richard, with his accomplice Buckingham, of murdering the princes.[34] A London citizen, in some historical notes written before the end of 1488, noted that 'they were put to death in the Tower of London' in the mayoral year ending November 1483.[35] John Rous, writing in 1489, reported that Richard killed the princes within three months of welcoming Edward V at Stony Stratford on 30 April; Richard, he wrote, 'received his lord king Edward V blandly with embraces and kisses, and within three months or a little more he killed him with his brother'.[36] Rumours to similar effect reached France. In a speech to the estates general in 1484 the chancellor of France, Guillaume de Rochefort, reminded his audience how Edward IV's sons had been murdered and the crown seized by the murderer.[37]

More specific information suggesting Edward V's early death is given in two English sources which are near contemporary. In the first of these, the Anlaby family cartulary, a scribe writing after 1509 states categorically that Edward V died on 22 June 1483.[38] The reliability of the Anlaby document may be questioned given the writer's misdating of the death of the princes' father, Edward IV. Yet, on the other hand, an accurate record is made not only of the dates of all other kings but also the birth and accession dates of Edward V himself. In the second source, a king list now in the Middleton Collection in Nottingham University Library, Edward is said to have been murdered on the day after his uncle took possession of the throne – in other words, 27 June.[39] There are difficulties in reconciling these sources with the evidence of Mancini and the London chronicler that the princes were alive in early July. Mancini's chronology, however, is imprecise: he simply says the princes were seen less and less by the time that he left – which was no later than mid July; and it is undeniable that he was already fearful for their safety by then. But the Middleton king list itself raises problems. It gives, in addition to the date of the king's death, the strange information that Edward V's body 'submersum fuit' – meaning, perhaps, 'was drowned'. There is no other mention of such action, and it is hard to reconcile with More's account of the bodies being buried. The safest approach is probably to interpret the note – and that in the Anlaby cartulary – as evidence of rumour rather than of hard fact. What is undeniable is that all the sources point to one thing: the widespread suspicion in the summer of 1483 that the princes were dead.

But were they indeed dead? And, if they were, did their uncle have them despatched? Or were others involved? These are questions to which it is almost impossible to give a satisfactory answer. The evidence is not only inadequate and inconclusive; it is also muddled and highly contradictory. No modern jury would be convinced by it. Yet at the same time the issue continues to fascinate. The one thing that can be said for certain is that after 1483 the princes were never seen again. The argument of Richard's defenders is that someone else was responsible for their despatch. The name most often mentioned is that of Henry Stafford, duke of Buckingham.[40] Buckingham certainly had a motive, for he had a claim to the throne himself through his great-grandmother, Thomas of Woodstock's daughter.[41] But it is unlikely that Buckingham would have taken so drastic a step as assassination without seeking the king's prior approval. To accuse Buckingham is thus indirectly to accuse Richard himself again. Richard's defenders have often suggested that Henry VII was responsible. Henry, it is true, had no more interest in seeing the princes alive than Richard himself had. But, were he the murderer, would Elizabeth of York have been content, as she was, to marry him – she being none other than the princes' sister? It seems unlikely, to say the least. Any dispassionate observer, reviewing the evidence, is bound to conclude that Richard himself is the likeliest candidate for the crime. Perhaps the most telling argument against him is that he never once produced the princes in public. In the summer of 1483, when rumours that he had despatched the princes were rife, fatally undermining his kingship, he could have silenced the talk by putting the two boys on show. Yet he never did so. His failure in this respect is damning. It may also be significant that, when the southern rebels rose against him in the autumn of 1483, they quickly switched their support from the princes to Henry Tudor. The rebels obviously believed the princes to be dead. There can hardly be any doubt as to whom they held responsible.

In politics, it is said, perception is all. And rarely is this truer than in respect of the murder of the princes. Richard was fatally discredited by his association with their disappearance. People in London felt enormous sympathy for the boys. Mancini tells us of public displays of grief in the capital. 'Many men', he said, 'burst into tears and lamentations when mention was made [of Edward V] after his removal from men's sights'.[42] Another contemporary, John Argentine, the king's physician, expressed his feelings in Old Testament terms. He said dramatically that the young Edward V was like 'a victim prepared for sacrifice'.[43] To others, another biblical analogy – the Massacre of the Innocents – sprang to mind. In a marginal note in the *Great Chronicle of London* a scribe entered the words 'Mors innocentium', the death of the innocents. Henry VII, in his indictment of Richard in his first parliament, spoke of

Richard 'shedding infants' blood'. With the princes cast in the role of the biblical innocents, Richard was inevitably seen as the new Herod. In 1486 a Welsh bard, lamenting what he called 'the boar's' murder of Christ's angels, spoke ironically of 'the bravery of cruel Herod'.[44] For Richard, the identification with Herod was damning. Herod was the ultimate biblical model for tyranny. The implication was that Richard himself was a tyrant.

The charge of infanticide effectively undermined Richard's search for legitimacy. He could not shake off the mantle of the wicked uncle. To compound his problems, by 1484 he faced charges of tyranny on a different score – 'administrative tyranny'. The criticism was made that he had trampled on the rights of the nobility and the gentry. In fifteenth-century England there was a long and well-established tradition of 'self-government at the king's command' – that is to say, of local men being left to run local affairs. Richard challenged this. In the aftermath of Buckingham's revolt, he intruded northerners into positions of authority in the south. The problem which he faced was his acute lack of grass-roots support in the south. Buckingham's revolt had left the counties of southern England bereft of their natural leaders. The revolt's heartland had been the long belt of counties from Cornwall to Kent. Once the rebellion was over, as it was by October, Richard had to find new leaders for southern society. To do so, he turned to his northern retainers. As the Crowland Continuator wrote,

> [In the parliament of 1484] attainders were made of so many lords and men of high rank ... that we do not read of the like being issued by the Triumvirate even of Octavian, Antony and Lepidus. What immense estates and patrimonies were collected into the king's treasury in consequence of this measure! All of which he distributed among his northern adherents whom he planted in every spot throughout his dominions to the disgrace and lasting sorrow of all the people in the south who daily longed more and more for the hoped for return of their ancient rulers, rather than the present tyranny of these people.[45]

But those 'ancient rulers' to whom the Crowland writer referred were gone – the victims of Richard's sweeping Act of Attainder. In their places came men from the north. Richard divided southern England into three main areas, in which he deployed different groups of men.[46] In the south-eastern counties – Kent and Sussex – he deployed some of his closest intimates: Sir Robert Brackenbury, the constable of the Tower, from County Durham, and Robert Percy, Ralph Ashton, William Mauleverer and Marmaduke Constable, all from Yorkshire. Into the central southern counties of Berkshire, Wiltshire and Hampshire he intruded John Hoton, William Mirfield and John Saville, all of them again Yorkshiremen; and in the four south-western counties, John, Lord Scrope, Richard, Lord Fitzhugh, Robert Markenfield and Edward Redman, all Yorkshiremen, and Ralph, Lord Neville, from County Durham. As a consequence of their acquisition of estates in southern England, these men were quickly appointed to offices and commissions in their counties of adoption. In November 1483 William Mauleverer was appointed escheator and justice of the peace in Kent, Edward Redman sheriff of Somerset and Dorset, and Thomas Huddleston sheriff of Gloucestershire. In the following year Thomas Mauleverer was appointed sheriff of Devon and John Musgrave sheriff of Wiltshire, while a Yorkshireman, Sir Thomas Fulford took over from Edward Redman in Somerset and Dorset. Among the many other northerners granted lands in the south and whose names appear on the commissions of the peace and other local commissions were Richard's close ally and counsellor Richard Ratcliffe, Thomas, Lord Stanley, and the Yorkshire knights, John Nesfield, John Broughton and John Savage.[47] These intrusions and appointments not only upset the balance of local society; they also violated the time-honoured tradition of local government by local men. Richard was challenging the interests of those on whom the 'politic rule' of the realm was held to depend. In this sense, as well as in the sense of being a usurper, he could be seen as ruling without popular consent. To many, his undermining of the local elites was part of what constituted tyranny.[48]

Richard's alienation of the southern gentry was a major element in his defeat at Bosworth. Bereft of support in a key area of his realm, he lacked the strength to see off his challenger. Henry thus found himself the unlikely beneficiary of Richard's regional policy. In the middle ages, particularly from the twelfth century, there was much debate about what to do with a ruler who was a tyrant. Was it legitimate, thinkers asked, for his subjects to kill him? Or was it their duty always to obey him? The answers given to these questions were various. In France the position most commonly taken was that obedience was unconditional.

According to Jean Masselin writing in the 1480s, the good subject did
not rebel; rebellion was no option for him; his only hope was to be
found in submission and the working of God's wrath on the tyrant's
will. Jean de Terre-Vermeille, half a century earlier, arguing for the obedience of the members of the body politic to the head and the will, said
that rebellion was unnatural: more than that, it was sacrilegious. Jean
Gerson agreed with him.[49] In England, however, opinion was divided.
In the fifteenth century there were some like the author of the *Somnium
Vigilantis* who believed that nothing but unquestioning obedience could
be justified.[50] Some three centuries earlier, however, at least one English
writer had advocated tyrannicide. This was John of Salisbury, Becket's
secretary and the most able English thinker of his day. In his celebrated
Policraticus, a wide-ranging political tract, John on several occasions
urged the killing of tyrants. Near the beginning, John cited Cicero – not
to mention St Matthew's Gospel – in support of the argument for the
killing of tyrants; later, retreating a little from this position, he justified
tyrannicide as a last resort. There were times, admittedly, when John
seemed worried by what he said. At one point he warned that poison
was on no account to be used, while at another he maintained that
prayer was the most effective weapon against a tyrant. Even so, in his
tract we find evidence of a different kind of thinking from that in
France. In John's defence of tyrant-slaying some would have found a
justification for the slaying of the tyrant king, Richard.

What conclusions can be drawn from this survey of kingly regicide in
late medieval England? A couple of lessons stand out. The most obvious
of these is that the deaths of the second and the third Richards were
connected. The deposition of Richard II inaugurated nearly a century of
political instability, which reached its climax in 1485 in the death of
Richard III. Had Richard II not been deposed, there would have been
no Richard III, or at least not a Richard III in 1483. This is not to say
that there would have been no Yorkist dynasty. Almost certainly, there
would have been. If Richard had remained childless, the crown would
have passed on his death to his Mortimer heir, and from the Mortimers
on their extinction in the male line to the Yorks. Richard, earl of Cambridge, and not Richard of Gloucester, would have become Richard III,
and his son Richard, duke of York, Richard IV. The Yorkist dynasty, in

all likelihood, would have enjoyed a far longer period in possession of the throne. Duke Richard of York would have lived his full span (avoiding death in civil war), delaying the accession of his son, Edward IV. Edward, spared the pains of exile, would probably have been less given to excess in later life and would have lived longer. Richard, duke of Gloucester, would then have been unlikely to have seized the throne. If we accept this counter-factualised narrative of events, we can see that Richard II's deposition changed everything. By opening the dynastic question, it paved the way for the later depositions.

A second obvious conclusion is that to rule England in the late middle ages was to live dangerously. England's kings in this period proved singularly vulnerable to political challenge. Because of the considerable resources of which they disposed, they wielded immense power: Richard II's reshaping of the territorial map of England after 1397 was witness to that. Yet that great power was simultaneously a strength and a weakness. When a king had the capacity to affect the lives of his subjects as directly as a king of England did, the question arose of how his exercise of his authority was to be limited. In the thirteenth century, the mechanism generally employed by baronial oppositions had been to impose a council – in other words, to curb the king's powers by constitutional means. But the speed and completeness with which successive kings had recovered the initiative had shown that mechanism to be ineffective. By the fourteenth and fifteenth centuries a different solution to the problem was found – that of deposition: of changing the king, not restraining him. Although the language used in fifteenth-century deposition processes was the language of dynasticism, the real issue at stake was the king's fitness to hold office.

Yet there is also a less obvious lesson to be learned. Shakespeare in his history cycle portrayed fifteenth-century England as a kingdom at odds with itself. Towards the end of *Richard II*, the bishop of Carlisle utters this prophetic warning:

> My Lord of Herford here, whom you call king,
> Is a foul traitor to proud Herford's king,
> And if you crown him, let me prophesy –
> The blood of English shall manure the ground,
> And future ages groan for this foul act,
> Peace shall go sleep with Turks and infidels,

And, in this seat of peace, tumultuous wars
Shall kin with kin, and kind with kind, confound.
Disorder, horror, fear, and mutiny,
Shall here inhabit, and this land be call'd
The field of Golgotha and dead men's skulls –
O, if you raise this house against this house,
It will the woefullest division prove
That ever fell upon this cursed earth.
Prevent it, resist it, let it not be so,
Lest child, child's children, cry against you woe.[51]

In Shakespeare's view, the bishop's prophecy was fulfilled in the blood-letting and strife of the fifteenth century.

In reality, however, the history of fifteenth-century England was somewhat different from that which the bishop prophesied. England's soil may, indeed, have been manured by the shedding of her noblemen's blood. Yet the battles fought were relatively few, and the numbers involved in them, Towton apart, small. The physical damage caused by the fighting was slight. Towns were never subjected to siege and bombardment, as they commonly were on the Continent; nor were castles destroyed. Life, in both town and country, went on largely as normal. Parish churches and chapels were enlarged, rebuilt and embellished, and merchants' houses beautified. The export trade in woollen cloth went from strength to strength. People's standards of living steadily improved. The struggle within England's noble elite affected the mass of her population but little.

There is something of a paradox here. England was a highly centralised state – a country much governed by medieval standards. Yet the violent fates of her kings had little or no effect on the mass of her people. The explanation for the paradox is not too difficult to find. By the fifteenth century, England's governmental processes were sufficiently institutionalised to cope with the comings and goings of kings. The main administrative departments – the chancery, privy seal and exchequer – had, centuries before, gone out of court. They operated independently of the royal household. None of them was directly responsive any longer to the king's command. Away from Westminster, in the shires, the principal royal officials – the sheriffs, escheators and JPs – while appointed by the king, were not in any meaningful sense his men. They were not directly in royal pay; they were, for the most part, independent country gentlemen. Over time, as national government grew in depth and density, the impact of the royal will on the administrative machine became less. Jolts such as depositions could be withstood, absorbed and neutralised.

Later medieval England, despite appearances, was in many ways a remarkably mature and law-abiding society. It is instructive in this connection to compare her with late medieval France. Judged solely by the fates of her kings, England was a far more violent society than France. No fewer than five English kings in these years were deposed, three of them in just thirty years in the fifteenth century. In the whole of the medieval period no medieval French king was removed by deposition. The reason for the difference is that France was not racked by the dynastic instability that England was. But, equally, medieval England did not face the periodic explosions of discontent that France did. No English ruler, for example, was ever subjected to indignities comparable to those heaped on the Dauphin after his father's defeat at Poitiers. On 22 February 1358, with France on the brink of collapse, one of the Dauphin's councillors was hacked to death in his presence; and the Dauphin himself was forced to hide in disguise behind a couch. Weeks earlier, in another appalling scene, the Dauphin had been browbeaten into submitting to the demands of the leader of the Paris merchants, who had barged his way into his room at the head of a mob.[52] Events of this sort rarely, if ever, occurred in England. Even at the height of the Great Revolt, when the rebels, having occupied the capital, murdered the king's ministers, the king himself was treated with respect. The king – who was admittedly at this time a boy – was held beyond reproach by the rebels; it was his councillors who were blamed for the realm's ills. The French monarchy was in many ways the most prestigious in Europe. Since Clovis's time, the kings of France had been anointed with holy oil believed to have been brought down from heaven by a dove. Yet, when the monarchy was faced with its gravest crisis, the aura of mystique afforded the heir to the throne no protection. How very different was the position in late medieval England. Monarchy, the institutional expression of kingship, survived the misdeeds of individual kings. It even survived the depositions of the last two Richards.

Kings might come and go, then. And in the fifteenth century they did so with unnerving rapidity. Yet, in practical terms, the problems posed by the deposition of a king were little different from those posed by a normal succession to the crown. The problem in each case was to smooth over and to manage the transfer of power. Over the centuries political theologians had come up with a solution to this problem. It took the form of the doctrine of the king's two bodies: 'The king is dead; long live the king.' The king himself, a mortal, it was held, might die. The crown, however, the symbol of the permanence of the realm, would live on. In the late middle ages, elaborate funerary ceremonies for kings were arranged to give visual expression to this doctrine. Usually, an effigy of the deceased king was carried on parade through the streets. By the fourteenth century it was expected as well that the king would be given honourable burial; provided such burial were given, the old king's spirit would rest in peace. In the early 1400s Henry IV neglected these niceties in respect of his predecessor Richard II. Richard, after his murder at Pontefract, had been buried in obscurity at King's Langley Friary (Hertfordshire). His tomb in Westminster Abbey lay empty. In the eyes of some at least of his critics, Henry IV's troubles were attributable to his contempt for his predecessor's wishes.[53] Henry V, therefore, when he became king, moved the body from King's Langley to Westminster. With that deed done, he could set out in safety for France.

Three quarters of a century later after Bosworth, another Henry – Henry VII – faced the problem of what to do with the remains of a deposed predecessor. There was no question of the fallen Richard III being buried in a place of honour or distinction. Richard was a usurper. After the battle, his remains were tipped into an unmarked grave at the Greyfriars church, Leicester. In 1495, however, Henry somewhat unexpectedly paid for an alabaster effigy to be placed in his memory.[54] The gesture was in many ways a token one. It mattered less than if he had actually reburied Richard. None the less, the gesture was significant. Henry was concerned to come to terms with the past. If the times were discordant, then harmony had to be restored. Honouring a usurping predecessor was a way of healing the wounds which the usurper had torn open.

The tomb of Richard II and Anne of Bohemia in Westminster Abbey. (*A. F. Kersting*)

11

What's in a Face?

What did the three kings look like? Do we even know what they looked like? Have any likenesses of them come down to us? What can a knowledge of their physical features tell us about their personalities?

These are important questions, and not just because of our natural curiosity about the human physiognomy. By the central middle ages rulers devoted considerable energy to crafting their public images. They were concerned about how they were perceived by their subjects. In the sixteenth century the official portrait of the ruler formed part of his or her broader projection of majesty. Elizabeth I, as queen, took particular care to ensure that she was never shown ageing in her later portraits. When did this interest on the part of rulers in their public image begin? And can such an interest be traced back to the middle ages?

The earliest post-Classical individualised likenesses of rulers date from the third quarter of the fourteenth century. At the head of the list, dating from the early 1360s, is the famous panel of John II (the Good), king of France, now in the Louvre. Though now surviving in isolation, this probably formed part of a quadriptych representing, in addition, the king's son the future Charles V, Edward III of England and the Emperor Charles IV. From a generation later come a series of panel portraits of other members of the Valois family – John's younger son, Philip the Bold, duke of Burgundy, Philip's son, John the Fearless, and Louis II, duke of Anjou.[1] All four of these portraits are remarkably frank representations of their subjects. None is in the least flattering. The sitter is shown each time in profile, slightly hunched and round-shouldered, and with the long hooked nose characteristic of the Valois line. This same set of features is found in the many representations in manuscripts or in sculpture of King Charles V of France (1364–80).[2] The somewhat unattractive, but none the less forceful, Charles apparently made no attempt to seek flattery from his painters. Conscious of his royal dignity as he was, he insisted on Cromwell's 'warts and all'.

This first group of representations of rulers attest the absorption by the artist class of new naturalistic ideas from Italy. People began to be represented as they actually looked. The breakthrough marked a radical shift in the outlook of medieval artists and artisans. The art of portraiture had flourished back in Classical Antiquity. To the fifth century, images of the Roman emperors had been multiplied in statuary and on coins. But, with the waning of Antiquity, the art of portraiture had gone into decline. Likenesses of individuals became purely conventional. The sense of character and personality in a face was lost. When kings were represented in art, it was their office that was stressed. The person of the king was of little interest; the attributes of office were.

Richard the Lionheart lived well before the late medieval rediscovery of the art of portraiture. Accordingly, we lack any authentic likeness of him. Not even the descriptions of contemporaries help us a great deal. Somewhat strangely for an age so rich in historical writing, descriptions of Richard are few. The fullest description is Richard de Templo's in the narrative known as the *Itinerarium*: 'Richard was tall, of elegant build', de Templo says. 'The colour of his hair was between red and gold; his limbs were supple and straight. He had quite long arms, which were particularly suited to drawing a sword and wielding it to great effect. His long legs matched the rest of his body.'[3] This passage is of questionable historical value, however, being written twenty years after his death, by which time the king was passing into legend. It may be somewhat idealised. Against it should be set the suggestions in the chronicles that in middle age Richard was putting on weight. Coggeshall says that when the king was mortally wounded the excess fat made the surgeon's task difficult.[4] Beyond these vague observations, however, the contemporary narratives do not let us go.

Alongside the word pictures of the chroniclers we can set the representations, admittedly conventional, of the king that have come down to us on his tomb effigies. The most familiar of these is the effigy over his burial place at Fontevrault Abbey. Fontevrault, on the borders of Anjou and Poitou, was the family mausoleum of the Angevins. Henry II had been buried there in 1189, with Eleanor, his widow, joining him in 1204 and Isabella of Angoulême, John's widow, in 1246. The effigies of

Richard and his father are almost identical. Each king is shown with eyes closed, wearing coronation robes, crowned and holding a sceptre, and lying on a cloth-covered bier (plate 1). The plausible suggestion has been made that the intention was to evoke the deceased's lying in state.[5] The effigies are almost certainly the work of a Loire valley school of sculptors who had some knowledge of the sculptures at Chartres. It is hard to date them with any precision, for there is no extant documentation relating to their setting-up. Stylistically they appear to belong to the first quarter of the thirteenth century. A date of approximately that order would certainly accord with the historical evidence. Although the French took over Anjou in 1203, Fontevrault was ruled until 1219 by three abbesses in succession who had close connections with the Angevin royal house. Any one of these could have taken the initiative in commissioning the effigies.[6]

A second effigy was placed in the thirteenth century over the burial place of Richard's heart in Rouen Cathedral. The burial of the heart and viscera separately from the body was a regular characteristic of French and Angevin royal funerary rites in this period. Originally, Richard's heart was enclosed in a silver reliquary casket immediately south of the high altar. In the 1250s, however, this was melted down to help pay for Louis IX's ransom. A stone effigy was then commissioned by the canons to take its place. The effigy was a more conventional one than that at Fontevrault. Placed on a slab supported by four crouching lions, it showed Richard crowned and wearing a long robe belted at the waist, with a cloak over it, his left hand resting on his belt, and his right hand raised. A beast, apparently a lion, was shown trampled underfoot. The effigy was swept away in the late eighteenth century, sometime after being recorded by Richard Gough in the 1780s. It was recovered, however, in mutilated condition in 1838. It is now placed on a plain plinth in the south ambulatory. Gaignières recorded its appearance before mutilation.[7]

More informative in many ways than the tomb effigies are the images of the king on his seals. Richard used two successive great seals for his correspondence. The first of these was swept away in a shipwreck off Cyprus in 1191, when the vice-chancellor was drowned with it hanging round his neck. A second seal made in the following year was used for the rest of the reign. Both seals showed striking innovations in design.

In each case, on the obverse the king was shown enthroned in state, as on earlier royal seals. Interestingly, however, the decorative detail was greatly elaborated on both instruments.[8] The throne, for example, was made much richer: a row of arcaded panels was included on its back. And, most remarkably, there was resort to symbolism. On the first seal the Angevin family badge of the broom pod was shown on each side of the throne with, above it, on each side of the king's head a crescent enclosing an estoile of seven points. One authority has described this seal as revolutionary.[9] On the second seal, the badge emblem and the estoiles were replaced by representations of the sun and the crescent moon, symbolising day and night – the royal eye watching over all the king's subjects both sleeping and waking. Equally striking innovations were made on the reverse of this second seal. Since the Conquest the king had been shown on this side mounted in armour on horseback. But whereas earlier kings had been shown wearing just a mail hauberk, Richard was shown in coat armour, a surcoat being worn over the hauberk; and, most significantly, the shield held in the left hand was positioned in such a way as to show the king's arms, the three lions of England (plate 2). As Walter de Gray Birch pointed out in the 1880s, this is the first appearance on the great seal of the royal arms of England.[10] In the century after Richard's death, his kingship was to be closely associated in men's minds with the image of the three lions. When in the 1250s Matthew Paris drew a portrait of the king in his *Abbreviatio Chronicorum*, he showed him with his shield displaying those lions (plate 1).[11] The king's promotion of this heraldic device was yet another way in which he influenced the character and development of later English kingship.

The interest which Richard took in the propagandist potential of emblematic language is amply demonstrated by his changes to his seals. Equipped with a strong visual sense, Richard was fascinated by the ways in which kingly power could be represented to his subjects. Indeed, in some respects, he could be said to anticipate the intense interest which his namesake Richard II was to take in these matters later.

The second Richard was one of the most image-conscious of all medieval rulers. It is no coincidence that more contemporary likenesses of him have come down to us than of any English ruler before the sixteenth century. Richard's interest in his self-image was partly narcissistic: he had a distinct taste for self-dramatising behaviour. But almost certainly there was another dimension to his interest. In the late fourteenth century, and particularly in England in Richard's reign, there was a shift in the human setting of kingship. To a greater extent than before, emphasis was placed on the personal or dynastic attributes of kingship. In the early middle ages, when kingship had been weaker, the sanctity inherent in the kingly office had been stressed. By Richard's time it was rather the more personal aspects of the sovereign's rule. The man and the office became virtually indistinguishable. Projecting appropriately regal images of the man became as important as projecting impersonal images of his authority.

The multiplication of images of Richard is also connected with developments in representation. By Richard's lifetime the ancient art of portraiture was being rediscovered. A new interest was shown in capturing the individuality of the human face. The styles associated with Giotto, Simone Martini and the other pioneering artists of Italy were now sweeping across Europe. In England the impact of artistic change can first be seen in the effigy of Edward III in Westminster Abbey (c. 1386). The dead king was no longer represented in idealised form, the perfect icon of a king, as his predecessors had been. Rather, he was shown aged and careworn. His forehead is lined, his face slightly misshapen, and he sports a long beard. The likeness was probably based on a death mask. Edward had died a very old man, and he was shown as such.

In Richard II's reign, the production and manipulation of the royal image were both carefully controlled. Nothing was left to chance. When we gaze on representations of the royal physiognomy, it is all too easy to suppose that we know what Richard looked like: his appearance has become so familiar to us. It is important to remember, however, that royal images were produced under royal supervision: Richard was concerned to present himself as an icon of regality. We see him as he wanted us to see him. We may not be seeing him as he actually looked.

The most finely executed, and almost certainly the most authentic image of the king, is that on his monument in Westminster Abbey. The tomb, on the south side of the Confessor's chapel, was commissioned shortly after Anne of Bohemia's death in 1394. It was the first double tomb in the abbey: all previous royal monuments there had comprised single figures. The commission was entrusted to two London copper-smiths, Nicholas Broker and Godfrey Prest. According to the contract, the effigies were to be produced according to a 'patron', a model.[12] From this, it can be assumed that the king gave his approval to the design. Richard was depicted with striking, but slightly feminine, features (p. 230). He has unusually high cheekbones and a long, straight nose ending in flared nostrils. The eyes are large and heavy-lidded. On either side of the chin appear the tufts of a goatee beard, while a small moustache droops over the extremities of the lips. The hair is short and relatively wavy and around the temples is held in place by a circlet. Many of the characteristics found in this likeness appear in other con-temporary portraits of the king. The grand, but heavily restored, 'state' portrait in Westminster Abbey, for example, shows the same youthful looking, but slightly epicene, features (plate 3). Richard is again shown with a long nose, narrow eyes, high arched eyebrows and a short goatee beard. In an illumination (p. 48) in the Shrewsbury borough charter of 1389, a smaller but finely executed image, he is shown yet again with the same long nose, high arched eyebrows and goatee beard, but this time with longer flowing hair.[13] There are features in all these likenesses which are without doubt highly stylised. The narrowed, oriental-looking eyes, for example, are a stylistic trait deriving from the conventions of Italian art: they appear on London-made brasses of the period. The high, arched eyebrows may be a stylised convention too. None the less, it remains the case that an attempt was made to capture a likeness of the king. There are portraits from outside the 'official' group which confirm the essential features of Richard's physiognomy. The portrait of the king in the Book of Statutes presented to him (St John's College, Cambridge MS A.7) is almost identical to that in the Shrewsbury borough charter: Richard is once again shown mousta-chioed and with a goatee beard, and his face exhibits the same elongated features. Two other portraits with broadly the same characteristics are found in the Ipswich borough charter and Dymock's treatise against the Lollards.[14] In both of these Richard is shown bearded and with a long, narrow face.

The one major image which portrays the king differently is the one so familiar to us in the Wilton Diptych (plate 2). In this, Richard is shown clean-shaven. The Diptych probably dates from c. 1395–97. It was executed around the same time as, or shortly after, the tomb. Richard was entering his thirties. Yet he is shown as little more than a boy. He lacks both a beard and a moustache, and his features have the elegant smoothness of a choirboy. There can be little doubt that Richard was sporting a beard by this date: the evidence of the tomb effigy and the Westminster portrait makes this almost certain. So why is he shown so much younger? It has been suggested that the Diptych portrait was deliberately idealised. It was by no means uncommon in the pre-modern period for rulers to be represented younger than they were. In miniatures painted in the 1590s Queen Elizabeth was habitually shown as if she were thirty years younger. Richard can hardly be said to have been approaching the elderly Elizabeth in years. Yet there was a reason why his manhood needed to be understated. In 1396 a marriage was being arranged between him and the six-year-old Isabella, daughter of the king of France. The artist could possibly have wanted to gloss over the age difference between Richard and his bride-to-be.[15]

If we lay aside the Diptych, we find a broad consistency in the representations of the king in his extant portraits. Richard is shown long faced and with high cheekbones. In virtually all the portraits from the 1390s he is moustachioed and with a goatee beard. His hair was reddish and slightly wavy; in his younger years it was probably worn long.

The descriptions of contemporaries add little to what these likenesses tell us. The fullest and most vivid description to have come down to us is that in the *Historia Vitae et Regni* of the monk of Evesham. 'King Richard', the monk says, 'was of average height. He had shining hair, a face which was white, rounded and feminine, and which sometimes flushed red.'[16] The writer adds that he stammered. Richard's 'femininity' (as the monk puts it) is hinted at by other writers. A number of them describe him as 'beautiful' rather than handsome. Gower, writing near the beginning of the reign, pictures him as a 'most beautiful king'.[17] Adam of Usk in an obituary recalled him as 'beautiful as Absalom'.[18] The ardently pro-Lancastrian John Lydgate, writing in the 1430s, said that he was 'of great beauty'.[19] Implicit in these barbed tributes is the view that he was lacking in manliness. The author of the *Historia Vitae et Regni* commented on his faint-heartedness in war.[20] Conceivably, contemporaries were judging him against his aggressively manly father. Yet there is actually no evidence that he was a weakling. Such evidence as we have suggests that he was physically impressive. When his tomb was opened in 1871, his skeleton was found to be six feet tall.[21] He is known to have been healthy, vigorous and active. Like his predecessors, he was fond of the chase: every summer he spent five or six weeks at forest lodges hunting game. There is evidence that he could ride well. Walsingham says that in 1383 he made the journey from Daventry to London in one night, switching horses as he went.[22] When occasion demanded, he could don the mantle of a general. He led three expeditions in the British Isles, two to Ireland and one to Scotland; and, as the two Irish expeditions showed, he could endure the rigours of long weeks in the field. If, as is perfectly true, he did not lead an expedition to France, as his father and grandfather had, it was not because he could not; it was because he did not want to.

In the fifteenth century it became increasingly common for princes and notables to commission likenesses of themselves. All four of the Valois dukes of Burgundy are known to us from extant portraits. Members of the Burgundian nobility and civil servant class began commissioning portraits from painters in the Low Countries. By the 1430s, if not earlier, wealthy townsmen, merchants and financiers in Italy and the Low Countries were following in their wake. Men like the banker Giovanni Arnolfini were commissioning portraits as mementoes or keepsakes. By the middle of the century, we know what a fair number of Europe's leaders looked like.

There is evidence that the new fascination with portraiture was felt in England as elsewhere. English patrons regularly sat to painters in the Low Countries. Edward Grimston's likeness was captured by Petrus Christus, and Cardinal Beaufort's, so it seems, by Jan Van Eyck.[23] There is strong evidence that some at least of England's kings joined in the rush to commission portraits. A series of likenesses of England's kings and queens has come down to us in the Royal Collection. Among the portraits are likenesses of Henry V, Henry VI, Edward IV and Elizabeth Woodville, and Richard III. All but one of these, however, are copies of lost originals. It is particularly unfortunate that the famous Royal Collection portrait of Richard III is a copy (plate 6). The portrait has been dated on tree-ring evidence to c. 1518–23.[24] By this time, likenesses of Richard were already being distorted; the historical Richard was being turned into the twisted hunchback. How close can we in fact come to visualising what Richard was like?

The Royal Collection portrait of Richard is one of a pair which derive from lost originals. The companion to it is the portrait in the Society of Antiquaries. This latter may in fact may be slightly the earlier of the two. It has been given a date on tree-ring evidence of *c.* 1516–22.[25] Arguably, the Antiquaries portrait is the most authentic likeness of the king to have come down to us. Both its early date and the relative independence of its treatment of clothing establish for it a primacy among early paintings of the king. Richard is shown as very different in appearance from his brother. Edward IV in his likeness in the Royal Collection is shown blandly self-confident, with a faint smile on his face; Richard in the Antiquaries portrait is portrayed as anguished but determined (plate 7). He fiddles nervously with the ring on his finger. His features are unprepossessing. His face is thin, even emaciated, in contrast to his brother's well-fed appearance; his chin, however, is prominent and strongly formed. He looks older than his years. He is slightly built, and his neck, like his face, is thin. The shoulders are slightly hunched, while the head juts forward intently, suggesting someone round-shouldered. The image is unflattering. But no hint of deformity is to be detected. The hands, indeed, are delicately rendered. The painting carries an air of authenticity.

The portrait in the Royal Collection shows the king from a different angle: he looks to the left rather than to the right. But the features of the face are the same. The king is nervous and worried. He gazes into the middle distance. His brow is knitted and his lips are tightly drawn. He again fingers the ring on his hand nervously. Less gaunt than in the Antiquaries portrait, he is still slightly built. He lacks his brother's strong physique. But, as Ross said, he is not 'uncomely'.[26] We are looking at a real man. Already, however, in this portrait the process of character assassination has begun. At some stage fairly soon after the painting was finished a number of alterations were made to the king's figure. Firstly, the right eye was narrowed, by making the lower edge virtually straight, to give him a more villainous appearance. Secondly, the outline of the right shoulder was raised by extending the gown to suggest that the king was deformed. In other words, at just the time that Sir Thomas More was at work, Richard was turned in his portraits into

a hunchback. The myth of the ogre was launched. Innumerable copies
of the Windsor portrait were made, each one more villainous-looking
than the one before.[27] The depths were plumbed at the turn of the sixteenth and seventeenth centuries. In portraits of Shakespeare's time
Richard was turned into a caricature. These poorly produced panels
were ornaments for Elizabethan long galleries. No one expected them to
bear much resemblance to reality; and it is clear that they did not.

A century before, however, things were different. When we look at the
earliest portraits, particularly that in the Society of Antiquaries, we are
probably looking at faithful copies of lost originals. We are likely to see
the king much as he had been in life. The accuracy of the representations is confirmed by contemporaries' descriptions of him. The
Crowland Continuator, for example, tells us that he was pale. Describ-
ing his appearance on the eve of Bosworth, he says that his face 'though
always thin, was more deathly pale than ever'.[28] Nicholas von Poppelau,
a German traveller whom Richard received at Middleham in 1484, con-
firms that he was thin: he describes him as leaner than his visitor and
with thin arms and legs.[29] Von Poppelau also tells us that he was short.
Other contemporaries were struck by Richard's lack of physique.
Archibald Whitelaw, a Scottish envoy, for example commented on the
'remarkable powers' which Richard held in so small a body, while John
Stow later commented on his shortness of stature.[30] Ralph Shaw, indeed,
in his sermon in 1483, claimed Richard as his father's true heir on the
grounds that, like his father, he was short.[31] The physical contrast
between Richard and his tall, handsome brother was notable. Possibly
the fact that he was the eleventh surviving child of his mother helps to
account for that slightness which was later interpreted as deformity.

Was Richard himself conscious of his lack of good looks? Is there
any evidence that he sought to manipulate the visual representations of
his person? Can we see him anticipating the concern later shown by
Charles I, a similarly short monarch, for the production of grand
images? The answer to all these questions appears to be no. It is hard
to see any official campaign to build up or magnify the king's image.
We have seen that the two earliest likenesses of him probably show him
much as he was. There was no attempt to portray him otherwise. And
this is probably what we would expect. Neutrality to the sitter is characteristic of the age. Earlier in the century, the Valois dukes of Burgundy

had been shown just as they looked. Duke Philip and Duke John, for example, were shown with their long noses, and Duke John with his angular jutting chin. Later in the century, in the 1470s Duke René of Anjou was shown stocky and ageing, his face a little lopsided.[32] In medieval 'state' portraiture the emphasis was put not on the person but on the attributes of rank and status. Sitters were shown wearing collars, rings, badges or other distinguishing insignia that marked their superiority. Richard III, for example, in his early portraits is shown wearing a rich collar and a jewel or badge on his hat. It is true that in the fifteenth century rulers no longer commissioned 'king enthroned' images, as Richard II had. Nonetheless, they still wanted images which stressed their wealth and power. In his two earliest portraits Richard is shown as finely arrayed as any ruler could be. In the Antiquaries portrait he is in an elegant black velvet gown with striped doublet peeping through, while in the Royal Collection panel he is in cloth-of-gold. We know that Richard kept a large and magnificent wardrobe: the record of the finery which he wore on his coronation day amply attests to that. For Richard, as for other rulers, impressing people meant laying on a good show and appearing kingly. Richard may not have cut an impressive figure physically. But there is no doubt that he knew how to play the part of the king in public.

In an age which set such store by appearances, looking like a king was essential to actually being a king. Of the three kings, Richard II was probably the one who most assiduously cultivated an extravagant image: his court was well known for its size and magnificence. But Richard I hardly lagged far behind. More than anyone, he knew how to impress the crowd. Yet, as the three kings' fates show, style by itself was insufficient to assure success. Other qualities had to be on display too. A king had to inspire confidence and trust. He had to heed wise counsel. He had to offer his people effective leadership. In one or other of these respects, the two later Richards failed. The three Richards had many things in common: they were all pious, and they all met violent ends. But at the same time, in their careers they point up a contrast. They highlight for us, in extreme form, the strengths and the weaknesses, the success and the failures, of English medieval kingship. They highlight the role of personality in the shaping of England's medieval destiny.

Appendix

In Bodleian Library, Oxford, MS Ashmole 1448, folios 285–87 is a transcription of a genealogy of the kings of England down to Richard III. The compiler or author is unknown. Most of the genealogy was written in the reign of Edward IV. The final section on Richard III appears to have been added shortly afterwards because Henry VII is referred to as earl of Richmond. The narrative is of value as a near contemporary piece of history. Particularly striking is the author's conviction that Richard murdered the two princes in the Tower. Also of interest is the clear evidence that, like others who noted the deaths, he felt their loss deeply.

Here follows the passage on Richard III's reign. It was first published in *Catalogue of the Manuscripts of Elias Ashmole*, ed. W. H. Black (Oxford, 1845), p. 1231.

Invidia diaboli et in insaciabili appetitu succedendi in regnum Ricardus dux Gloucestr' postquam Rex Edwardus Quartus frater dicti ducis viam universe carnis ingressus fuit, dolose Edwardum principum Wallie et Ricardum ducem Ebor' fratrem eius, filios invictissimi Regis Edward Quarti in sua custodia mancipavit donec seipsum in regnum fraudulentis circumstanciis cum instigacione et consilio et auxilio Henrici ducis de Bokyngham diademate regni coronaret. Brevo tempore succedente dominum Antonium comitem de Rivers et Ricardum fratrem eius necnon dominum Thomam Vaughan ea occasione apud Pontefractum gladio sine aliquo iuris processu capita truncabat. Necnon vero in turri Londoniarum maligne concilium vocari instituit et ibidem dominum Willelmum Hastynges quia coronandi ipsum non preberet assensum sine aliqua intermissione super truncum arboris gladio peremptus est; et seipsum coronari fecit apud Westmonasterium die dominica post passionem Sancti Petri apostoli. Perterritus nepotes, ne ut regnaret favore regni eum impedirent inito concilio cum duce de Bokyngham, ut prefertur, eos de lumine huius seculi, qualiter vel quomodo nequiter et homicide abstrahebat. Heu dolor!

Tam nobiles principes tam fecudi [*sic*] et regni heredes, taliter vitam finiri, qui nullo crimine seu transgressione vel merito violari meruerunt.

Rex Edwardus Quintus exercebat regna [*sic*] gubernacula vii [*sic*] die Aprilis ad festum passionis sancti Petri apostolici.

Rex Ricardus iii, frater Edwardi Quarti: primo anno regni sui decessit eius filius; secundo anno Regina sua, apud Westmonasterium tumulata; tercio anno iuxta sua merita, secundum Dei providentiam, miserrime per Henricum Comitem de Richemonde et alios exulatos iuxta Leycestriam bello peremptus est.

Notes

Notes to Chapter 1: What's in a Name?

1. William had died in 1156, aged three, and Henry 'the Young King' in 1183.
2. In the event, his hopes of a son were to be disappointed: J. L. Laynesmith, *The Last Medieval Queens: English Queenship, 1445–1503* (Oxford, 2004), p. 135.
3. *Rotuli Parliamentorum* (6 vols, London, 1767–77), vi, p. 240; *English Historical Documents*, iv, *1327–1485*, ed. A. R. Myers (London, 1969), p. 341.
4. M. Aston, 'Richard II and the Wars of the Roses', *The Reign of Richard II: Essays in Honour of May McKisack*, ed. F. R. H. du Boulay and C. M. Barron (London, 1971), p. 289.
5. A verse history of the Third Crusade, quoted by R. V. Turner and R. R. Heiser, *The Reign of Richard Lionheart* (Harlow, 2000), p. 3.
6. J. Gillingham, *Richard I* (New Haven and London, 1999), p. 16. Gillingham looks at Richard 'Through Muslim Eyes' in his chapter 2.
7. Ibid., p. 8.
8. This theme is picked up below, chapter 6.
9. S. Daniel, *The Collection of the Historie of England* (London, 1621), pp. 101–2.
10. W. Churchill, *Divi Britannici* (London, 1675), pp. 215–16. This writer is not of course to be confused with the later Prime Minster.
11. L. Echard, *The History of England* (London, 1707), p. 229, quoted by Gillingham, *Richard I*, p. 2n.
12. D. Hume, *History of England* (London, 1786; repr. 1871), p. 162.
13. A. L. Poole, *From Domesday Book to Magna Carta* (2nd edn, Oxford, 1955), p. 350.
14. F. Barlow, *The Feudal Kingdom of England, 1042–1216* (3rd edn, London, 1972), p. 367.
15. J. Brundage, *Richard Lionheart* (New York, 1974), p. 263.
16. Turner and Heiser, *Reign of Richard Lionheart*, pp. 244–45.

17. For discussion, see E. M. W. Tillyard, *Shakespeare's History Plays* (London, 1946).

18. Aston, 'Richard II and the Wars of the Roses', pp. 308–9.

19. Ibid., p. 311.

20. For a survey of Richard's changing reputation, see P. W. Hammond, 'The Reputation of Richard III', *Richard III: A Medieval Kingship*, ed. J. Gillingham (London, 1993), chapter 8.

21. Rous's account of Richard III's reign is printed in A. Hanham, *Richard III and his Early Historians, 1483–1535* (Oxford, 1975), pp. 118–24.

22. P. M. Kendall, *Richard III* (London, 1955), p. 421.

23. T. More, *The History of King Richard III*, ed. R. S. Sylvester (New Haven, 1963), pp. 7–8.

24. P. Vergil, *Three Books of Polydore Vergil's English History*, ed. H. Ellis, Camden Society (1844); idem, *The Anglica Historia of Polydore Vergil, AD 1485–1537*, ed. D. Hay, Camden Society, 74 (1950). For discussion, see D. Hay, *Polydore Vergil: Renaissance Historian and Man of Letters* (Oxford, 1952).

25. G. Buck, *The History of King Richard III*, ed. A. N. Kincaid (Gloucester, 1979).

26. H. Walpole, *Historic Doubts on the Life and Reign of Richard III* (London; repr. 1965).

27. J. Lingard, *History of England* (London, 1819); J. Gairdner, *History of the Life and Reign of Richard the Third* (2nd edn, Cambridge, 1898).

28. S. Turner, *History of England in the Middle Ages* (London, 1830).

29. C. Halsted, *Life of Richard III* (2 vols, London, 1844); A. O. Legge, *The Unpopular King* (2 vols, London, 1885).

30. C. Ross, *Richard III* (London, 1981), p. l.

31. J. Tey, *The Daughter of Time* (London, 1951).

32. Kendall, *Richard III*. 'Over-imaginative' may be an understatement. As Charles Ross wrote, Kendall's account of the battle of Bosworth 'remains an astonishing mixture of imagination, speculation and purple prose, and his description of Richard's last moments seems to suggest that he was perched on the crupper of the king's horse', Ross, *Richard III*, p. 215n. None the less, as Ross also wrote, 'the book is soundly based on a wide range of sources, for which it shows a proper respect', ibid., p. li. Kendall was professor of English at Ohio University.

33. Hanham, *Richard III and his Early Historians*.

34. *The Crowland Chronicle Continuations, 1459–1486*, ed. N. Pronay and J. Cox (London, 1986). For discussion of this source, see A. Gransden, *Historical Writing in England*, ii, *c. 1307 to the Early Sixteenth Century* (London, 1982), pp. 265–74.

35. Ross, *Richard III*, p. xliv.

36. Pronay and Cox, in *Crowland*, p. 90, suggest Sharp. They are supported by M. Hicks, *Richard III* (Stroud, 2000), p. 43.

37. So he was less well placed to gather information. On the other hand, it is noticeable that his reporting is patchy. He was stronger on domestic affairs than foreign. This may be taken as evidence in support of his authorship. In general, it can be argued that a writer retired from government is more likely to speak frankly than one still employed.

38. *Crowland*, p. 149.

39. Ibid., p. 159.

40. Ibid., p. 159.

41. Ibid., p. 161.

42. Ibid., pp. 159–61.

43. Ibid., p. 171.

44. Ibid., p. 173.

45. Ibid., p. 175.

46. Hicks, *Richard III*, p. 95.

Notes to Chapter 2: The Kingship in Medieval England

1. Quoted by G. L. Harriss, in *Henry V: The Practice of Kingship*, ed. G. L. Harriss (Oxford, 1985), p. 10.

2. *Chronicles of the Revolution, 1397–1400*, ed. C. Given-Wilson (Manchester, 1993), pp. 177–78.

3. For discussion, see D. Carpenter, 'King, Magnates and Society: The Personal Rule of King Henry III', in idem, *The Reign of Henry III* (London, 1996), pp. 77–78; and J. Dunbabin, 'Government', *The Cambridge History of Medieval Political Thought, c. 350–c. 1450*, ed. J. H. Burns (Cambridge, 1988), pp. 506–7. The treatise which goes by the name of 'Bracton' probably originated in the circle of the justice William de Raleigh in the 1230s and was then edited by Bracton a decade or two later.

4. For Fortescue's ideas, see Dunbabin, 'Government', p. 508.

5. For this paragraph, see G. L. Harriss, 'The King and his Subjects', *Fifteenth-Century Attitudes: Perceptions of Society in Late Medieval England*, ed. R. Horrox (Cambridge, 1994), p. 13; and M. Hicks, *English Political Culture in the Fifteenth Century* (London, 2002), p. 38.

6. For counsel, see in particular J. L. Watts, 'Ideas, Principles and Politics', *The Wars of the Roses*, ed. A. J. Pollard (Basingstoke, 1995), pp. 110–33.

7. For the structure of government in late medieval England, see A. L. Brown, *The Governance of Late Medieval England, 1272–1461* (London, 1989).

Notes to Chapter 3: Richard I

1. The nickname 'Coeur de Lion' was coined by Ambroise, the verse chronicler of the Third Crusade.
2. Another son, William, had died aged three.
3. For Richard's early years, see J. Gillingham, *Richard I* (New Haven and London, 1999), chapters 3–6.
4. Though Eleanor herself still remained in custody.
5. For Richard's movements in England at this time, see L. Landon, *Itinerary of King Richard I* (Pipe Roll Society, new series, 13, 1935), pp. 2–23.
6. *Chronica Rogeri de Hovedene*, ed. W. Stubbs, 4 vols, Rolls Series (1868–87), iii, p. 15.
7. C. Tyerman, *England and the Crusades, 1095–1588* (Chicago, 1988), p. 81.
8. *Gesta Henrici II et Ricardi I*, ed. W. Stubbs, 2 vols, Rolls Series (1867), ii, p. 90.
9. Richard's revenue in 1190, according to the accounts on the pipe roll, was £31,000, more than twice that for the year before or the year after: N. Barratt, 'The English Revenue of Richard I', *English Historical Review*, 116 (2001), p. 637.
10. For his itinerary, see Landon, *Itinerary*, pp. 29–38.
11. For affairs in Sicily, see Gillingham, *Richard I*, pp. 131–39.
12. For Richard's marriage to Berengaria, see below, pp. 138–39.
13. *Chronica Rogeri de Hovedene*, iii, pp. 105–6.
14. Narratives of the Third Crusade are found in Howden, iii, pp. 112–85 passim; Ambroise, *L'estoire de la Guerre Sainte*, ed. G. Paris (Paris, 1897), translated by M. J. Hubert and J. La Monte, *The Crusade of Richard Lionheart* (New York, 1941); and the narrative known as the *Itinerarium* in *Chronicles and Memorials of the Reign of Richard I*, ed. W. Stubbs, Rolls Series (1864), translated by Helen Nicholson, *Chronicle of the Third Crusade* (Aldershot, 1997).
15. Richard had been betrothed to Philip's sister Alice before his marriage to Berengaria. For the complex story of Richard's marital history, see below, pp. 137–38.
16. *Chronica Rogeri de Hovedene*, iii, pp. 129–30; *Chronicle of the Third Crusade*, pp. 246–59.
17. For the final stages of the crusade, see Howden, iii, pp. 182–84; *Chronicle of the Third Crusade*, pp. 348–59.
18. Henry's main potential rivals were Richard's nephews Henry and Otto, the sons of his sister Matilda and her husband, Duke Henry of Saxony.
19. Ibid., pp. 215–16.

20. For the significance of Winchester, see below, pp. 169–70.

21. The fullest account of the years from 1194 is Gillingham, *Richard I*, chapters 16–18.

22. For a positive evaluation of Richard's defence of Normandy, see V. Moss, 'The Defence of Normandy, 1193–1198', *Anglo-Norman Studies*, 24, *Proceedings of the Battle Conference, 2001*, ed. J. Gillingham (Woodbridge, 2002).

23. Gillingham, *Richard I*, p. 334.

24. But it also reflected the wide distribution of Angevin power. Nothing, however, was sent to England. For discussion, see M. Evans, *The Death of Kings: Royal Deaths in Medieval England* (London, 2003), pp. 30–31, 83.

Notes to Chapter 4: Richard II

1. For Richard's childhood and upbringing, see N. E. Saul, *Richard II* (New Haven and London, 1997), chapter 2.

2. *The St Albans Chronicle, i, 1376–1394: The Chronica Maiora of Thomas Walsingham*, ed. J. Taylor, W. Childs, L. Watkiss (Oxford, 2003), p. 120.

3. *The Anonimalle Chronicle, 1333 to 1381*, ed. V. H. Galbraith (Manchester, 1927), pp. 107–14, offers the fullest description.

4. In 1388, in letters confirming the gift of a gold ring to the Confessor's shrine, he recalled that it was in the Confessor's church that he had received his royal anointing (Westminster Abbey Muniment, 9473).

5. For the opening years of the reign, see Saul, *Richard II*, chapter 3.

6. The sources for the Great Revolt are conveniently brought together in translation in *The Peasants' Revolt of 1381*, ed. R. B. Dobson (2nd edn, London, 1983).

7. Ibid., pp. 362–63.

8. *Rotuli Parliamentorum*, 6 vols (1767–77), iii, pp. 124–25; *CPR 1385–9*, p. 430.

9. *The Westminster Chronicle, 1381–1394*, ed. L. C. Hector and B. F. Harvey (Oxford, 1982), p. 114.

10. Ibid., pp. 68–80, 112–14.

11. *Knighton's Chronicle, 1337–1396*, ed. G. H. Martin (Oxford, 1995), p. 354.

12. The questions are printed in *Westminster*, pp. 196–202.

13. The fullest accounts of the Merciless Parliament are found in ibid., pp. 234–342.

14. Again, the fullest account is in ibid., pp. 354–68.

15. *Rotuli Parliamentorum*, iii, pp. 301–2.

16. N. E. Saul, 'Richard II and the Vocabulary of Kingship', *English Historical Review*, 110 (1995), pp. 854–77.

17. *Chronicles of the Revolution, 1397–1400*, ed. C. Given-Wilson (Manchester, 1993), p. 68.
18. Ibid., p. 71.
19. *Rotuli Parliamentorum*, iii, p. 347.
20. For this and other examples, see Saul, *Richard II*, pp. 283–85.
21. J. H. Harvey, 'The Wilton Diptych: A Re-Examination', *Archaeologia*, 98 (1961), appendix 2.
22. *Chronicles of the Revolution*, pp. 86–87. The judgement of 1327 had restored Henry of Lancaster to the inheritance which his elder brother Thomas had forfeited five years before for treason.
23. The main narratives of Richard's overthrow are conveniently brought together in ibid., part 2. The fullest modern account is M. Bennett, *Richard II and the Revolution of 1399* (Stroud, 1999).

Notes to Chapter 5: Richard III

1. M. K. Jones, 'Somerset, York and the Wars of the Roses', *English Historical Review*, 104 (1989), pp. 285–307.
2. H. Kleineke, 'Alice Martyn, Widow of London: An Episode from Richard's Youth', *The Ricardian*, 14 (2004), pp. 32–36. From London he fled briefly to the Low Countries before returning with his brother: L. Visser-Fuchs, 'Richard in Holland, 1461', *The Ricardian*, 6 (1983), pp. 182–89.
3. Richard initially went to Zealand with Anthony Woodville, later joining his brother at Bruges: L. Visser-Fuchs, 'Richard in Holland, 1470–1', *The Ricardian*, 6 (1983), pp. 220–29.
4. For Edward's grants to Richard, see C. D. Ross, *Richard III* (London, 1981), pp. 24–25.
5. The complex story of the division of the Warwick inheritance is told by M. Hicks, 'Descent, Partition and Extinction: The Warwick Inheritance', idem, *Richard III and his Rivals: Magnates and their Motives in the Wars of the Roses* (London, 1991), pp. 323–36.
6. M. Hicks, 'Richard III as Duke of Gloucester: A Study in Character' and 'Richard III's Cartulary in the British Library: MS Cotton Julius BXII', both in his *Richard III and his Rivals*, pp. 247–80, 281–90.
7. D. Mancini, *The Usurpation of Richard III*, ed. C. A. J. Armstrong (2nd edn, Oxford, 1969) p. 92. See also Ross, *Richard III*, p. 71.
8. Henry VI had become king at the age of nine months. It was agreed that Gloucester, his uncle, be Protector in England, giving way to his elder brother Bedford, the English commander in France, when the latter was in England.

9. For the arrangements for Richard II's minority, see above, pp. 51–52.

10. C. Richmond, '1483: The Year of Decision (or Taking the Throne)', *Richard III: A Medieval Kingship*, ed. J. Gillingham (London, 1993), pp. 39–56.

11. Ross, *Richard III*, p. 74.

12. On a block, according to the compiler of the genealogical notes in Bodleian Library, Oxford, MS Ashmole 1448: see Appendix.

13. *Richard III: A Source Book*, ed. K. Dockray (Stroud, 1997), p. 56.

14. *Rotuli Parliamentorum*, 6 vols (London, 1767–77), vi, pp. 240–42. Michael K. Jones has recently treated as credible an argument that Richard put forward at the time, and which was reported by Mancini, but was not incorporated in the *Titulus Regius*, that Edward was a bastard, and not the son of the duke of York. Jones argues that when Edward was conceived in 1441 his parents were almost certainly living apart; Edward must therefore have been the offspring of an illegitimate liaison by Cecily: M. K. Jones, *Bosworth, 1485: Psychology of a Battle* (Stroud, 2002), pp. 67–68. Jones certainly argues his case with conviction and, on the evidence that he musters, his hypothesis is at least possible. But it needs to be said that Edward's illegitimacy cannot be proved. It might also be added that contemporaries apparently did not attach much importance to it. Richard, in his search for arguments to justify his title, switched to the story about the pre-contract with Eleanor Butler.

15. The documentation relating to Richard's coronation is brought together in *The Coronation of Richard III*, ed. A. Sutton and P. Hammond (Gloucester, 1983).

16. A point made by C. Richmond, '1485 and All That: or What was Going on at the Battle of Bosworth', *Richard III: Loyalty, Lordship and Law*, ed. P. W. Hammond (London, 1986), p. 183.

17. C. Richmond, 'The Death of Edward V', *Northern History*, 25 (1989), pp. 278–80; P. Morgan, 'The Death of Edward V and the Rebellion of 1483', *Historical Research*, 68 (1995), pp. 229–32; *Richard III: A Source Book*, ed. Dockray, p. 80.

18. P. Fleming and M. Wood, *Gloucestershire's Forgotten Battle: Nibley Green, 1470* (Stroud, 2003), p. 98.

19. For accounts of the rebellion, see Ross, *Richard III*, chapter 6; and R. Horrox, *Richard III: A Study in Service* (Cambridge, 1989), chapter 3; L. Gill, *Richard III and Buckingham's Rebellion* (Stroud, 1999).

20. *Richard III: A Source Book*, ed. Dockray, pp. 103–7.

21. A. J. Pollard, 'The Tyranny of Richard III', *Journal of Medieval History*, 3 (1977), pp. 147–65. And see below, pp. 223–24.

22. *The Crowland Chronicle Continuations, 1459–1486*, ed. N. Pronay and J. Cox (London, 1986), pp. 171, 175.

23. For this paragraph, see A. Grant, 'Foreign Affairs under Richard III', *Richard III: A Medieval Kingship*, ed. J. Gillingham (London, 1993), pp. 113–32.

24. C. Richmond, 'The Battle of Bosworth, August 1485', *History Today*, 35 (August 1985), pp. 17–22.

25. Jones, *Bosworth*, pp. 149–57.

26. Ibid., p. 166.

27. See below, p. 229.

28. Richmond, '1485 and All That', pp. 186–91.

29. J. Hughes, *The Religious Life of Richard III: Piety and Prayer in the North of England* (Stroud, 1997), chapter 2.

Notes to Chapter 6: Kingship, Chivalry and Warfare

1. The characterisation of M. T. Clanchy, *England and its Rulers, 1066–1272* (2nd edn, London, 1998), p. 98.

2. J. R. S. Phillips, 'Edward II and the Prophets', *England in the Fourteenth Century*, ed. W. M. Ormrod (Woodbridge, 1986), p. 189.

3. 'Brute force' is the phrase of J. Campbell, *The Anglo-Saxon State* (London, 2000), p. 40.

4. G. L. Harriss, *King, Parliament and Public Finance in Medieval England to 1369* (Oxford, 1975), p. 7.

5. R. W. Kaeuper, *War, Justice and Public Order: England and France in the Later Middle Ages* (Oxford, 1988).

6. J. Gillingham, 'Some Legends of Richard the Lionheart: Their Development and Influence', idem, *Richard Coeur de Lion: Kingship, Chivalry and War in the Twelfth Century* (London, 1994), p. 183.

7. S. Lloyd, *English Society and the Crusade, 1216–1307* (Oxford, 1988), pp. 199–200.

8. Gillingham, 'Some Legends of Richard the Lionheart', p. 184.

9. Gillingham, 'The Unromantic Death of Richard I', *Richard Coeur de Lion: Kingship, Chivalry and War in the Twelfth Century*, chapter 6.

10. Gillingham, *Richard I* (New Haven and London, 1999), pp. 153, 315.

11. J. Gillingham, 'The Art of Kingship: Richard I, 1189–99', idem, *Richard Coeur de Lion: Kingship, Chivalry and War in the Twelfth Century*, p. 101.

12. For Newburgh's account and its context, see *Historia Rerum Anglicarum* in *Chronicles of the Reigns of Stephen, Henry II and Richard I*, ed.

R. Howlett, 4 vols, Rolls Series (1884–90), ii, pp. 422, and Gillingham, *Richard I*, pp. 278–79.

13. Lloyd, *English Society and the Crusade*, p. 198, citing a poem in praise of the young Edward.

14. *Vita Edwardi Secundi*, ed. N. Denholm-Young (London, 1957), p. 40.

15. Edward was compared to Brutus and Richard the Lionheart in a eulogy written by John of London: M. Prestwich, *Edward I* (London, 1988), p. 558.

16. *Der mittelenglische Versroman über Richard Löwenherz*, ed. K. Brunner (Vienna, 1913); *The Auchinleck Manuscript*, ed. D. Pearsall and I. C. Cunningham (London, 1977).

17. For these stories, see above, p. 88.

18. *King Arthur's Death*, ed. B. Ford (Harmondsworth, 1988).

19. For these examples, see L. A. Hibbard, *Medieval Romance in England* (Oxford, 1924), pp. 147–54.

20. London, National Archives (Public Record Office), E101/408/19, an inventory compiled in 1435.

21. Those of the Pastons, for example: *Paston Letters and Papers of the Fifteenth Century*, ed. N. Davis (Oxford, 1971, 1976), i, p. 517; and of an East Anglian neighbour of theirs, Thomasin Graa: C. Richmond, *The Paston Family in the Fifteenth Century: Endings* (Manchester, 2000), p. 125n.

22. Sir William Carrington, a knight of no particular distinction, claimed that his ancestor Michael had been Richard I's standard-bearer in the Holy Land, a claim for which there is no foundation: Oxford, Bodleian Library, MS Dugdale 15, fo. 281. In like manner, the Cobhams of Cobham (Kent), another knightly family, maintained that Henry, son of Serlo de Cobham, the first traceable member of the line, had fought alongside Richard at Acre. The family's Saracen's head armorial crest was explained by reference to this myth: J. G. Waller, 'The Lords of Cobham, their Monuments and the Church', *Archaeologia Cantiana*, 11 (1877), p. 53.

23. *The Chronicle of Pierre de Langtoft*, ed. T. Wright, 2 vols, Rolls Series (1886), ii, pp. 26–124.

24. *Polychronicon Ranulphi Higden Monachi Cestrensis*, ed. C. Babington and J. R. Lumby, 9 vols, Rolls Series (1865–86), i, pp. 70–78.

25. *Vita Edward Secundi*, pp. 36–7. Edward was also a keen collector of chronicles: W. M. Ormrod, *The Reign of Edward III: Crown and Political Society in England, 1327–1377* (New Haven and London, 1990), p. 44.

26. N. H. Nicolas, 'Expenses of the Great Wardrobe of Edward III', *Archaeologia*, 31 (1846), p. 103.

27. For this legend, and its appearance in the Black Book of the Order of the

Garter in the sixteenth century, see O. de Laborderie, 'Richard the Lion-heart and the Birth of a National Cult of St George: Origins and Development of a Legend', *Nottingham Medieval Studies*, 39 (1995), pp. 37–53, in particular 45–46.

28. For the importance of Edward III's legacy, see D. A. L. Morgan, 'The Political After-Life of Edward III: The Apotheosis of a Warmonger', *English Historical Review*, 112 (1997), pp. 856–81.

29. W. Shakespeare, *Richard II*, ed. P. Ure (5th edn, London, 1961), Act 2, Scene 1, lines 51–54.

30. For Richard's negotiation with the past, see W. M. Ormrod, 'Richard II's Sense of English History', *The Reign of Richard II*, ed. G. Dodd (Stroud, 2000), pp. 97–110.

31. *Collection of the Wills of the Kings and Queens of England*, ed. J. Nichols (London, 1780), p. 72.

32. For Richard's encouragement of tournaments, see N. E. Saul, *Richard II and Chivalric Kingship*, Royal Holloway, University of London, Inaugural Lecture (1999).

33. J. Froissart, *Chronicles*, ed. T. Johnes, 2 vols (London, 1862), ii, pp. 580–81; J. Gillespie, 'Richard II: Chivalry and Kingship', *The Age of Richard II*, ed. J. L. Gillespie (Stroud, 1997), pp. 115–38.

34. *Boke of Noblesse*, ed. J. G. Nichols (London, 1860; repr. 1972), pp. 4–5, 10.

35. The next generation of Yorkists were to make much of the duke's success at Pontoise. The episode was celebrated on his tomb epitaph at Fotheringhay (1476). Michael Jones argues that 'York's example may have been a touchstone for his son': Michael K. Jones, *Bosworth 1485: Psychology of a Battle* (Stroud, 2002), p. 51.

36. At least two of his esquires – men who would have been close to him – were killed in the battle, Thomas Apar and John Mylwater: E. B. S. Shepherd, 'The Church of the Friars Minor in London', *Archaeological Journal*, 59 (1902), p. 274.

37. *Crowland*, p. 149.

38. See above, p. 67.

39. For both statements: J. Hughes, *The Religious Life of Richard III: Piety and Prayer in the North of England* (Stroud, 1997), p. 39.

40. Ibid., pp. 31–55; R. J. Mitchell, *John Tiptoft, 1427–1470* (London, 1938), pp. 176–78.

41. *Chronicle of Pierre de Langtoft*, ii, pp. 26–124. Langtoft gives disproportionate coverage to the reign, relative to its length. His admiration for Richard was shared by Robert Mannyng of Bourne, who translated his chronicle in the 1330s. For discussion, see T. Summerfield, *The Matter of*

Kings' Lives: The Design of Past and Present in the Early Fourteenth-Century Verse Chronicles by Pierre de Langtoft and Robert Mannyng (Amsterdam, 1998), pp. 64, 88, 183–84.

42. The Anglo-Norman contingent on the First Crusade (1096–99), because it was led by Robert, duke of Normandy, was more Norman than English. William Rufus, the king of England, did not take part. An English contingent participated in the Second Crusade in the 1140s. However, the fact that England was torn apart by the war between Stephen and Matilda at the time meant that the contingent was small: C. Tyerman, *England and the Crusades, 1095–1588* (Chicago, 1988), pp. 24–35.

43. See above, p. 94.

44. For de Mézières' crusading initiatives, see J. J. N. Palmer, *England, France and Christendom, 1377–99* (London, 1972), chapter 11.

45. Mancini, *Usurpation of Richard III*, p. 137. For discussion, see Tyerman, *England and the Crusades*, p. 302.

46. A. F. Sutton, '"A Curious Searcher for our Weal Public": Richard III, Piety, Chivalry and the Concept of the "Good Prince"', *Richard III: Loyalty, Lordship and Law*, ed. P. W. Hammond (London, 1986), p. 72.

47. Jones, *Bosworth*, pp. 106, 209.

48. *The Hours of Richard III*, ed. A. F. Sutton and L. Visser-Fuchs (Stroud, 1990), p. 65.

49. The tradition is recorded by John Stow: 'On the north side (of All Hallows) was sometime builded a fayre Chappel, founded by King Richard the first, some have written that his heart was buried there under the high Altar', John Stow, *A Survey of London* (2 vols, Oxford, 1908; repr. 2000), i, p. 130. For discussion, see R. Horrox, 'Richard III and All Hallows Barking by the Tower', *The Ricardian*, 6 (1982), pp. 38–40.

Notes to Chapter 7: Every Inch a King

1. P. Meyer, 'L'entrevue d'Ardres', *Annuaire Bulletin de la Société de France*, 18 (1881), pp. 209–24.

2. *The Household of Edward IV: The Black Book and the Ordinance of 1478*, ed. A. R. Myers (Manchester, 1959).

3. The details which follow are taken from L. Landon, *Itinerary of Richard I*, Pipe Roll Society, new series, 13 (1935), pp. 81–100.

4. For Richard's itinerary, see N. E. Saul, *Richard II* (New Haven and London, 1997), pp. 468–74.

5. R. A. Brown, H. M. Colvin, A. J. Taylor, *History of the King's Works: The Middle Ages*, 2 vols (London, 1963), ii, pp. 864–88; C. Wilson, 'The Royal

Lodgings of Edward III at Windsor Castle: Form, Function, Representation', *Windsor: Medieval Archaeology, Art and Architecture of the Thames Valley*, ed. L. Keen and E. Scarff, British Archaeological Association Transactions, 25 (2002), pp. 15–94.

6. For Westminster and the other palaces, see *History of the King's Works*, i, pp. 491–552; ii, pp. 910–18, 930–37, 994–1002.

7. D. Crouch, *William Marshal: Court, Career and Chivalry in the Angevin Empire, 1147–1219* (Harlow, 1990), pp. 59–60.

8. J. Gillingham, *Richard I* (New Haven and London, 1999), p. 131.

9. D. A. Carpenter, 'The Burial of King Henry III, the *Regalia* and Royal Ideology', idem, *The Reign of Henry III* (London, 1996), p. 436. Richard is the first king whom we know for certain to have been buried in coronation robes. The evidence for his father is less certain. Richard is shown in coronation robes on his tomb at Fontevrault.

10. A. Gransden, *Historical Writing in England*, i, *c. 550 to c. 1307* (London, 1974), p. 241.

11. *The Westminster Chronicle, 1381–1394*, ed. L. C. Hector and B. F. Harvey (Oxford, 1982), pp. 155–57.

12. *Chronicles of the Revolution, 1397–1400*, ed. C. Given-Wilson (Manchester, 1993), p. 68.

13. A. F. Sutton, 'The Court and its Culture in the Reign of Richard III', *Richard III: A Medieval Kingship*, ed. J. Gillingham (London, 1993), p. 78. Edward of Middleham, Richard's son, was invested as Prince of Wales on this visit.

14. Ibid., pp. 78–79.

15. For the size of the English royal household, see C. Given-Wilson, *The Royal Household and the King's Affinity: Service, Politics and Finance in England, 1360–1413* (New Haven and London, 1986), pp. 258–59. For courts generally in the thirteenth and fourteenth centuries, see M. Vale, *The Princely Court: Medieval Courts and Culture in North-West Europe, 1270–1380* (Oxford, 2001).

16. *Hautesse* and *mageste*, in the French of the parliament rolls.

17. 'Annales Ricardi Secundi et Henrici Quarti', in *Chronica et Annales*, ed. H. T. Riley, Rolls Series (1866), p. 210.

18. In the original: 'A tres excellent et tres redoute et tres puissant Prince, et tres gracious Seigneur, nostre Seignour le Roi, supplient voz povres liges, Communes de vostre Roialme d'Engleterre, que please a vostre Hautesse et Roiale Mageste, en ese et supportation de voz ditz Communes … granter les Petitions souz escripte …' (*Rotuli Parliamentorum*, 6 vols (London, 1767–77), iii, p. 290. The subject of the language of address to

the king is discussed by N. E. Saul, 'Richard II and the Vocabulary of Kingship', *English Historical Review*, 110 (1995), pp. 854–77.

19. *Anglo-Norman Letters and Petitions*, ed. M. D. Legge, Anglo-Norman Text Society, 3 (1941), no. 24.

20. For examples of bowing, see *Westminster*, pp. 112, 226.

21. J. E. Powell and K. Wallis, *The House of Lords in the Middle Ages* (London, 1968), pp. 437–38, 453–54.

22. 'John Russell's Boke of Nurture', *The Babees Book*, ed. F. J. Furnivall, Early English Text Society, original series, 32 (1868), pp. 115–228.

23. *The Anonimalle Chronicle, 1333 to 1381*, ed. V. H. Galbraith (Manchester, 1927), pp. 107–8.

24. *The Brut, or the Chronicles of England*, ii, ed. F. W. D. Brie, Early English Text Society, original series, 136 (1908), pp. 338–39; Saul, *Richard II*, p. 343.

25. F. Bacon, *History of the Reign of King Henry VII*, ed. J. R. Lumby (Cambridge, 1902), pp. 214–15.

26. This is the categorisation used by D. Starkey, 'Introduction: Court History in Perspective', *The English Court from the Wars of the Roses to the Civil War*, ed. D. Starkey (London, 1987), pp. 7–8.

27. A. Gransden, *Historical Writing in England*, i, *c. 550 to c. 1307*, p. 241.

28. Gillingham, *Richard I*, pp. 258–59.

29. Ibid., p. 260.

30. *Historia Vitae et Regni Ricardi Secundi*, ed. G. B. Stow (Philadelphia, 1977), p. 132.

31. *Westminster*, p. 451.

32. C. M. Barron, 'Centres of Conspicuous Consumption: The Aristocratic Town House in London 1200–1500', *London Journal*, 20 (1995), p. 10.

33. *Westminster*, pp. 505–7.

34. *Historia Vitae et Regni*, p. 66; M. V. Clarke, *Fourteenth Century Studies*, ed. L. S. Sutherland and M. McKisack (Oxford, 1937; repr. 1968), p. 98.

35. 'Annales Ricardi Secundi', p. 307.

36. Sutton, 'The Court and its Culture', pp. 78–79.

37. J. Milles, 'Observations on the Wardrobe Accounts for the Year 1483', *Archaeologia*, 1 (1779), pp. 363–87; and, more generally, Ross, *Richard III*, pp. 140–41.

38. Sutton, 'The Court and its Culture', pp. 78–79.

39. W. L. Warren, *Henry II* (London, 1973), p. 208.

40. Gillingham, *Richard I*, p. 256.

41. Ibid., p. 254. Richard also showed an interest in Arabic music. At a meeting with al-Adil, Saladin's brother, in 1191, he asked if he could hear some

Arabic singing, and al-Adil had a woman brought in who accompanied herself on the guitar: ibid., p. 23.

42. J. Harvey, *The Plantagenets, 1154–1485* (London, 1948), p. 98.

43. For discussion of the Diptych, see D. Gordon, *Making and Meaning: The Wilton Diptych* (London, 1993), and *The Regal Image of Richard II and the Wilton Diptych*, ed. D. Gordon, L. Monnas and C. Elam (London, 1997).

44. For the effigy of Edward III, which shows him as an old man, and which was probably based on a death mask, see below, p. 235.

45. For Richard's appearance, see below chapter 11.

46. *Age of Chivalry: Art in Plantagenet England, 1200–1400*, ed. J. Alexander and P. Binski (London, 1987), no. 446.

47. For discussion, see *Age of Chivalry*, no. 713; F. Hepburn, *Portraits of the Later Plantagenets* (Woodbridge, 1986), pp. 13–26.

48. S. Whittingham, 'The Chronology of the Portraits of Richard II', *Burlington Magazine*, 113 (1971), pp. 12–21.

49. Saul, *Richard II*, p. 451 and plate 15.

50. C. M. Barron, 'The Quarrel of Richard II with London 1392–7', *The Reign of Richard II: Essays in Honour of May McKisack*, ed. F. R. H. Du Boulay and C. M. Barron (London, 1971), pp. 195–96.

51. P. Lindley, 'Absolutism and Regal Image in Ricardian Sculpture', *The Regal Image of Richard II and the Wilton Diptych*, pp. 61–84.

52. For a survey of the field, see Saul, *Richard II*, and the references there given.

53. J. Stratford, 'Gold and Diplomacy: England and France in the Reign of Richard II', *England and the Continent in the Middle Ages: Studies in Memory of Andrew Martindale* (Stamford, 2000), pp. 218–37.

54. J. Gower, *Confessio Amantis*, ed. R. A. Peck (Toronto, 1980), p. 494.

55. It is fair to add, however, that the chamber accounts, in which payments of a more personal nature would have been recorded, have not survived for this period.

56. Oxford, Bodleian Library, MS 581. For discussion of this work and other texts of a varying nature which can loosely be associated with Richard, see P. J. Eberle, 'Richard II and the Literary Arts, *Richard II: The Art of Kingship*, ed. A. Goodman and J. L. Gillespie (Oxford, 1999), chapter 11.

57. This is a point made by T. Jones and others, *Who Murdered Chaucer? A Medieval Mystery* (London, 2003), pp. 25–31. My own thinking on the subject owes much to this discussion.

58. *Lak of Stedfastnesse*, lines 22–28.

59. P. Strohm, *Hochon's Arrow: The Social Imagination of Fourteenth-Century Texts* (Princeton, 1992), pp. 57–74.

60. Chaucer, *The Legend of Good Women*, lines 230–1.

61. The sunburst appears on Richard's tomb effigy in Westminster Abbey.

62. Chaucer, *The Legend of Good Women*, lines 495–7.

63. The *Tale of Melibee* was a close translation of the *Livre de Melibee et de Dame Prudence* written by Reynaud de Louens sometime after 1336, which was itself a free translation of the *Liber consolationis et consilii* of 1246 by Albert of Brescia: *The Riverside Chaucer*, ed. L. D. Benson (Oxford, 1987), pp. 923–24. For the omitted lines, see ibid., pp. 925–26. Chaucer's poem probably dates from the mid 1380s.

64. A stimulating case for a more active royal role is, however, argued by M. J. Bennett, 'The Court of Richard II and the Promotion of Literature', *Chaucer's England: Literature in Historical Context*, ed. B. A. Hanawalt (Minneapolis, Minnesota, 1992), pp. 3–20.

65. D. Pearsall, 'The *Troilus* Frontispiece and Chaucer's Audience', *Yearbook of English Studies*, 7 (1977), pp. 68–77.

66. Richard's use of a piece of cloth for wiping his nose – what today we call the handkerchief – is attested from 1384: see G. B. Stow, 'Richard II and the Invention of the Pocket Handkerchief', *Albion*, 27 (1995), pp. 221–35.

67. C. D. Ross, *Edward IV* (London, 1975), pp. 264–66; A. F. Sutton and L. Visser-Fuchs, 'Choosing a Book in Late Fifteenth-Century England and Burgundy', *England and the Low Countries in the Late Middle Ages*, ed. C. M. Barron and N. E. Saul (Stroud, 1995), pp. 61–98.

68. The most recent discussion of Edward IV's chantry is A. Fehrmann, 'The Chantry Chapel of King Edward IV', *Windsor: Medieval Archaeology, Art and Architecture of the Thames Valley*, pp. 177–91. Fehrmann identifies further Burgundian influence in the choice of position for the chantry – the north side of the altar. The oratory of the dukes of Burgundy at their now destroyed mausoleum, the Champmol, near Dijon, was also in this position.

69. M. G. A. Vale, 'An Anglo-Burgundian Nobleman and Art Patron: Louis de Bruges, Lord of la Gruthuyse and Earl of Winchester', *England and the Low Countries*, pp. 115–31.

70. *The Household of Edward IV*, ed. A. R. Myers.

Notes to Chapter 8: Marriage and Family

1. *The Crowland Chronicle Continuations, 1459–1486*, ed. N. Pronay and J. Cox (London, 1986), p. 184.

2. For discussion of the tangled affair of Richard's non-marriage to Alice, see

J. Gillingham, *Richard I* (New Haven and London, 1999), pp. 77–78, 81–82, 87–88, 125–26, 141–43, to which the present discussion is heavily indebted.

3. *Gesta Henrici II et Ricardi I*, ed. W. Stubbs, 2 vols, Rolls Series (1867), ii, p. 160; Giraldus Cambrensis, 'Liber de Principis Instructione Praefatio Prima', *Opera Historica*, ed. J. S. Brewer, J. S. Dimock, G. F. Warner, 8 vols, Rolls Series (1861–91), viii, p. 232.

4. A. Trindade, *Berengaria: In Search of Richard the Lionheart's Queen* (Dublin, 1999), pp. 111–12.

5. *The Ecclesiastical History of Orderic Vitalis*, ed. M. Chibnall, 6 vols (Oxford, 1969–81), iii, pp. 114–15.

6. For these matches and Anglo-Iberian relations more generally, see A. Goodman, 'England and Iberia in the Middle Ages', *England and her Neighbours, 1066–1453*, ed. M. Jones and M. Vale (London, 1989), pp. 73–96.

7. For Gaunt's campaign in Spain, see P. E. Russell, *The English Intervention in Spain and Portugal in the Time of Edward III and Richard II* (Oxford, 1955).

8. N. E. Saul, *Richard II* (New Haven and London, 1997), pp. 83–84.

9. For discussions of the marriage, see E. Perroy, *L'Angleterre et le Grand Schisme d'Occident* (Paris, 1933), chapter 4; Saul, *Richard II*, chapter 5; A. Tuck, 'Richard II and the House of Luxemburg', *Richard II: The Art of Kingship*, ed. A. Goodman and J. L. Gillespie (Oxford, 1999), pp. 205–30.

10. 'King of the Romans' was the title given to the emperor before his actual coronation.

11. *The Westminster Chronicle, 1381–1394*, ed. L. C. Hector and B. F. Harvey (Oxford, 1982), p. 24. Similar sentiments were expressed some years later by Adam Usk: *The Chronicle of Adam Usk, 1377–1421*, ed. C. Given-Wilson (Oxford, 1997), p. 6.

12. *Westminster*, p. 24.

13. It had been rumoured in 1485 that Richard III was keen to seek Elizabeth's hand after his wife's death – and for the same reason that Henry was to seek it.

14. For the marriage, see J. L. Laynesmith, *The Last Medieval Queens: English Queenship, 1445–1503* (Oxford, 2003), pp. 69–70,

15. A. Crawford, 'The King's Burden? The Consequences of Royal Marriage in Fifteenth-Century England', *Patronage, the Crown and the Provinces in Later Medieval England*, ed. R. A. Griffiths (Gloucester, 1981), p. 39.

16. R. H. C. Davis, 'What Happened in Stephen's Reign, 1135–54', *History*, 49 (1964), pp. 1–12.

17. For discussion of John's activities during his brother's reign, see

A. L. Poole, *From Domesday Book to Magna Carta, 1087–1216* (2nd edn, Oxford, 1955), pp. 354–55, 362–64.

18. It is worth noting that neither the king of Scots nor the Welsh princes accepted the invitation. The king of Scots, indeed, contributed to Richard's ransom.

19. W. L. Warren, *King John* (3rd edn, New Haven and London, 1997), pp. 48–49.

20. Ibid., p. 49.

21. For the events covered in this and the following paragraph, see J. Gillingham, *The Angevin Empire* (2nd edn, London, 2001), pp. 89–94.

22. Radulphi de Coggeshall, *Chronicon Anglicanum*, ed. J. Stevenson, Rolls Series (1875), pp. 139–40.

23. *Eulogium Historiarum sive Temporis*, ed. F. S. Haydon, 3 vols, Rolls Series (1858–63), iii, p. 361.

24. See above, pp. 55–56.

25. *Westminster*, pp. 192–94.

26. *Chronicles of the Revolution, 1397–1400*, ed. C. Given-Wilson (Manchester, 1993), p. 196.

27. *Eulogium*, iii, pp. 369–70.

28. A point well made by L. Staley, 'Gower, Richard II, Henry of Derby and the Business of Making Culture', *Speculum*, 75 (2000), pp. 68–96.

29. *Chronicle of Adam Usk*, pp. 38–40.

30. *Chronicles of the Revolution*, p. 211.

31. *Crowland*, p. 170.

32. John Rous in the *Historia Regum Anglie*: Ross, *Richard III*, pp. 158–59.

33. Saul, *Richard II*, pp. 455–57.

34. See above, p. 39.

35. Prestwich, 'Richard Coeur de Lion: *Rex Bellicosus*', *Richard Coeur de Lion in History and Myth*, ed. J. L. Nelson, King's College, London, Medieval Studies, 7 (1992), pp. 6–7, quoting Ambroise, lines 7377–84.

36. R. A. Griffiths, 'The Crown and the Royal Family in Later Medieval England', *Kings and Nobles in the Later Middle Ages*, ed. R. A. Griffiths and J. Sherborne (Gloucester, 1986), p. 16.

37. London, National Archives (Public Record Office), E403/555, 6 June.

38. For this paragraph, see P. Strohm, 'Queens as Intercessors', idem, *Hochon's Arrow: The Social Imagination of Fourteenth-Century Texts* (Princeton, 1992), pp. 95–119; and, more generally, *Medieval Queenship*, ed. J. C. Parsons (Stroud, 1994). For revisionist comment, see Laynesmith, *The Last Medieval Queens*.

39. *Westminster*, p. 24.

40. Judith M. Bennett, *Queens, Whores and Maidens: Women in Chaucer's England*, Royal Holloway, University of London: Hayes Robinson Lecture Series, 6 (2002), p. 13.

41. For these examples, see *Westminster*, pp. 92, 330, 502. For discussion of the ceremony in Westminster hall, see Strohm, 'Queens as Intercessors', pp. 105–11.

42. She and Richard travelled back separately from the Holy Land. When in 1194 he visited England, and went to Winchester for his second coronation, she was not with him. His mother accompanied him in the ceremony: *Chronica Rogeri de Hovedene*, ed. W. Stubbs, 4 vols, Rolls Series (1868–87), iii, p. 248. She was not at his bedside when he died. For what is known of Berengaria, see Trindade, *Berengaria: In Search of Richard the Lionheart's Queen*. See above, p. 140, for discussion of whether or not Richard was homosexual.

43. H. E. Maurer, *Margaret of Anjou: Queenship and Power in Late Medieval England* (Woodbridge, 2003).

44. *Paston Letters and Papers of the Fifteenth Century*, ed. N. Davis (2 vols, Oxford, 1971, 1976), ii, no. 575.

Notes to Chapter 9: Kingship and Piety

1. J. Gillingham, *Richard I* (New Haven and London, 1999), p. 103.

2. R. V. Turner, 'Richard Lionheart and English Episcopal Elections', *Albion*, 29 (1997).

3. For Richard II's ecclesiastical policies, see R. G. Davies, 'Richard II and the Church', *Richard II: The Art of Kingship*, ed. A. Goodman and J. L. Gillespie (Oxford, 1999), chapter 5.

4. Gillingham, *Richard I*, p. 258; E. M. Hallam, 'Henry II, Richard I and the Order of Grandmont', *Journal of Medieval History*, 1 (1975), pp. 171–82.

5. A. Gransden, *Historical Writing in England*, i, *c. 550 to c. 1307* (London, 1974), p. 325.

6. *Radulphi de Coggeshall Chronicon Anglicanum*, ed. J. Stevenson, Rolls Series (1875), pp. 97–98.

7. Gillingham, *Richard I*, p. 258.

8. Ibid., p. 257.

9. Ibid., p. 259.

10. *Chronica Rogeri de Hovedene*, ed. W. Stubbs, 4 vols, Rolls Series (1868–87), iii, p. 108. Richard had stayed at Bury St Edmunds on his itinerary of England in the autumn of 1189: L. Landon, *Itinerary of King Richard I*, Pipe Roll Society, new series, 13 (1935), p. 16.

11. *Coggeshall*, pp. 97–8.

12. He stayed at St Albans in September 1189: Landon, *Itinerary*, p. 5.

13. As if to emphasise the spiritual aspect of the ceremony, he stayed at St Swithun's priory (the cathedral priory), not at the castle: *Chronica Rogeri de Hovedene*, iii, p. 246.

14. *The Historical Works of Gervase of Canterbury*, ed. W. Stubbs, 2 vols, Rolls Series (1879–80), i, p. 524. For Richard's itinerary on this English visit, see Landon, *Itinerary*, pp. 85–92.

15. *Victoria County History of Hampshire*, iii, ed. W. Page (London, 1908), p. 197.

16. For Richard's granting of a charter to Portsmouth on 2 May 1194, while he was staying there, see ibid., pp. 174, 176.

17. For an architectural description, see N. Pevsner, *Hampshire and the Isle of Wight* (Harmondsworth, 1967), pp. 393–99. Pevsner suggests that Southwick Priory, which held the living, was responsible for the building – which is certainly possible. But Southwick was not a particularly wealthy foundation. Given Richard's role in the foundation of Portsmouth, royal assistance with the cost of building is more than likely. See also the discussion in J. Gillingham, 'Richard I, Galley-Warfare and Portsmouth: The Beginnings of a Royal Navy', *Thirteenth Century England*, 6, ed. M. Prestwich, R. H. Britnell and R. Frame (Woodbridge, 1997).

18. O. de Laborderie, 'Richard the Lionheart and the Birth of a National Cult of St George in England: Origins and Development of a Legend', *Nottingham Medieval Studies*, 39 (1995).

19. J. Catto, 'Religion and the English Nobility in the Later Fourteenth Century', *History and Imagination: Essays in Honour of H. R. Trevor-Roper*, ed. H. Lloyd-Jones, V. Pearl and B. Worden (London, 1981), pp. 43–55.

20. J. Hughes, *Pastors and Visionaries: Religion and Secular Life in Late Medieval Yorkshire* (Woodbridge, 1988).

21. M. G. A. Vale, *Piety, Charity and Literacy among the Yorkshire Gentry, 1370–1480*, Borthwick Papers, 50 (1976).

22. R. Pfaff, *New Liturgical Feasts in Late Medieval England* (Oxford, 1970).

23. *The Westminster Chronicle, 1381–1394*, ed. L. C. Hector and B. F. Harvey (Oxford, 1982), p. 42; *Calendar of Patent Rolls, 1396–99*, p. 24. For further discussion, see S. Mitchell, 'Richard II: Kingship and the Cult of Saints', *The Regal Image of Richard II and the Wilton Diptych*, ed. D. Gordon, L. Monnas and C. Elam (London, 1997), pp. 115–24.

24. *Westminster*, p. 454.

25. Ibid., p. 42.

26. *Political Songs and Poems Relating to English History*, ed. T. Wright, 2 vols, Rolls Series (1859–61), i, p. 293.

27. *Wykeham's Register*, ed. T. F. Kirby, Hampshire Record Society, 2 vols (1896–9), ii, p. 481.

28. *Calendar of Close Rolls, 1392–96*, p. 473.

29. N. E. Saul, *Richard II* (New Haven and London, 1997), pp. 311–16.

30. Prestwich, 'Richard Coeur de Lion: *Rex Bellicosus*', *Richard Coeur de Lion in History and* Myth, ed. J. L. Nelson, King's College, London, Medieval Studies, 7 (1992), pp. 6–7.

31. *Westminster*, p. 372.

32. *Calendar of Charter Rolls, 1341–1417*, p. 311; Westminster Abbey Muniments 5262A.

33. For discussion, see N. E. Saul, 'Richard II and Westminster Abbey', *The Cloister and the World: Essays in Medieval History in Honour of Barbara Harvey*, ed. W. J. Blair and B. Golding (Oxford, 1996), pp. 196–218.

34. *Westminster*, p. 508.

35. For Wyclif and Lollardy, see K. B. McFarlane, *John Wycliffe and the Beginnings of English Nonconformity* (London, 1952); M. Keen, 'Wyclif, the Bible and Transubstantiation', *Wyclif in his Times*, ed. A. Kenny (Oxford, 1986), pp. 1–16; R. Rex, *The Lollards* (Basingstoke, 2002).

36. For discussion of the 'Lollard Knights', see K. B. McFarlane, *Lancastrian Kings and Lollard Knights* (Oxford, 1972), part 2; and Saul, *Richard II*, pp. 297–99.

37. *Rotuli Parliamentorum*, iii, pp. 124–25.

38. Ibid.

39. *Literae Cantuarienses*, ed. J. B. Sheppard, 3 vols, Rolls Series (1887–9), iii, pp. 26–28.

40. Ibid., p. 50.

41. *Calendar of Close Rolls, 1396–99*, p. 158.

42. *Chronicles of the Revolution, 1397–1400*, ed. C. Given-Wilson (Manchester, 1993), p. 211.

43. *Calendar of Close Rolls, 1392–96*, pp. 437–38.

44. *Calendar of Close Rolls, 1389–92*, p. 453; *Calendar of Close Rolls 1392–96*, p. 434.

45. *Annales Ricardi Secundi et Henrici Quarti*, in J. de Trokelowe et Anon., *Chronica et Annales*, ed. H. T. Riley, Rolls Series (1866), p. 183.

46. H. G. Richardson, 'Heresy and the Lay Power under Richard II', *English Historical Review*, 51 (1936), p. 18.

47. *Calendar of Close Rolls, 1396–99*, p. 37.

48. Cambridge, Trinity Hall, MS 17. For an edition of the volume, see *Rogeri Dymmok Liber contra XII Errores et Hereses Lollardorum*, ed. H. S. Cronin (London, 1922).

49. E. Duffy, *The Stripping of the Altars: Traditional Religion in England, 1400–1580* (New Haven and London, 1992), chapter 5; R. Marks, *Image and Devotion in Late Medieval England* (Stroud, 2004).

50. P. Strohm, *England's Empty Throne: Usurpation and the Language of Legitimation, 1399–1422* (New Haven and London, 1998), chapter 2.

51. London, Lambeth Palace Library, MS 474, published as *The Hours of Richard III*, ed. A. F. Sutton and L. Visser-Fuchs (Stroud, 1990). The quotation is from C. D. Ross, *Richard III* (London 1981), p. 129.

52. Ibid, p. 128.

53. J. Hughes, *The Religious Life of Richard III: Piety and Prayer in the North of England* (Stroud, 1997).

54. J. Hughes, *Pastors and Visionaries: Religion and Secular Life in Late Medieval Yorkshire* (Woodbridge, 1988), p. 259.

55. Ibid., pp. 57–58.

56. Lambeth Palace Library, MS 474, published as *The Hours of Richard III*.

57. *The Hours of Richard III*, pp. 76–78.

58. Hughes, *Religious Life of Richard III*, p. 139.

59. Rex, *The Lollards*, pp. 12–13.

60. N. E. Saul, *Death, Art and Memory in Medieval England: The Cobham Family and their Monuments, 1300–1500* (Oxford, 2001), pp. 220–23.

61. *The Hours of Richard III*, pp. 67–69; Hughes, *Religious Life of Richard III*, p. 128.

62. J. Raine, ' Statutes Ordained by Richard, Duke of Gloucester, for a College at Middleham, *Archaeological Journal*, 14 (1857), pp. 160–70.

63. McFarlane, *Lancastrian Kings and Lollard Knights*, pp. 214–15.

64. A. Fehrmann, 'The Chantry Chapel of King Edward IV', *Windsor: Medieval Archaeology, Art and Architecture of the Thames Valley*, ed. L. Keen and E. Scarff, British Archaeological Association Transactions, 25 (2002), pp. 177–78.

65. For Richard's movements, see *The Itinerary of King Richard III, 1483–1485*, ed. R. Edwards (Gloucester, 1983).

66. R. B. Dobson, 'Richard III and the Church of York', *Kings and Nobles in the Later Middle Ages*, ed. R. A. Griffiths and J. Sherborne (Gloucester, 1986), pp. 130–54.

67. It seems that he envisaged burial in York Minster.

68. Richard could have arranged for his wife, Anne Neville, to be buried at Windsor, to stress her association with the Yorkist royal line, but he did not; he had her buried in Westminster Abbey, a location conferring a different kind of legitimation.

Notes to Chapter 10: Sad Stories of the Death of Kings

1. *The Crowland Chronicle Continuations, 1459–1486*, ed. N. Pronay and J. Cox (London, 1986), p. 185.

2. For a general study of the deaths of England's medieval kings, see M. Evans, *The Death of Kings: Royal Deaths in Medieval England* (London, 2003). The subject of Evans's book is the manner of the kings' deaths and the way in which those deaths were interpreted. The main concern of the present chapter, however, is with the events that led up to the three kings' deaths.

3. Though it is fair to add that Æthelred was actually deposed by Swein in 1013, only to be reinstated shortly afterwards, on Swein's death.

4. In 1216 the supporters of Louis maintained that John had been deposed, but that he had died before deposition had been completed. John's supporters would have disputed their view.

5. J. C. Holt, *Magna Carta* (2nd edn, Cambridge, 1992), p. 53.

6. For disafforestation, see ibid., pp. 60–64.

7. J. C. Holt, *Magna Carta and Medieval Government* (London, 1985), chapter 7.

8. The terms used by J. E. A. Jolliffe, *Angevin Kingship* (2nd edn, London, 1963), heading of chapter 3.

9. D. A. Carpenter, 'King, Magnates and Society: The Personal Rule of King Henry III', *Speculum*, 60 (1985), reprinted in idem, *The Reign of Henry III* (London, 1996), pp. 75–106, quotation at p. 77. The law book which goes by the name 'Bracton' is now thought to have been produced in the 1220s or 1230s by the circle around Judge William de Raleigh and later revised and edited by Bracton.

10. R. F. Treharne, *The Baronial Plan of Reform, 1258–1263* (Manchester, 1932), p. 101.

11. C. Valente, 'The Deposition and Abdication of Edward II', *English Historical Review*, 113 (1998), pp. 852–81.

12. *The Chronicle of Adam Usk, 1377–1421*, ed. C. Given-Wilson (Oxford, 1997), pp. 59–77, parts of which are printed in *Chronicles of the Revolution, 1397–1400*, ed. C. Given-Wilson (Manchester, 1993), pp. 157–61.

13. G. E. Caspary, 'The Deposition of Richard II and the Canon Law', *Proceedings of the Second International Congress of Medieval Canon Law* (Boston, 1965), pp. 189–201.

14. *Chronicles of the Revolution*, pp. 172–84.

15. J. Dunbabin, 'Government', *The Cambridge History of Medieval Political Thought, c. 350–c. 1450*, ed. J. H. Burns (Cambridge, 1988), pp. 495–96.

16. *Chronicles of the Revolution*, p. 71.

17. For discussion of late medieval ideas on tyranny, see P. S. Lewis, 'Jean Juvenal des Ursins and the Common Literary Attitude towards Tyranny in Fifteenth-Century France', idem, *Essays in Later Medieval French History* (London, 1985), pp. 169–87.

18. For Bartolus's discussion, see M. Schlauch, 'Chaucer's Doctrine of Kings and Tyrants', *Speculum*, 20 (1945), pp. 133–56, at p. 47.

19. Ibid., p. 148.

20. Bennett, *Richard II and the Revolution of 1399* (Stroud, 1999), p. 182.

21. Chaucer, *Legend of Good Women*, prologue G, lines 353–76; for discussion, see *The Riverside Chaucer*, ed. L. D. Benson (3rd edn, Oxford, 1987), pp. 1059–65. For Arundel's meeting with Salutati, see M. Aston, *Thomas Arundel* (Oxford, 1967), pp. 319n., 374.

22. Lewis, 'Jean Juvenal des Ursins and the Common Literary Attitude towards Tyranny'; idem, *Later Medieval France: The Polity* (London, 1968), p. 374.

23. For the succession problem in Richard's reign, see above, pp. 153–56.

24. D. Mancini, *The Usurpation of Richard III*, ed. C. A. J. Armstrong (2nd edn, Oxford, 1969), pp. 94–95. The argument has recently been given support by Michael K. Jones: *Bosworth, 1485*, pp. 67–68. For details, see above, p. 76 and note.

25. *Crowland*, p. 161.

26. *Rotuli Parliamentorum*, 6 vols (London, 1767–77), vi, pp. 240–42.

27. Stillington was a canon lawyer and is likely to have advised on the bastardy claim and not originated it.

28. C. D. Ross, *Richard III* (London, 1981), p. 173.

29. M. Hicks, *Richard III* (Stroud, 2000), p. 151; *Richard III: A Source Book*, ed. K. Dockray (Stroud, 1997), p. 71.

30. Mancini, *The Usurpation of Richard III*, p. 93.

31. *The Cely Letters, 1472–1488*, ed. A. Hanham, Early English Text Society, 273 (1975), pp. 184–85.

32. *Crowland*, p. 163.

33. A. J. Pollard, *Richard III and the Princes in the Tower* (Stroud, 1991), p. 122.

34. *Catalogue of the Manuscripts of Elias Ashmole*, ed. W. H. Black (Oxford, 1845), p. 1231. This document has not previously been considered in debates about Richard III's culpability. It is printed below in the Appendix, below, p. 243.

35. R. F. Green, 'Historical Notes of a London Citizen, 1483–1488', *English Historical Review*, 96 (1981), pp. 585–90.

36. Ibid.

37. Mancini, *The Usurpation of Richard III*, p. 22.

38. C. F. Richmond, 'The Death of Edward V', *Northern History*, 25 (1989), pp. 278–80.

39. P. Morgan, 'The Death of Edward V and the Rebellion of 1483', *Historical Research*, 68 (1995), pp. 229–32.

40. The Londoner who compiled the set of historical notes in the late 1480s maintained that the princes were murdered on Buckingham's orders: Green, 'Historical Notes of a London Citizen', p. 588.

41. He also had a claim, albeit a weak one, through his mother Margaret, who was a Beaufort. Her father was Edmund, duke of Somerset (d. 1455).

42. Mancini, *The Usurpation of Richard III*, p. 93.

43. Argentine reported by Mancini, *The Usurpation of Richard III*, ibid, p. 93.

44. For these examples, see Pollard, *Richard III and the Princes in the Tower*, pp. 135–37.

45. *Crowland*, p. 171.

46. A. J. Pollard, 'The Tyranny of Richard III', *Journal of Medieval History*, 3 (1977), pp. 147–66.

47. Ibid.; R. Horrox, *Richard III: A Study in Service* (Cambridge, 1989), pp. 188–97.

48. Richard II had likewise intruded retainers of his into local government. In his last two years, the years of his 'tyranny', he had appointed household men as sheriffs, escheators and justices of the peace. This policy added to his unpopularity. In 1399 his actions formed the basis of charges in the deposition articles: *Chronicles of the Revolution*, pp. 177–78. Richard II, however, unlike his namesake, did not transplant gentlemen from one part of the country to another.

49. P. S. Lewis, 'Jean Juvenal des Ursins and the Common Literary Attitude towards Tyranny in Fifteenth-Century France', idem, *Essays in Later Medieval French History*, pp. 170–71.

50. The tract, which was written in 1459 by someone of strongly Lancastrian sympathy, is discussed by J. Watts, 'Ideals, Principles and Politics', *The Wars of the Roses*, ed. A. J. Pollard (Basingstoke, 1995), pp. 128–31, and J. P. Gilson, 'A Defence of the Proscription of the Yorkists in 1459', *English Historical Review*, 26 (1911), pp. 512–25.

51. W. Shakespeare, *Richard II*, IV, 1, 134–49.

52. For these episodes, see J. Sumption, *The Hundred Years War, II: Trial by Fire* (London, 2000), pp. 296, 312.

53. P. Strohm, *England's Empty Throne: Usurpation and the Language of Legitimation, 1399–1422* (New Haven and London, 1998), chapter 4.

54. R. Edwards, 'King Richard's Tomb at Leicester', *The Ricardian*, 3 (1975),

reprinted in *Richard III. Crown and People*, ed. J. Petre (London, 1985), pp. 29–30.

Notes to Chapter 11: What's in a Face?

1. M. Meiss, *French Painting in the Time of Jean de Berry: The Late Fourteenth Century and the Patronage of the Duke*, 2 vols (London, 1967), i, p. 75.

2. C. R. Sherman, *The Portraits of Charles V of France (1338–1380)* (New York, 1969).

3. Quoted by J. Gillingham, *Richard I* (New Haven and London, 1999), p. 266.

4. *Radulphi de Coggeshall Chronicon Anglicanum*, ed. J. Stevenson, Rolls Series (1875), p. 95.

5. P. Williamson, *Gothic Sculpture, 1140–1300* (New Haven and London, 1995), p. 54.

6. T. S. R. Boase, 'Fontevrault and the Plantagenets', *Journal of the British Archaeological Association*, 3rd series, 34 (1971), pp. 1–9.

7. For discussion of the Rouen effigy, see E. M. Hallam, 'Royal Burial and the Cult of Kingship in France and England, 1060–1330', *Journal of Medieval History*, 8 (1982), pp. 364–65; and M. Duffy, *Royal Tombs of Medieval England* (Stroud, 2003), pp. 58–59. For its rediscovery in 1838, see A. Way, 'Effigy of King Richard Coeur de Lion in the Cathedral at Rouen', *Archaeologia*, 29 (1842), pp. 202–16. The effigy was accompanied by a silver shrine containing the heart.

8. For discussion of Richard's seals, see J. H. Bloom, *English Seals* (London, 1906), pp. 64–66.

9. T. A. Heslop, 'Seals', *English Romanesque Art, 1066–1200*, ed. G. Zarnecki, J. C. Holt, T. Holland (London, 1984), no. 334.

10. *Catalogue of Seals in the Department of Manuscripts in the British Museum*, ed. W. de Gray Birch, 6 vols (London, 1887–1900), i, nos 80, 87.

11. British Library, Cotton MS Claudius D VI, fo. 9v. For discussion, see R. Vaughan, *Matthew Paris* (Cambridge, 1958), p. 223.

12. *Age of Chivalry: Art in Plantagenet England, 1200–1400*, ed. J. Alexander and P. Binski (London, 1987), no. 446. For general discussion of the tomb, see Duffy, *Royal Tombs of Medieval England*, pp. 163–73.

13. S. Whittingham, 'The Chronology of the Portraits of Richard II', *Burlington Magazine*, 113 (1971), pp. 14–15.

14. For these, see ibid., pp. 14–17.

15. For discussion of the Diptych, see D. Gordon, *Making and Meaning: The Wilton Diptych* (London, 1993).

16. *Historia Vitae et Regni Ricardi Secundi*, ed. G. B. Stow (Philadelphia, 1977), p. 166; *Chronicles of the Revolution, 1397–1400*, ed. C. Given-Wilson (Manchester, 1993), p. 241.

17. *The Complete Works of John Gower*, ed. G. C. Macaulay, 4 vols (Oxford, 1899–1902), iv, pp. 265–66.

18. *The Chronicle of Adam Usk, 1377–1421*, ed. C. Given-Wilson (Oxford, 1997), p. 90.

19. *The Minor Poems of John Lydgate*, ed. H. N. MacCracken, Early English Text Society, old series, 192 (1934), p. 721.

20. *Historia Vitae et Regni*, p. 166.

21. A. P. Stanley, 'On an Examination of the Tombs of Richard II and Henry III in Westminster Abbey', *Archaeologia*, 45 (1880), p. 323.

22. *The St Albans Chronicle*, i, *1376–1394: The Chronica Maiora of Thomas Walsingham*, ed. J. Taylor, W. Childs, L. Watkiss (Oxford, 2003), p. 702.

23. For the portrait of Edward Grimston, in the National Gallery, London, see *Gothic: Art for England, 1400–1547*, ed. R. Marks and P. Williamson (London, 2003), p. 44. In supposing that the portrait in the Kunsthistorisches Museum, Vienna, long attributed to Cardinal Albergati, is in fact of Henry Beaufort, I am following M. G. A. Vale, 'Cardinal Henry Beaufort and the "Albergati" Portrait', *English Historical Review*, 105 (1990), pp. 337–54.

24. P. Tudor-Craig, *Richard III* (London, 1973), p. 93.

25. Ibid., p. 92 and plate 25; F. Hepburn, *Portraits of the Later Plantagenets* (Woodbridge, 1986), pp. 78–81 and plate 55.

26. C. D. Ross, *Richard III* (London, 1981), p. 140.

27. For examples, see Tudor-Craig, *Richard III*, plates 30–39.

28. *The Crowland Chronicle Continuations, 1459–1486*, ed. N. Pronay and J. Cox (London, 1986), p. 181.

29. D. Mancini, *The Usurpation of Richard III*, ed. C. A. J. Armstrong (2nd edn, Oxford, 1969), p. 137.

30. Hepburn, *Portraits of the Later Plantagenets*, p. 83.

31. Ross, *Richard III*, p. 139.

32. Hepburn, *Portraits of the Later Plantagenets*, plate 51.

Bibliography

MANUSCRIPT SOURCES

London, British Library
MS Egerton 3510
Cotton MS Claudius D VI

London, Lambeth Palace Library
MS 474

London, National Archives (Public Record Office)
E101 Exchequer, Various Accounts

London, Westminster Abbey
Muniments 5262A, 9473

Oxford, Bodleian Library
MS Bodley 581
MS Dugdale 15
MS Ashmole 1448

PRINTED SOURCES

Ambroise, *L'estoire de la Guerre Sainte*, ed. G. Paris (Paris, 1897).

Anglo-Norman Letters and Petitions, ed. M. D. Legge, Anglo-Norman Text Society, 3 (1941).

'Annales Ricardi Secundi et Henrici Quarti', in *Chronica et Annales*, ed. H. T. Riley, Rolls Series (1866).

The Anonimalle Chronicle, 1333–1381, ed. V. H. Galbraith (Manchester, 1927).

The Auchinleck Manuscript, ed. D. Pearsall and I. C. Cunningham (London, 1977).

Boke of Noblesse, ed. J. G. Nichols (London, 1860; repr. 1972).

The Brut, or the Chronicles of England, ii, ed. F. W. D. Brie, Early English Text Society, original series, 136 (1908).

Calendar of Charter Rolls.

Calendar of Close Rolls.

Calendar of Patent Rolls.

Catalogue of the Manuscripts of Elias Ashmole, ed. W. H. Black (Oxford, 1845).

Catalogue of Seals in the Department of Manuscripts in the British Museum, ed. W. de Gray Birch, 6 vols (London, 1887–1900).

The Cely Letters, 1472–1488, ed. A. Hanham, Early English Text Society, 273 (1975).

Chronica Rogeri de Hovedene, ed. W. Stubbs, 4 vols, Rolls Series (1868–87).

The Chronicle of Adam Usk, 1377–1421, ed. C. Given-Wilson (Oxford, 1997).

Chronicle of Pierre de Langtoft, ed. T. Wright, Rolls Series (1886).

Chronicle of the Third Crusade, ed. H. Nicholson (Aldershot, 1997).

Chronicles and Memorials of the Reign of Richard I, ed. W. Stubbs, Rolls Series (1864).

Chronicles of the Reigns of Stephen, Henry II and Richard I, ed. R. Howlett, 4 vols, Rolls Series (1884–90).

Chronicles of the Revolution, 1397–1400, ed. C. Given-Wilson (Manchester, 1993).

Collection of the Wills of the Kings and Queens of England, ed. J. Nichols (London, 1780).

The Complete Works of John Gower, ed. G. C. Macaulay, 4 vols (Oxford, 1899–1902).

The Coronation of Richard III, ed. A. Sutton and P. Hammond (Gloucester, 1983).

The Crowland Chronicle Continuations, 1459–1486, ed. N. Pronay and J. Cox (London, 1986).

Eulogium Historiarum sive Temporis, ed. F. S. Haydon, 3 vols, Rolls Series (1858–63).

Froissart, J., *Chronicles*, ed. T. Johnes, 2 vols (London, 1862).

Gesta Henrici II et Ricardi I, ed. W. Stubbs, 2 vols, Rolls Series (1871).

Giraldus Cambrensis, 'Liber de Principis Instructione Praefatio Prima', *Opera Historica*, ed. J. S. Brewer, J. S. Dimock, G. F. Warner, 8 vols, Rolls Series (1861–91).

Gower, J., *Confessio Amantis*, ed. R. A. Peck (Toronto, 1980).

Historia Vitae et Regni Ricardi Secundi, ed. G. B. Stow (Philadelphia, 1977).

The Historical Works of Gervase of Canterbury, ed. W. Stubbs, 2 vols, Rolls Series (1879–80).

The Hours of Richard III, ed. A. F. Sutton and L. Visser-Fuchs (Stroud, 1990).

The Household of Edward IV: The Black Book and the Ordinance of 1478, ed. A. R. Myers (Manchester, 1959).

'John Russell's Boke of Nurture', *The Babees Book*, ed. F. J. Furnivall, Early English Text Society, original series, 32 (1868).

King Arthur's Death, ed. B. Ford (Harmondsworth, 1988).

Knighton's Chronicle, 1337–1396, ed. G. H. Martin (Oxford, 1995).

Literae Cantuarienses, ed. J. B. Sheppard, 3 vols, Rolls Series (1887–89).

Mancini, D., *The Usurpation of Richard III*, ed. C. A. J. Armstrong (2nd edn, Oxford, 1969).

The Minor Poems of John Lydgate, ed. H. N. MacCracken, Early English Text Society, old series, 192 (1934).

Der mittelenglische Versroman über Richard Löwenherz, ed. K. Brunner (Vienna, 1913).

The Peasants' Revolt of 1381, ed. R. B. Dobson (2nd edn, London, 1983).

Political Songs and Poems Relating to English History, ed. T. Wright, 2 vols, Rolls Series (1859–61).

Polychronicon Ranulphi Higden Monachi Cestrensis, ed. C. Babington and J. R. Lumby, 9 vols, Rolls Series (1865–86).

Radulphi de Coggeshall Chronicon Anglicanum, ed. J. Stevenson, Rolls Series (1875).

Richard III: A Source Book, ed. K. Dockray (Stroud, 1997).

The Riverside Chaucer, ed. L. D. Benson (3rd edn, Oxford, 1987).

Rogeri Dymmok Liber contra XII Errores et Hereses Lollardorum, ed. H. S. Cronin (London, 1922).

Rotuli Parliamentorum, 6 vols (London, 1767–77).

Vita Edwardi Secundi, ed. N. Denholm-Young (London, 1957).

The St Albans Chronicle, i, *1376–1394: The Chronica Maiora of Thomas Walsingham*, ed. J. Taylor, W. Childs, L. Watkiss (Oxford, 2003).

The Westminster Chronicle, 1381–1394, ed. L. C. Hector and B. F. Harvey (Oxford, 1982).

Wykeham's Register, ed. T. F. Kirby, 2 vols, Hampshire Record Society (1896–99).

SECONDARY SOURCES

The Age of Chivalry: Art and Society in Plantagenet England, 1200–1400, ed. J. Alexander and P. Binski (London, 1987).

Aston, M., *Thomas Arundel* (Oxford, 1967).

—, 'Richard II and the Wars of the Roses', *The Reign of Richard II: Essays in Honour of May McKisack*, ed. F. R. H. du Boulay and C. M. Barron (London, 1971).

Barlow, F., *The Feudal Kingdom of England, 1042–1216* (3rd edn, London, 1972).

Barratt, N., 'The English Revenue of Richard I', *English Historical Review*, 116 (2001).

Barron, C. M., 'The Quarrel of Richard II with London, 1392–7', *The Reign of Richard II: Essays in Honour of May McKisack* (London, 1971).

—, 'Centres of Conspicuous Consumption: The Aristocratic Town House in London, 1200–1500', *London Journal*, 20 (1995).

Bennett, J. M., *Queens, Whores and Maidens: Women in Chaucer's England*, Royal Holloway, University of London: Hayes Robinson Lecture Series, 6 (2002).

Bennett, M., 'The Court of Richard II and the Promotion of Literature', *Chaucer's England: Literature in Historical Context*, ed. B. A. Hanawalt (Minneapolis, Minnesota, 1992).

—, *Richard II and the Revolution of 1399* (Stroud, 1999).

Bloom, J. H., *English Seals* (London, 1906).

Boase, T. S. R., 'Fontevrault and the Plantagenets', *Journal of the British Archaeological Association*, 3rd series, 34 (1971).

Brown, A. L., *The Governance of Late Medieval England, 1272–1461* (London, 1989).

Brown, R. A., Colvin, H. M., Taylor, A. J., *History of the King's Works: The Middle Ages*, 2 vols (London, 1963).

Brundage, J., *Richard Lionheart* (New York, 1974).

Buck, G., *The History of King Richard III*, ed. A. N. Kincaid (Gloucester, 1979).

Carpenter, D. A., 'The Burial of King Henry III, the *Regalia* and Royal Ideology', idem, *The Reign of Henry III* (London, 1996).

Caspary, G. E., 'The Deposition of Richard II and the Canon Law', *Proceedings of the Second International Congress of Medieval Canon Law* (Boston, 1965).

Catto, J., 'Religion and the English Nobility in the Later Fourteenth Century', *History and Imagination: Essays in Honour of H. R. Trevor-Roper*, ed. H. Lloyd-Jones, V. Pearl and B. Worden (London, 1981).

Churchill, W., *Divi Britannici* (London, 1675).

Clanchy, M. T., *England and its Rulers, 1066–1272* (2nd edn, London, 1998).

Clarke, M. V., *Fourteenth Century Studies* (Oxford, 1937; repr. 1968).

Crawford, A., 'The King's Burden? The Consequences of Royal Marriage in Fifteenth-Century England', *Patronage, the Crown and the Provinces in Later Medieval England*, ed. R. A. Griffiths (Gloucester, 1981).

Crouch, D., *William Marshal: Court, Career and Chivalry in the Angevin World, 1147–1219* (Harlow, 1990).

Daniel, S., *The Collection of the Historie of England* (London, 1621).

Davies, R. G., 'Richard II and the Church', *Richard II: The Art of Kingship*, ed. A. Goodman and J. L. Gillespie (Oxford, 1999).

Davis, R. H. C., 'What Happened in Stephen's Reign, 1135–54', *History*, 49 (1964).

Dobson, R. B., 'Richard III and the Church of York', *Kings and Nobles in the Later Middle Ages*, ed. R. A. Griffiths and J. Sherborne (Gloucester, 1986).

Duffy, M., *Royal Tombs of Medieval England* (Stroud, 2003).

Dunbabin, J., 'Government', *The Cambridge History of Medieval Political Thought, c. 350–c. 1450* (Cambridge, 1988).

Eberle, P. J., 'Richard II and the Literary Arts', *Richard II: The Art of Kingship*, ed. A. Goodman and J. L. Gillespie (Oxford, 1999).

Echard, L., *The History of England* (London, 1707).

Edwards, R., 'King Richard's Tomb at Leicester', *Richard III. Crown and People*, ed. J. Petre (Gloucester, 1985).

Evans, M., *The Death of Kings: Royal Deaths in Medieval England* (London, 2003).

Fehrmann, A., 'The Chantry Chapel of King Edward IV', *Windsor: Medieval Archaeology, Art and Architectureof the Thames Valley*, ed. L. Keen and E. Scarff, British Archaeological Association Transactions, 25 (2002).

Gairdner, J., *History of the Life and Reign of Richard the Third* (2nd edn, Cambridge, 1898).

Gill, L., *Richard III and Buckingham's Rebellion* (Stroud, 1999).

Gillespie, J. L., 'Richard II: Chivalry and Kingship', *The Age of Richard II*, ed. J. L. Gillespie (Stroud, 1997).

Gillingham, J., 'Some Legends of Richard the Lionheart: Their Development and Influence', idem, *Richard Coeur de Lion. Kingship, Chivalry and War in the Twelfth Century* (London, 1994).

—, 'The Art of Kingship: Richard I, 1189–99', ibid.

—, 'The Unromantic Death of Richard I', ibid.

—, 'Richard I, Galley-Warfare and Portsmouth: The Beginnings of a Royal Navy', *Thirteenth Century England*, 6, ed. M. Prestwich, R. H. Britnell and R. Frame (Woodbridge, 1997).

—, *Richard I* (New Haven and London, 1999).

—, *The Angevin Empire* (2nd edn, London, 2001).

Given-Wilson, C., *The Royal Household and the King's Affinity: Service, Politics and Finance in England, 1360–1413* (New Haven and London, 1986).

Goodman, A., 'England and Iberia in the Middle Ages', *England and her Neighbours, 1066–1453*, ed. M. Jones and M. Vale (London, 1989).

Gordon, D., *Making and Meaning: The Wilton Diptych* (London, 1993).

Gransden, A., *Historical Writing in England*, i, *c. 550 to c. 1307* (London, 1974).

Gransden, A., *Historical Writing in England*, ii, *c. 1307 to the Early Sixteenth Century* (London, 1982).

Grant, A., 'Foreign Affairs under Richard III', *Richard III: A Medieval Kingship*, ed. J. Gillingham (London, 1993).

Green, R. F., 'Historical Notes of a London Citizen, 1483–1488', *English Historical Review*, 96 (1981).

Griffiths, R. A., 'The Crown and the Royal Family in Later Medieval England', *Kings and Nobles in Later Medieval England*, ed. R. A. Griffiths and J. Sherborne (Gloucester, 1986).

Hallam, E. M., 'Henry II, Richard I and the Order of Grandmont', *Journal of Medieval History*, 1 (1975).

—, 'Royal Burial and the Cult of Kingship in France and England, 1060–1330', *Journal of Medieval History*, 8 (1982).

Halsted, C., *Life of Richard III* (2 vols, London, 1844).

Hammond, P. W., 'The Reputation of Richard III', *Richard III: A Medieval Kingship*, ed. J. Gillingham (London, 1993).

Hanham, A., *Richard III and his Early Historians, 1483–1535* (Oxford, 1975).

Harriss, G. L., 'The King and his Subjects', *Fifteenth-Century Attitudes: Perceptions of Society in Late Medieval England* (Cambridge, 1994).

Harvey, J. H., *The Plantagenets, 1154–1485* (London, 1948).

—, 'The Wilton Diptych: A Re-Examination', *Archaeologia*, 98 (1961).

Hepburn, F., *Portraits of the Later Plantagenets* (Woodbridge, 1986).

Heslop, A., 'Seals', *English Romanesque Art, 1066–1200*, ed. G. Zarnecki, J. C. Holt, T. Holland (London, 1984).

Hibbard, L. A., *Medieval Romance in England* (Oxford, 1924).

Hicks, M., 'Descent, Partition and Extinction: The Warwick Inheritance', idem, *Richard III and his Rivals: Magnates and their Motives in the Wars of the Roses* (London, 1991).

—, 'Richard III as Duke of Gloucester: A Study in Character', ibid.

—, 'Richard III's Cartulary in the British Library: MS Cotton Julius BXII', ibid.

—, *Richard III* (Stroud, 2000).

—, *English Political Culture in the Fifteenth Century* (London, 2002).

Holt, J. C., *Magna Carta and Medieval Government* (London, 1985).

—, *Magna Carta* (2nd edn, Cambridge, 1992).

Horrox, R., 'Richard III and All Hallows Barking by the Tower', *The Ricardian*, 6 (1982).

—, *Richard III: A Study in Service* (Cambridge, 1989).

Hughes, J., *Pastors and Visionaries: Religion and Secular Life in Late Medieval Yorkshire* (Woodbridge, 1988).

—, *The Religious Life of Richard III: Piety and Prayer in the North of England* (Stroud, 1997).

The Itinerary of King Richard III, 1483–1485, ed. R. Edwards (Gloucester, 1983).

Jolliffe, J. E. A., *Angevin Kingship* (2nd edn, London, 1963).

Jones, Michael K., 'Somerset, York and the Wars of the Roses', *English Historical Review*, 104 (1989).

—, *Bosworth 1485: Psychology of a Battle* (Stroud, 2002).

Jones, T. and others, *Who Murdered Chaucer? A Medieval Mystery* (London, 2003).

Kendall, P. M., *Richard III* (London, 1955).

Kleineke, H., 'Alice Martyn, Widow of London: An Episode from Richard's Youth', *The Ricardian*, 14 (2004).

Laborderie, O. de, 'Richard the Lionheart and the Birth of a National Cult of St George in England: Origins and Development of a Legend', *Nottingham Medieval Studies*, 39 (1995).

Landon, L., *Itinerary of King Richard I*, Pipe Roll Society, new series, 13 (1935).

Laynesmith, J. L., *The Last Medieval Queens: English Queenship, 1445–1503* (Oxford, 2004).

Legge, A. O., *The Unpopular King* (2 vols, London, 1885).

Lewis, P. S., *Later Medieval France. The Polity* (London, 1968).

—,'Jean Juvenal des Ursins and the Common Literary Attitude towards Tyranny in Fifteenth-Century France', idem, *Essays in Later Medieval French History* (London, 1985).

Lindley, P., 'Absolutism and Regal Image in Ricardian Sculpture', *The Regal Image of Richard II and the Wilton Diptych*, ed. D. Gordon, L. Monnas and C. Elam (London, 1997).

Lloyd, S., *English Society and the Crusade, 1216–1307* (Oxford, 1988).

Maurer, H. E., *Margaret of Anjou: Queenship and Power in Late Medieval England* (Woodbridge, 2003).

McFarlane, K. B., *John Wycliffe and the Beginnings of English Nonconformity* (London, 1952).

—, *Lancastrian Kings and Lollard Knights* (Oxford, 1972).

Medieval Queenship, ed. J. C. Parsons (Stroud, 1994).

Meiss, M., *French Painting in the Time of Jean de Berry: The Late Fourteenth Century and the Patronage of the Duke*, 2 vols (London, 1967).

Meyer, P., 'L'entrevue d'Ardres', *Annuaire Bulletin de la Société de France*, 18 (1881).

Milles, J., 'Observations on the Wardrobe Accounts for the Year 1483', *Archaeologia*, i (1779).

Mitchell, S., 'Richard II: Kingship and the Cult of Saints', *The Regal Image of Richard II and the Wilton Diptych*, ed. D. Gordon, L. Monnas and C. Elam (London, 1997).

More, T., *The History of King Richard III*, ed. R. S. Sylvester (New Haven, 1963).

Morgan, P., 'The Death of Edward V and the Rebellion of 1483', *Historical Research*, 68 (1995).

Moss, V., 'The Defence of Normandy, 1193–1198', *Anglo-Norman Studies*, 24, *Proceedings of the Battle Conference, 2001*, ed. J. Gillingham (Woodbridge, 2002).

Nicolas, N. H., 'Expenses of the Great Wardrobe of Edward III', *Archaeologia*, 31 (1846).

Ormrod, W. M., *The Reign of Edward III: Crown and Political Society in England, 1327–1377* (New Haven and London, 1990).

—, 'Richard II's Sense of English History', *The Reign of Richard II*, ed. G. Dodd (Stroud, 2000).

Palmer, J. J. N., *England, France and Christendom, 1377–99* (London, 1972).

Pearsall, D., 'The *Troilus* Frontispiece and Chaucer's Audience', *Yearbook of English Studies*, 7 (1977).

Perroy, E., *L'Angleterre et le Grand Schisme d'Occident* (Paris, 1933).

Pfaff, R., *New Liturgical Feasts in Late Medieval England* (Oxford, 1970).

Phillips, J. R. S., 'Edward II and the Prophets', *England in the Fourteenth Century*, ed. W. M. Ormrod (Woodbridge, 1986).

Pollard, A. J., 'The Tyranny of Richard III', *Journal of Medieval History*, 3 (1977).

—, *Richard III and the Princes in the Tower* (Stroud, 1991).

—, *The Wars of the Roses* (Basingstoke, 1995).

Poole, A. L., *From Domesday Book to Magna Carta, 1097–1216* (2nd edn, Oxford, 1955).

Powell, J. E., and Wallis, K., *The House of Lords in the Middle Ages* (London, 1968).

Prestwich, J. O., 'Richard Coeur de Lion: *Rex Bellicosus*', *Richard Coeur de Lion in History and Myth*, ed. J. L. Nelson, King's College, London, Medieval Studies 7 (1992).

Prestwich, M., *Edward I* (London, 1988).

Raine, J., 'Statutes Ordained by Richard, Duke of Gloucester, for a College at Middleham', *Archaeological Journal*, 14 (1857).

The Regal Image of Richard II and the Wilton Diptych, ed. D. Gordon, L. Monnas and C. Elam (London, 1997).

Rex, R., *The Lollards* (Basingstoke, 2002).

Richardson, H. G., 'Heresy and the Lay Power under Richard II', *English Historical Review*, 51 (1936).

Richmond, C., ''The Battle of Bosworth, August 1485', *History Today*, 35 (August 1985).

—, '1485 and All That: or What was Going on at the Battle of Bosworth', *Richard III: Loyalty, Lordship and Law*, ed. P. W. Hammond (London, 1986).

—, 'The Death of Edward V', *Northern History*, 25 (1989).

—, '1483: The Year of Decision (or Taking the Throne)', *Richard III: A Medieval Kingship*, ed. J. Gillingham (London, 1993).

Ross, C., *Richard III* (London, 1981; 2nd edn, 1999).

Russell, P. E., *The English Intervention in Spain and Portugal in the Time of Edward III and Richard II* (Oxford, 1955).

Saul, N. E., 'Richard II and the Vocabulary of Kingship', *English Historical Review*, 110 (1995).

—, 'Richard II and Westminster Abbey', *The Cloister and the World: Essays in Medieval History in Honour of Barbara Harvey*, ed. W. J. Blair and B. Golding (Oxford, 1996).

—, *Richard II* (New Haven and London, 1997).

—, *Richard II and Chivalric Kingship*, Royal Holloway, University of London, Inaugural Lecture (1999).

—, *Death, Art and Memory in Medieval England: The Cobham Family and their Monuments, 1300–1500* (Oxford, 2001).

Schlauch, M., 'Chaucer's Doctrine of Kings and Tyrants', *Speculum*, 20 (1945).

Shakespeare, W., *Richard II*, ed. P. Ure (5th edn, London, 1961).

—, *Richard III*, ed. A. Hammond (London, 1981).

Sherman, C. R., *The Portraits of Charles V of France (1338–1380)* (New York, 1969).

Staley, L., 'Gower, Richard II, Henry of Derby and the Business of Making Culture', *Speculum*, 75 (2000).

Stanley, A. P., 'On an Examination of the Tombs of Richard II and Henry III in Westminster Abbey', *Archaeologia*, 45 (1880).

Starkey, D., 'Introduction: Court History in Perspective', *The English Court from the Wars of the Roses to the Civil War*, ed. D. Starkey (London, 1987).

Stow, G. B., 'Richard II and the Invention of the Pocket Handkerchief', *Albion*, 27 (1995).

Stow, J., *A Survey of London*, ed. C. L. Kingsford, 2 vols (Oxford, 1908; repr. 2000).

Stratford, J., 'Gold and Diplomacy: England and France in the Reign of Richard II', *England and the Continent in the Middle Ages: Studies in Memory of Andrew Martindale*, ed. J. Mitchell (Stamford, 2000).

Strohm, P., *Hochon's Arrow: The Social Imagination of Fourteenth-Century Texts* (Princeton, 1992).

—, *England's Empty Throne: Usurpation and the Language of Legitimation, 1399–1422* (New Haven and London, 1998).

Summerfield, T., *The Matter of Kings' Lives: The Design of Past and Present in the Early Fourteenth-Century Verse Chronicles by Pierre de Langtoft and Robert Mannyng* (Amsterdam, 1998).

Sumption, J., *The Hundred Years War*, ii, *Trial by Fire* (London, 2000).

Sutton, A. F., '"A Curious Searcher for our Weal Public": Richard III, Piety, Chivalry and the Concept of the "Good Prince"', *Richard III: Loyalty, Lordship and Law*, ed. P. W. Hammond (London, 1986).

—, 'The Court and its Culture in the Reign of Richard III', *Richard III: A Medieval Kingship*, ed. J. Gillingham (London, 1993).

Sutton, A. F. and Visser-Fuchs, L., 'Choosing a Book in Late Fifteenth-Century England and Burgundy', *England and the Low Countries in the Late Middle Ages*, ed. C. M. Barron and N. E. Saul (Stroud, 1995).

Tey, J., *The Daughter of Time* (London, 1951).

Tillyard, E. M. W., *Shakespeare's History Plays* (London, 1946).

Trindade, A., *Berengaria: In Search of Richard the Lionheart's Queen* (Dublin, 1999).

Tuck, A., 'Richard II and the House of Luxemburg', *Richard II: The Art of Kingship*, ed. A. Goodman and J. L. Gillespie (Oxford, 1999).

Tudor-Craig, P., *Richard III* (London, 1973).

Turner, R. V., 'Richard Lionheart and English Episcopal Elections', *Albion*, 29 (1997).

Turner, R. V., and Heiser, R. R., *The Reign of Richard Lionheart* (Harlow, 2000).

Tyerman, C., *England and the Crusades, 1095–1588* (Chicago, 1988).

Vale, M., 'An Anglo-Burgundian Nobleman and Art Patron: Louis de Bruges, Lord of la Gruthuyse and Earl of Winchester', *England and the Low Countries in the Late Middle Ages*, ed. C. M. Barron and N. E. Saul (Stroud, 1995).

—, *The Princely Court: Medieval Courts and Culture in North-West Europe, 1270–1380* (Oxford, 2001).

Valente, C., 'The Deposition and Abdication of Edward II', *English Historical Review*, 113 (1998).

Vaughan, R., *Matthew Paris* (Cambridge, 1958).

Vergil, P., *The Anglica Historia of Polydore Vergil, AD 1485–1537*, ed. D. Hay, Camden Society, 74 (1950).

Vergil, P., *Three Books of Polydore Vergil's English History*, ed. H. Ellis, Camden Society (1844).

Victoria County History of Hampshire, iii, ed. W. Page (London, 1908).

L. Visser-Fuchs, 'Richard in Holland, 1461', *The Ricardian*, 6 (1983).

—, 'Richard in Holland', *The Ricardian*, 6 (1983).

Waller, J. G., 'The Lords of Cobham, their Monuments and the Church', *Archaeologia Cantiana*, 11 (1877).

Walpole, H., *Historic Doubts on the Life and Reign of Richard III* (London; repr. 1965).

Watts, J., 'Ideals, Principles and Politics', *The Wars of the Roses*, ed. A. J. Pollard (Basingstoke, 1995).

Warren, W. L., *King John* (3rd edn, New Haven and London, 1997).

Way, A., 'Effigy of King Richard Coeur de Lion in the Cathedral at Rouen', *Archaeologia*, 29 (1842).

Whittingham, S., 'The Chronology of the Portraits of Richard II', *Burlington Magazine*, 113 (1971).

Index

10510178R20174

Made in the USA
San Bernardino, CA
19 April 2014